Dub Sub Confidential

Dub Sub Confidential

A Goalkeeper's Life with – and
without – the Dubs

JOHN LEONARD

PENGUIN
IRELAND

PENGUIN IRELAND

UK | USA | Canada | Ireland | Australia
India | New Zealand | South Africa

Penguin Ireland is part of the Penguin Random House group of companies
whose addresses can be found at global.penguinrandomhouse.com.

First published 2015
001

Set in 12/14.75 pt Bembo Book MT Std
Typeset by Jouve (UK), Milton Keynes
Printed in Great Britain by Clays Ltd, St Ives plc

A CIP catalogue record for this book is available from the British Library

ISBN: 978–1–844–88356–1

www.greenpenguin.co.uk

MIX
Paper from
responsible sources
FSC® C018179

Penguin Random House is committed to a
sustainable future for our business, our readers
and our planet. This book is made from Forest
Stewardship Council® certified paper.

For Serena my love

Keep your eye on the ball, son, and roar like a bull.

Jim Leonard

Prologue

16 July 2006

The bus turns off the Malahide Road and out on to Fairview Strand. In front of us the sirens of the Garda bikes wail as they clear a path for us through the traffic. The streets are lined with people cheering and waving flags. In the park, groups of youngsters are lazing around, drinking cans and flagons. When they see the bus they get up on their feet and start shouting and roaring. Kids are pointing. Cars are honking. Drunken young lads run alongside, shouting mad stuff, banging the side of the bus, trying to keep up.

Inside the bus the mood is calm. I feel good. I feel relaxed. Driving along these roads brings back old memories. I close my eyes to gather myself, take some deep breaths.

I think about my dad, who died two years ago. Just a year before that I was pushing his wheelchair along Clonliffe Road, watching this very bus drive by. Tears well up in my eyes. He took me to my first Dublin game. Football was something we shared with each other. I miss him and know that he would be proud of where I am right now. I nod to myself and take on that energy.

As Croke Park looms we see the first Offaly supporters in their green, white and gold jerseys. That's another psychological trigger. My concentration ups a little more. There is a battle to be won today. Sentiment and memory count for nothing. Big, ugly, melon-headed bogmen are grabbing their crotches and making suggestive sexual motions towards us. I am flattered, but they're not my type.

The bus drives slowly through the stadium gates and leaves us right to the door of the dressing room. It is like any dressing room I have ever been in – except that it is bigger, with a better paint job, and everything has been laid out for us. I take my seat under my jersey, number 16. We sit in sequence, which means I'm beside Mossy

Quinn. I am the only member of the subs who sits on the first-team side of the room – and yet, because I'm a keeper, I'm the sub least likely to get on the pitch.

One or two lads chuckle and chat. Others sit with eyes closed, going through their mental preparations. I have already done a 40-minute warm-up with Stephen Cluxton and our keeper coach, Gary Matthews, in Parnell Park. But that doesn't mean much, and Clucko is first into the warm-up room.

This is my first Leinster final. I should be nervous, but being a sub takes a lot of the pressure away. You prepare, but your adrenalin is in check. You are ready, but mentally you don't – and shouldn't – switch on completely. You need to keep something in reserve, so that you'll be ready to make an impact. It's important to be tuned in to the tactics that are being employed, but you don't need to be storming around the dressing room screaming at lads or psyching yourself up.

The opening 20 minutes of the match are pretty uneventful. The Offaly boys are up for the challenge and it's a cagey game. Questions are being asked. We are the favourites, but Offaly don't give a monkey's about that. The heat is slowing the game down. I'm feeling hot – and I'm only sitting in the dugout. The Croke Park subs benches must be as good as any in the world. The seats are built with comfort in mind – like upright La-Z-Boys. There's a little bit of give in the cushion, but it's firm enough so you don't get sleepy. And lots of leg room too.

The subs bench is at the front of the stand, so you are surrounded by fans. It is humbling when little kids come up before kick-off, looking for autographs and photos. They have no idea who I am, but that's OK. I am one of the Dubs. And then there are the girls who fill the stadiums these days: young ladies wearing designer sunnies, in slinky light-blue Dublin tops, smiling and giggling in our general direction. I try to stay focused, but the occasional sunglassed eye is still caught.

Most of my life I have been a number 1 – the first name on the team sheet – and I haven't quite got used to sitting on the bench. Being a sub keeper means twiddling thumbs and shouting at your teammates. It means warming up Clucko and trying to keep my mind right in case something happens. It means being positive and focused and in the right frame of mind. Being a sub keeper means you train harder than every other person on the squad, knowing you have less chance than everyone of playing.

If you don't train harder than the number 1, then how can you be better than him? Unless his form takes a massive dip or he gets injured, then the reality is that when the big games come around, you will be watching it from the sidelines. You bust your guts to be a substitute. It is a tough mental adjustment and a hard equation to balance. And on match days all this comes to a head. This is what you spent nine months training for: sitting on this bench in a stadium with 70,000 people screaming.

The subs are organized into groups of three or four. During the match these groups rotate between sitting, watching and warming up. Today I'm in group 3 with Darren 'Geezer' Magee and Senan Connell, two legends of the game and great men to warm up with. After group 2 comes back in, we get up and ready ourselves to go through the warm-up routine.

It's not easy getting the run down the sideline right. Some lads will burst off down on their own at an incredible rate. I hate warming up with these sorts. They make you look bad. Other lads will jog along gently, letting the crowd savour their slow-motion grace, their puffed-out chests, their steely game faces. They ham it up for the galleries. They do lots of nonchalant lunges and gaze away into the distance. They project confidence and stability.

Myself, Geezer and Seno take it middle of the road, speed-wise. We get down to the corner and start doing a leisurely stretch.

We are close to the action. The crowd are metres away and they love to shout at the subs. I can hear shouts of 'Lenny, ya big bleedin' bollix' and 'Lenny, Lenny give us a wave'. I'm trying not to smile but the energy is intoxicating. I love it, being here in Croke Park. I would give anything to be out on the pitch, but can only bide my time.

We jog slowly back towards the dugouts, but pick up the pace as we come into management's view. I sit back down and crack open another Powerade. We drink so much of this that some of the lads joke about sending their dental bills to the County Board. Every week at training there is an abundant supply and you take what you need. I have cases of the stuff at home and in my car. Every man and his dog knows the importance of rehydration these days.

A few weeks ago, on a Tuesday before training, we had random drug tests in the camp. Pee into a cup and off you went. A couple of days later the results were back. After training, Mark Vaughan and Conal Keaney and I were called to the side of the gym by the manager, Pillar Caffrey, and the team doctor, Gerry McElvaney.

'Lads, the results are back from your samples,' Pillar said. 'All of your results came back as extremely dehydrated. What's the reason for this?'

'Eh, not sure, Pillar, I had some problems with some food so hadn't been drinking enough fluids that day,' answered Vaughny.

Vaughny was a real character. You never quite knew what he was going to say in his classic southside accent. I was a bit disappointed by the lack of imagination in his excuse.

'Conal?' Pillar asked.

'Sorry, Pillar, I was driving all day, down to Kerry and back, and didn't drink enough.'

Pillar shook his head, but Keaney was calm and had a semi-valid excuse.

'Lenny?'

'Sorry, Pillar, I was in the saddle for four hours the night before and lost a lot of fluid.'

Myself, Vaughny and Keaney all started chuckling. Even Pillar cracked a smile and shook his head. We were all a little confused when the Doc said, 'Well, if you are on a bike in your room at night, just make sure you have some liquids ready to go.'

Now, as I guzzle down the sweet electrolyte concoction, my attention turns back to the Leinster final. I observe the kick-outs and notice an even distribution, with Offaly enjoying some good possession. I'm keeping an eye on their full forwards, but no one has me worried that much. I played with Ciaran McManus many moons ago in UCD, and nothing much has changed. I imagine him bursting through and lashing one of his piledrivers into the top corner – all the more spectacular would be the save I'd be making.

The first half is winding up. Six points all. A response will be needed at half-time. The ball is moved down the wing to Offaly's left corner forward, Thomas Deehan. He has a shot blocked by our defender Davey Henry, but he picks up the rebound. Beyond Deehan I can see Clucko out on his six-yard line. I see what he sees. He starts moving, anticipating a cross-field pass. Sure enough Deehan launches it forty yards over towards the figure of Cathal Daly, in full flight on the 21-yard line.

Everything slows down. Clucko takes off, arms and knees pumping. The ball hovers in the air. I can see Clucko straining every muscle in his body. I can see he isn't going to get there in time. The crowd, seeing it too, gasps collectively. Daly catches the ball and Clucko is way out of position. Daly, ball in hand, tries to run past Clucko, who rugby-tackles him to the ground: a horrendous-looking professional foul.

The referee marches over. Time seems to slow down. There is a moment of complete silence, and then we're at full surround-sound volume. The Dubs on the Hill are screaming. Every Offaly man, woman and beast in the stadium is screaming. They bellow 'OFF OFF OFF OFF' in unison in their big, thick accents. I clench my cheeks a little. I feel my fists go into balls. I hold my breath and hear my heart lashing through my chest as I wait and hope. It pumps so deep and loud that I hear it reverberate through my skull. Come on, ref, I think: send him off.

I'm ready, ref. I'm ready for it.

Send him fucking off.

I pushed the back door open, hopped up on the little metal props at the back of the wheelchair and gained a good gallop of speed: down the ramp, around into the driveway. My dad, the passenger, didn't flinch. He was used to it.

My older brother James followed behind, football in hand. We set up around the front of our house: two jackets as goalposts and Dad positioned at the penalty spot. James handed him the ball.

Dad double-checked his brakes and then placed the ball into his right hand. With his left hand he gripped the left-hand side brace of the wheelchair. He looked up and asked, were we ready? When we nodded yes he would slowly lower his right arm with the ball in hand, then lob it gently into the air. As it hovered for a split second, he lashed it with his fist in our general direction.

Dad suffered from multiple sclerosis, and he had lost the ability to walk. But his arms still worked well. His shots fizzed and flew past us.

We were only eight and nine at the time and it was the perfect training for us. My dad would bury us if he needed to, if we were getting too big for our boots. It was there, in our front garden, that I found my love for goalkeeping. It was there that I first imagined being a professional.

I was competitive from the get-go. We would have five shots taken on us at a time. I would call the scores, call James's scores. I would call for rematches and tie breakers. I always wanted there to be a winner and I never liked to lose. James was less bothered by it all. He could take it or leave it. He would look away sometimes, distracted by the smell of the sea or some curious little bird hopping through the garden.

We'd play until my mother called out to us that dinner was ready. After dinner we'd return to the front garden to practise our long jump. We had a ten-metre run-up to a little portion of softer grass. We planted coloured markers into the ground to mark each foot of distance. As the sun dropped lower in the western sky, Dad would coach us through the nuances of the long jump. He worked on our timing, our spring, our speed and the jump itself.

Dad was somewhat militant in his training. He took us running around local football pitches. From the car he would watch us, noting the times it took us to do laps. He would push us on and monitor how we performed. He took us training with other young lads – not playing and messing around, but practising our catching and kicking skills. He made me practise kicking balls against a wall, wearing a slipper on my right foot so I would strengthen my left. From a young age I was pushed to try my best and work hard. I had a mentor who was relentless in his attention to detail.

Having a dad in a wheelchair seemed natural – I didn't know any different. Having a dad who drove you to fields and timed you running around them was normal. Having a dad who punched footballs at you for hours on end seemed like regular life. As a child I just accepted my father's MS. But I understand now how much it drove him on. It drove him on something chronic. When he was first diagnosed, in his late twenties, they gave him fifteen years to live. He was now in his late forties and every day was precious to him. He knew the clock was ticking. So he trained us. He was strict but knew that it took more than talent to make it.

'Remember, son, it takes 10 per cent talent, 10 per cent luck and 80 per cent hard work to make it. You have the talent, but it is up to you to put the hard work in.'

At Baldoyle Boys' National School I soon became captain of the Gaelic football team. I joined a local GAA club called Na Piarsaigh, which has long since ceased to be. We played at the back of St Fintan's School in Sutton. We had some great young players from Sutton, Bayside and Baldoyle, and we were able to put it up to the big clubs in north Dublin. I had established myself as a tricky forward, getting trials for the North Dublin U/13 team.

When Na Piarsaigh folded I joined the local soccer club, Baldoyle United, who needed a goalkeeper. Lots of the lads I was in school with played there. I'd never played soccer seriously before, but I had the handling skills from GAA to play in nets.

I settled right in to playing soccer and forgot all about the GAA for a few years. Baldoyle United got to two All-Ireland quarter-finals. We dominated the Brenfer North Dublin Leagues and I was selected as one of the North Dublin keepers on representative teams from U/14 through to U/18. Our team was loaded with some real tough characters from Baldoyle. We had skill, guts and an incredible manager in Paddy 'Dungeon Master' Morrissey. Paddy was a builder by trade, and on match days he would pick up the majority of the team in his beat-up mustard-coloured Hiace van. Many were the cold mornings when we would have to jump out and give it a push start.

Things changed a little when I went to secondary school in St Nessan's, Baldoyle. It was a bigger pond than I was used to, but it was not long before I settled in. I joined every sports team I could. There was soccer, GAA and tennis. Anything was better than going to class. In my second year I was playing midfield and captaining the junior GAA team, playing half forward for the senior GAA team, and in goal for the only soccer team we had. Most weeks would involve two or three half-days as we travelled around playing matches.

I captained our team in a 'B' final in the old Croke Park. The build-up to the game had been exciting, a coming-of-age moment. The whole school came to support us. Banners with 'Lenny's Army' hung along the advertising hoardings. My extended family came to watch the game. I led the team out and was as proud as any captain who ever stood on that hallowed turf. But all that feeling, all that occasion, all that emotion and ceremony counted for nothing after the final whistle blew. Losing had not been part of the plan. Losing overshadowed all that positive sentiment. It was a simple lesson I learned that day: winning was all that mattered.

I loved school, but not because of anything to do with the curriculum. For me, secondary school meant playing sports and being around girls all day. It was an exciting time for an innocent young lad as I was until then. One time, in second year, a teacher failed to show up for a class. I decided to impress the ladies by piling desk upon desk and chair upon chair, climbing my way to the top, making monkey sounds and slapping the ceiling. Everyone was giggling and laughing until the door opened. There stood our headmaster, 'Spud' Murphy.

The class went quiet. I balanced in suspended animation on top of the tower of desks.

He had a fearsome reputation, did Spud, and I was bricking it as I made my way down to earth and then walked along the corridor towards his office. Spud walked a few steps behind me, and then I felt his powerful grip on my shoulder, forcing me to stop and turn around. We were in the canteen area, halfway between the classrooms and the offices. All was quiet. He took a long look out over the canteen area and then turned to address me.

'Now, Mr Leonard,' he bellowed, 'what club are you going to play for outside of school?'

'Sorry, sir?'

'Are you going to play club GAA outside of school, Mr Leonard?'

'Eh, I think so, sir.'

'With whom, Mr Leonard?' he demanded in his booming, rolling voice.

'Eh, Naomh Barróg I think, sir.' Naomh Barróg was the closest team to my house and I was going to train with them that very weekend.

'Well, have you thought about coming out to Malahide to play for St Sylvester's? They are a fine group of lads and I think you will really benefit from playing there.'

Malahide was a posh suburb, around five miles north of my house. I had never considered playing for them, but in light of my current situation I was open to persuasion.

'Eh, OK, sir.'

'Now, what do you think our chances are for the Under Sixteens this year? Have we missed any players from your old school?'

We took to talking about all things sport-related, and my transgression was not referred to. This was my first glimpse into the power of sport. I was blessed that our headmaster was a GAA man!

I tried training in Kilbarrack on a rainy Saturday afternoon with Naomh Barróg. There was no trainer, no manager and only seven other stragglers. I hung around for a while and then left. One week later I was picked up in a Mercedes and driven to Malahide to play my first game for St Sylvester's. I quickly realized that they were not just a very well-run club but also, as Spud Murphy had said, a fine group of lads. I slotted in nicely playing in goals.

I hadn't played goal in Gaelic football before, but the transition from soccer was pretty smooth. While I had to make some adjustments to the way I played, the same basic principles applied: organize your defence and distribute the ball when you had to. There was no 'box' or offside and you didn't need to cover through balls. I felt very confident in my new role. On top of that, the GAA goals were a couple of feet narrower. This made pulling off saves a lot easier. Throughout my GAA career, before the throw in, I always loudly encouraged the corner backs to let their opponent in for a one-on-one. The opposing forwards were always within earshot and I liked them to know I was not just your average keeper.

I was playing two or three games during the week in school, and then club soccer and GAA at the weekend. It was non-stop action and I loved it. Being selected as captain and on representative teams was great for my confidence. I was naturally outgoing and was making friends in school. Life was good.

In my first year playing for St Sylvester's we got to the minor championship final, where we played against a Ballyboden team spearheaded by Eric Miller — who would go on to win forty-eight international rugby caps for Ireland. Miller was an immense athlete and he gave us an absolute battering that day. Ballyboden destroyed us all over the park.

I wasn't at fault for any of their scores, but I was not in the greatest of condition playing the game.

The night prior to the final, my mother's family were having a celebration in Galway. My dad, meticulous thinker that he was, thought it would be detrimental to my preparation to have me travel an eight-hour round trip in the twenty-four hours before a game. So my parents decided to leave me behind. They left a seventeen-year-old boy at home alone on a Saturday night in Dublin.

Phone calls were made. Before I knew it, there was a party in full swing in the house. Friends came, friends of friends came, and girls who were friends of friends came. There was alcohol and hashish galore and I had my closest attempt at losing my virginity with a girl from school. At one stage this young lady and I were naked and wriggling around in my bedroom. I was having trouble maintaining stability, and the lack of sobriety was affecting my ability to get and maintain an erection.

Not that I would have known what to do with the erection once I had it up and running. The female genitals were a thing of myth and mystery. This was way before the days of the internet and the only porn I had seen until this time was a few big-titty magazines an old friend had snaffled from his dad's collection. So we learned about sex in Chinese whispers from other teenage boys. Where else could you learn?

The sex education I was taught in secondary school was so absurd it was funny. There was a particularly ridiculous day when Sister Bríd had the thankless job of explaining what the genitals were. Sr Bríd was a skinny, frail, timid, grey-haired old lady. She pointed out the vagina with a piece of chalk and asked us did we know other names for the male appendage. 'Purple-headed-warrior' was shouted a few times. She blushed and left the room.

My sex education with my dad wasn't much better. It happened one day when we were waiting for my brother to finish a karate class. We sat there in the car park and were listening to some music on the radio. He leaned over and turned down the volume a little bit. I could sense he was unusually uncomfortable.

'Eh son, now . . . eh . . . you know that eh . . . well, you know that eh . . . look tell me this . . . have you checked down below that you have both of your balls? Boys are meant to have two balls down near your . . . well, you know . . .'

I was just as embarrassed as he was.

'Eh, yeah, I know, Dad. I have them.'

'OK, son, that's great . . .'

My dad did give me a few nuggets of wisdom for dealing with women: things like 'Women are meant to be loved and not understood.' That was one of his favourites. Or 'Enjoy women, son, but always respect them.'

Neither of these nuggets helped me when, with a bellyful of drink, I was rubbing my flaccid penis against the midriff of a young girl. What also didn't help me were the people banging on the door and having a right old ruckus outside the room. No one went home satisfied, but there was beauty in trying.

My parents came home the next day and I thought I had gotten away with it. The final was an evening kick-off and I spent the morning scrubbing down the house. I was caught out by the fact that a couple had jumped into my little sisters' bedroom and had pulled the two single beds together. When one of my sisters opened the door and looked in she shouted for my mother. 'Mammy, someone has moved the two beds together and the pillow smells like perfume.'

It was not a good start to championship final day. Just as I was trying to cover up this little incident, a friend dropped back in the bike he had borrowed the night before. He met my mother in the driveway.

'Thanks for that, Mrs Leonard, I borrowed it last night to go home.'

Driving out to play that final was a sombre occasion. I slept most of the way, and my teammates in the car must have wondered why I was snoring away at five in the evening!

The desire to fit in with my peers, get drunk and lose my virginity had overridden the desire to prepare properly for a championship final. Up until recently, I had abstained from drinking and getting involved with any kind of drugs. But I had lost my innocence, and there were a number of factors that had combined to send me down a path which would take me fifteen years to get off.

It was around this time that I was being scouted to go over to England for soccer trials. Every game I played with Baldoyle brought more and more attention. We played Home Farm in the FAI Cup, a team full of underage internationals, and drew with them at home 0–0. I had a blinder and the replay went to penalties. Although I did manage to save one, we missed two and went out. I was gutted. We were all gutted.

After these games a scout approached me and came out to meet the family. He represented Oldham Athletic and he said they were really keen to get me to go over and sign up. I was excited beyond belief. For a month or two I was on cloud nine. Arrangements were being made for me to go over and spend some time at the club before hopefully signing a contract.

A week or so before I was to travel, the scout called and went through a few last details. When I told him my date of birth he paused for a second or two and asked me to say it again. When I repeated myself he went very quiet. Eventually he spoke.

'John, I'm not sure how to tell you this. There has been some mistake. This means that you are two months too old to play for the youth team next year in Oldham.'

The fabric of space and time unravelled there and then. The scout had been watching the U/17 Home Farm team who we played in the cup. But back then the cup was a mixed-age competition, and Baldoyle's side was an U/18 team. The scout had assumed I was young enough.

When I put down the phone that day it felt as though everything had changed. I was heartbroken. My way of dealing with the disappointment was that I started to care less. Whether it was a conscious decision or not I don't know, but I was happy to get drunk now. I was happy to get stoned. I wanted to feel the high and be part of the group. While I enjoyed the buzz of the alcohol and hash, it also helped numb me a little.

I became less interested in football. I had been drafted on to the Dublin minor GAA squad but was firmly down the pecking order. Graham Kinahan from St Vincent's was first choice. Graham was a tall and solid keeper. He had a safe kick-out and an underwhelming presence. He was the solid 6-out-of-10 performer every week. I was far more flamboyant and talented, but I was perceived as less reliable. So I trained hard and got nowhere. Damien Smith from St Brigid's was given the sub jersey and I had to deal with the rejection of not togging out on match days for the first time in my sporting life.

One summer's day a group of friends took a boat out to Ireland's Eye, a twenty-minute trip from Howth pier. We took with us some cans, some hashish and some girls. We ran around the island, getting drunk and stoned and kissing the girls. It was a great day – but I had to train for the Dublin minors that evening. By the time I got home, changed and up to training I was a giggly mess. I stumbled around St Anne's park. No one seemed to notice or care. I got away with it, and it signalled to me that I could function pretty well even when inebriated.

Towards the end of the summer my dad enrolled me in a summer camp for soccer keepers. It was run by the FAI, and the great Everton keeper Neville Southall came over to coach one of the days. On the first day I got to the final two of a shot-stopping competition. The coaches were using a machine that shot balls out from between two spinning wheels. With just myself and one keeper left, they turned it up full tilt, over 100 mph. I managed to save my shot and win – and broke two fingers in the process.

Instead of training for the week with some of the top keepers in Ireland, I went to hospital and had my fingers reset. Instead of winning keeper of the week, that honour went to none other than Nicky Byrne, who would go on to become famous as a member of Westlife. At that time, I knew Nicky as the guy who had been sub keeper to me in our school team. (Later that year he had trials for Leeds United and signed a contract. A few years later I was watching a match on TV in a pub in Dublin. The match was at Anfield. It was Leeds against Liverpool. There on the bench was none other than Nicky Byrne. No, I wasn't bitter – not at all!)

Suddenly life seemed to be one disappointment after another. Meanwhile, my friends were carrying on doing regular teenage things. It seemed like a massive space had opened up in my life. I wasn't going to be a professional footballer. I wasn't going to make it in the GAA. There was no one interested in bringing me into League of Ireland.

College was next on the list, but when my Leaving Cert results came in I hadn't got the points necessary to get the only course I had applied for (Journalism). So now I had no college offers, no job offers, no professional football offers. And still I had not lost my virginity. A few years previously, the world had seemed my oyster; now it seemed I was washed up.

And then something happened which would send me deep into a world of emotional pain. In order for you to get a good and credible picture I need to bring you right back.

2

I dragged my nine-year-old self out of bed. It was pitch black out, and it was cold. I pattered down to the kitchen and blinked heavily at the bright light. I looked inside the press for something to nibble on.

'Come on, lads, hurry up now — and don't eat anything before communion,' my mother called as she helped my dad into his wheelchair.

I scampered back down the hallway to our room. I put on my shoes and glanced at the clock: 7.05 a.m. My brother readied himself and we followed my parents out the house and down the ramp to the car. Above Howth Head there were faint purple and orange streaks rising through the black sky. We helped my dad into the car, put the wheelchair in the boot and were on our way.

My dad was able to drive an automatic until the later stages of his MS. He had a toggle attached to the steering wheel, which helped him steer with his left hand, and a hand control that allowed him to accelerate and brake using his right. We always got funny looks when people saw a man being helped out of the driver's seat into a wheelchair by two pre-teen boys. Those looks galvanized us.

The drive to St Fintan's Church took just a few minutes. We turned into the driveway which led to the side of the sacristy. The car park was nearly empty. This was normal for midweek mass. My dad slowed down and I hopped out. My brother stayed with him to help him out of the car.

I looked up to see Darragh, the sacristan, walking across the road from the parish priest's house. Darragh was a big rotund man. His skin was a deep grey colour, as though it had never been exposed to sunlight. He wore his hair parted to the right and giant horn-rimmed, semi-tinted glasses. He always wore the same clothes: the same black pants, the same black shoes and the same white shirt with black tie. The only possible variation came in his pullover: it was always light grey, but sometimes it had a V-neck and sometimes not. His belly hung heavily over his waistline. His fat face wobbled slowly when he talked. He looked like an oversized translucent piglet that was being primed for some dark feast. I never saw him smile.

He grunted a 'Morning' as he unlocked the door to the church. There was always a special feeling about being inside the church before others. It was as though I was in on some secret. I saw the machinations which whirred and clicked behind the spectacle that was presented to the public. I saw the plastic container where the communion wafers were stored before they were turned into the body of Christ. I saw the big, square, brown boxes that contained the wine which the priests were miraculously able to transform into the blood of Jesus using words and gestures.

I took a quick right and went into the altar boys' changing area, a small poky room at the back of the church. Inside were a few built-in cupboards where the special robes for big masses hung. There was a long bench on which to place your belongings. There was a tall window which looked out on to the car park. The window was tinted so you couldn't see in from the outside. I hung my altar boy costume on a hanger and began to get ready.

The door opened and I looked up to see Father Payne coming into the room. Father Payne was my favourite priest. He was nice and friendly and always happy to see us. He had a full head of greying blond hair, parted to the left, and a Roman nose. Even in winter he had a bit of a tan and he was always clean-shaven. He was not the tallest man in the world. He was a little pudgy. He had a nervous twitch whereby he blinked heavily, both eyes at once, then one on its own. He did this every twenty seconds or so.

'Well, hello, my little angel,' he exclaimed and approached me to give me a hug. When he saw me, Father Payne always liked to give me a hug. He always called me his little angel. I liked it. I thought it was a nice word to call someone. He wrapped his arms around me and pulled me in close to his body. I could feel the softness of his belly squashing against my face. It was a sensation I had not felt before meeting Fr Payne. I think that was why I preferred him to the other priests. They were colder and less friendly. When they saw me, they just said hello and good morning. Father Payne held me close. I was small for my age and my head reached just over his belly button. When he heard the creaking door opening in the background – this was Darragh letting in my brother, who had been helping my father into his wheelchair – he ended the hug.

Father Payne turned and left the room to get ready for saying mass. It was just James and me then. I took the black cassocks from the bag and handed one to my brother. I helped mine over my head and quickly buttoned up the little clip buttons. Then I took my white surplice and dropped that over my head. We always wore black shoes so they blended in with the bottom of our clothes. All set.

We hurried out through the corridor to the sacristy. It was 7.28 a.m. as we stood waiting just inside the doors. Father Payne put on the last of his vestments and turned to us and said, 'OK, my little angels, let's go.' This meant it was time to press the button to ring the bell and walk out to begin mass.

The church was practically empty, save for a handful of fanatical diehards. The mass passed without any glitches. I didn't drop anything. I rang the bell on time. I bowed at the correct moments. I genuflected graciously. I was happy with my performance.

After the mass was over we returned back into the sacristy. Father Payne was full of praise for us. 'Well done, my beautiful angels.' We thanked him and finished helping Darragh to tidy up. This meant returning to the altar and bringing in the books and wine and other ceremonial objects. Then we went back to the altar boys' room. My brother changed quickly and went out to help my dad get back into the car. I took my time, as there was no real hurry. A few seconds later the door to our room opened again. Father Payne's head appeared around the door frame. He stepped inside the room and didn't say a word. He stepped forward and opened his arms to give me a big hug.

The altar boy gown had big openings along the sides which meant you could access your pockets while serving. Father Payne's arms completely engulfed me and when his hands settled, I felt them slipping down inside the gown. One hand went around my back and over my bottom. The other circled around me and came to rest inside the front of my pants. I felt his hand sliding down the inside of my underpants and over the top of my penis. His other hand moved and pressed firmly against my back, pulling me into his belly and bloated midriff. His belly felt a lot lumpier than usual. It felt like something else was in there now. I didn't know what to do and just stood there as he rubbed me. I tried not to think about it. A car horn honked in the distance and he finished his hug. He gave one last squeeze as he left before returning to the parish priests' house across the road.

That was the first time, but not the last. Father Payne was always the opportunist. On big Sunday masses with other priests around, he would just say hello. When I was alone with him, I would expect a nice big hug. Sometimes he would rub his erection against my chest, my arms and my hands. Sometimes he would put his soft hands inside my pants. I did not know it was wrong. I had nothing to gauge it against.

The memories surfaced when I was a teenager – Father Payne's octopus arms, his big, evil smile, his teeth bared and his hands feeling. Conversations about religion and church would lead me to anger. As the years went on, I grew completely intolerant. Venomous vitriol poured from my mouth at any mention of Catholic priests.

In the summer, when I was sitting the Leaving Cert, a conversation began with my parents in the rickety old porch of our house. Reports of clerical abuse in certain parishes of Dublin had been surfacing in the media. People were talking about it.

My dad was aware of my complete disdain for the Church, my contempt for the idea that priests were paragons of virtue or that the Church had any claim to be purveyors of good and noble ideals. If I went with him to mass, I would wheel him up to receive communion, but would not receive communion myself. That day on our porch, he began a conversation about priests. I used some choice and colourful language to describe Father Payne. 'A dirty old perverted scumbag' might have been the phrase I used.

My parents were upset at my choice of language.

'Why would you say that, John? Did something ever happen with him?'

I thought about it for a moment or two and immediately realized I couldn't hide it. I let it out. I told my parents that he had rubbed me and made me touch him.

They looked at me in disbelief – and in that moment a deep and violent gap opened up in our life. I was crippled with sadness at ruining any illusions they may have had about the Church. I felt guilty on so many levels. By telling them what had happened, I was writing a new and shocking chapter in our lives.

It was a profound and devastating moment. My parents were shocked, but it didn't take long for that shock to turn to anger and rage. Their young son had been abused. I saw pain etched on their faces, the sort of pain I had never seen before and would never see again. Tears rolled down their faces. They tried to comfort me. They asked questions and I answered. They figured out what we needed to do.

My mother brought me to Howth Garda station, where I made a statement. The cops took it all down, and then made inquiries. These inquiries took a long time, but the results were astounding. It turned out that the Catholic Church had known for a long time about Father Ivan Payne's propensity for paedophilia. I was not the first person to complain about being abused. In 1981 Andrew Madden, a teenager from Cabra, told his school guidance counsellor that he had been abused by Father Payne. A formal complaint was lodged to Archbishop Ryan, who was in charge of the Dublin Diocese at that time. The resulting internal inquiry resulted in Father Payne being sent to a psychiatrist, who gave him the all-clear. The psychiatrist later claimed that the Church had not told him of the nature of the complaints against Payne. A short while later, in 1982, Payne was sent to my parish in Sutton, where he served mass until 1995. The Church later paid financial compensation to Madden, but still took no action against Payne.

In their investigations, the police got in touch with former altar boys who had served under Payne. More lads came forward. There were victims from when he was the chaplain in Our Lady's Hospital for Sick Children. There were victims from his time as a chaplain in Cabra. There were other victims from his time as a priest in Sutton.

The hierarchy of the Catholic Church knew of the serious allegations against him and did nothing. They compensated a victim yet allowed the predator to continue working with no restrictions. Meanwhile, Father Payne was also working all this time on the marriage tribunal in Dublin – a branch of the Church that counselled couples intending to be married. Imagine getting advice on your marriage from this perverted monster?

The revelations had a massive impact on me. I went from living in denial and secrecy, to living in denial but with some people now aware of what had happened. We felt it was so upsetting that we had to keep it secret from the rest of the family. A lack of trust in life and people surfaced in me. I had been a typical good little boy when young. I was shy and obedient. Now there was a latent anger that exploded from time to time. Now that it had come out in the open, I had to face up to memories which had stayed deep in the closet. They had been buried beyond the black noise of my mind. Now they were swimming just behind my eyes.

The investigations into Father Payne went on for a few years. The story was never far from my mind. Between talking to the cops, the lawyers and my parents I had a gentle refresher every once in a while. The whole saga crippled me emotionally. I dealt with it all in my head, by getting drunk or stoned. I never sought counselling or psychologists. My parents were happy that I seemed to be OK with it on the surface. And I was OK with it, on the surface. But inside I was corrupted. Inside I had been molested and abused by a sick, perverted paedophile. My first sexual experience was the Parish Priest rubbing my little boy penis.

The revelations of Father Payne coincided with a lot of disappointments in my normal life. I failed to get into college, I was rejected as a potential professional footballer and I was rejected as the Dublin Minor keeper. While I had been built and programmed by my parents to be confident and outgoing, all these events happening together had a tough effect on my mind. I couldn't handle the pain. I was a regular teenager who had high expectations for himself. But all these dreams and high ideas seemed to flitter away. So when there was talk of getting flagons of cider and drinking it in fields, I was more than ready for it. When there was talk of hashish and hypersonic giggling laughter, I was more than up for it. When there was a mention of a new drug called ecstasy it seemed like a perfectly reasonable thing to be interested in.

Now, most of my friends were into the same. Most teenagers experiment at some time with mind-altering substances. But for me there was something at work which was a little deeper than the standard. I was trying to mask the pain. I was trying to escape from the reality of my new world. I felt a failure. I felt a victim. I felt as though I was the one who was at fault. What better way to relieve these feelings than by drinking and taking drugs?

So that is what I did.

3

I had decided to repeat my Leaving Cert, having failed to get enough points the first time round to study journalism. My parents were very understanding in light of what had come about with Father Payne. They gave me some space and they knew that I would get there when I was ready. They knew I was a little wilder than I had been, but they just kept pushing me gently in the right direction. It appeared that I was getting on with things, and that needed to be encouraged.

I was still living at home with my older brother and three younger sisters. There had always been a warm and buzzing atmosphere in the house. We lived in a big old bungalow with lots of small rooms kitted out in dilapidated 1930s decor. My sisters were all in their early- and mid-teens and I was able to have some great laughs with them through those days. They were oblivious to me being stoned, drunk or otherwise, and no matter how shit or good I felt, I was always able to have a chuckle with them. We would imitate people, make up stories and speak in country accents for hours on end. Even though I was struggling with myself, I still had a lot of love around me. I was lucky in that respect.

We were always a close-knit family. We lived in our own detached house and never hung around in any estates or gangs growing up. I never really had any friends until secondary school, and I didn't feel I needed any; I had my family and the people I played sports with. That was just the way it was. We were slightly isolated in that respect but we got on well with each other.

My underage soccer and GAA days were finished. I decided to stop playing soccer completely: the adult amateur soccer leagues were too depressing to play in when I thought I should have been in England getting paid to play. The idea of togging out for Baldoyle Utd on a miserably cold and wet Sunday morning was not that appealing any more. The Sunday morning games also meant I couldn't go out on Saturday night. I had just discovered house music and ecstasy pills. House music and ecstasy worked very well on a Saturday night.

The reality now was that I was playing at most one game a week, on a Saturday afternoon, with the St Sylvester's U/21s. This in turn meant that I had a whole new world of freedom for myself. This could have meant more time preparing to re-sit the Leaving, but in my own mind it meant that I could put off studying for a long time.

My dad still came to any football matches I played. He began the year by pushing me to get involved with more teams, but when he saw that I wasn't interested he relented. Looking back now, I am amazed at how he managed to get into all the public parks around Dublin and drive up pitchside to watch the games. He was dedicated. He told me that his father had never been interested in what he achieved as a kid, and he was determined that he would not be like that. As my interest waned I felt a cutting guilt: he had expectations of me and I was letting him down.

Smoking hash had become a daily ritual. When supplies ran low I would walk under Bayside DART station and head over towards the 'Gap': a dark and muddy corner of Seagrange Park, where a series of blocks had been removed from a wall. The local Baldoyle dealers operated here. A 'ten spot' was a thin sliver of hash which cost ten quid. It came wrapped in a piece of tinfoil. I'd hand over my money, and the dealer would walk over to a bush, from which he'd kick out a cigarette packet containing his wares.

The weekends were reserved for pill-popping mayhem. The acid house scene in the UK was the stuff of legends, and clubs began to appear in Dublin which offered a slice of that loved-up madness. I remember taking my first proper pill when I was seventeen. The Ormond Multi-media Centre on Ormond Quay were running a night called 'The Magic Roundabout', based on the cartoon series from the '70s. There were giant characters from the cartoon walking around on stilts. The walls had been painted in fluoro murals to provide dramatic visual happiness. The place was packed with hundreds of young and excited pill-popping people. Just before I took my first pill I was intensely nervous. The drug could take up to half an hour or so to kick in, but when it did, I knew. As I stood to the sidelines of the crowds dancing and shouting at the DJ, I felt the tingle growing in my belly. Soon the tingle became a burst and I felt the energy surging through my system. I felt an overwhelming sensation of happiness and love. The room turned into a sparkling lollipop land. Every girl I saw was a supermodel with the most incredible glistening smile. Every bloke I saw was a sound lad I was about to become friends with. This was unlike any other sensation I had ever had in my life. And the music seemed to connect with this feeling at a deep and magical level. I was hooked. For three or four hours I danced and screamed, waffled and laughed, being tugged along by the most insanely good feeling.

The standard intake initially was one pill for the club and a half or possibly another full one for the after-party. Getting back to someone's house and chilling out was the best feeling ever. Stories were shared and spliffs were smoked. The most insanely tasty cups of tea were guzzled. Eyeballs were dilated and the tangy feeling of delight was heightened by giving and getting massages from new and old female friends. The spliffs combined with some booze, and another cheeky half would send the mind on the trippiest of journeys. In flats and houses all around Dublin we inhabited a world within a world.

I fell in love with the scene. I bought decks and began trawling through record shops and accumulating a large collection of techno and house music. I began playing DJ sets at parties and converted my bedroom at home into a mini studio. With no regard for the feelings of my family, I pounded dance music from the bedroom three or four nights a week. At the weekend I would carry records out with me just in case there was a chance to play at some stage. I was no Carl Cox, but I loved playing my music when I was off my face.

The year was becoming a real write-off for football. I was playing only an occasional game with Sylvester's, and I wanted nothing to do with ambitions of my old life. Drugs gave me the alternative reality I needed in order to deal with the emotions I felt. I managed to hide my descent pretty well from my family. There was little physical evidence that couldn't be hidden by retreating to my room for a few days. And in a family of five teenage kids there are an infinite number of issues to be dealt with at any one time. I was just another loud mouth to feed. I knew this and I felt entitled to do what I was doing; I was coping in the only way I knew how. They at least pretended they knew nothing and we all carried on loving each other in the Leonard Lunatic Asylum.

But this crazy and loving home was no substitute for getting out and up to mischief. And my nights out were becoming heavier and heavier. As the year rolled on, so did my intake of drugs. Instead of taking one or two pills a night, I was now popping three or four. And instead of paying for drugs up front, I would buy ten on tick and sell some of them on. After a while it seemed stupid to just buy ten. I mean, why buy ten when you could get fifty, have a great night out and make some money in the process?

I could not help myself when I was on the dance floor. In those days there was an innocence to the club scene. If there was a girl who smiled at you and you smiled back, you would normally dance beside each other. You would get talking. Or you mightn't even talk. She might just dance in front of you, and when a melodic breakdown happened in the music you would begin to massage her. If she liked you she would turn around and you would kiss each other. These kisses were spine-tinglingly erotic – drugs and tongues and horniness imploding and exploding.

When this happened I might pop a pill into the girl's mouth and she would happily take it. If a friend was near by, I might do the same for them. I was one loved-up goose who wanted to impress the girls as much as possible. The usual was that by the time I got back to the after-party, my bag of pills would be practically gone and I would have half the money I needed to pay back my dealer. Luckily enough he was a friendly guy, but I quickly realized I wasn't cut out to be a drug dealer.

At Christmas we went on a family holiday to the Costa del Sol. It was a real blast, the first time our complete family had ever gone overseas together. Myself, my brother and oldest sister were all over eighteen and we were given free rein to hit the town. Malibu and coke washed down by shots of tequila was the order of the day. We mingled and boogied and wandered from bar to bar.

Along the way I met a girl called Maggie from Finglas in Dublin. She said she had a bag of coke on her. We made our way upstairs to the toilets and went into a cubicle together. She handed me the bag and asked me to rack out a couple of lines. I began chopping out two big fat ones with a bank card on the top of a toilet roll holder. As I rolled up a note to get snorting I turned back around to Maggie. She had dropped pants and was sitting on the toilet.

'I have to go – you don't mind, do ya?' she asked.

I didn't mind. I thought it was dirty or sexy or something. Maggie had a flat face and sunken grey eyes. Her brown hair was straight and had a slick, oily sheen. I hoovered up my line of coke and felt a kicking surge, the likes of which I had never got from the coke I had tried in Ireland. As I coughed a little I heard what sounded like a spluttery and gaseous explosion coming from the toilet. I turned back to see Maggie scrunching up her face.

'Sorry, I needed to take a shite.'

I exited as quickly as I could and laughed to myself at the horror of Maggie taking a dump in front of me. The glamour of drugs! This should have been a warning sign for me. But the coke kicked in, the booze flowed and the night carried on. The Spanish cocaine was really strong. It lifted your eyeballs and gave you a heavy over-confidence and recklessness. It lasted for an initial surge of twenty minutes or so, and then petered away.

I asked Maggie for another line later on and she was happy to oblige. This time I went to the toilets on my own. I was charging now and got into a heavy conversation with her about drugs. She told me she smoked heroin back in Dublin. I was intrigued. I was off my face and open to suggestions. She told me her Spanish dealer could get some for us. I wanted to know how good heroin was, and I needed someone to show me what to do. It was a ritual. Whether you were shooting up or smoking it, you needed an expert to show you what to do.

Two days later I was in Maggie's apartment, in the complex next to ours. She took a piece of heroin – a sort of brown mush – and placed it on a piece of tinfoil, turned up at the edges so it wouldn't fall off. She took out a straw she had taken from a restaurant. She then took a lighter and told me to follow what she was doing. She lit the lighter underneath the lump of heroin and it began to melt with the heat. As it melted she moved it around the tinfoil and a smoky vapour was released. It was this vapour that she sucked up through the straw and into her lungs. When she had finished her lump, she slumped back a little on the couch. I sat there, waiting and watching her as she gurgled and murmured and made orgasmic noises.

She slowly opened her eyes. Her pupils had narrowed into tiny pinned irises. She was a long way away but coherent enough to help me through the process. I sucked up the vapour and inhaled it as deep into my lungs as possible. I blacked out then, eventually, came around, slumped on the couch. Maggie was looking at me and smiling and I could make out some of the words she spoke, but not all of them. I felt extremely light-headed and queasy. I ran to the toilet and hurled up some bile and food from earlier in the day. I clung on to the toilet seat in a deep, sickly trance.

By the time I returned to the living room, Maggie was chasing the dragon again. She said it was normal to get sick and not to worry about it. I went for round two. I took up my position above the foil and she lit the flame again. I followed the vapour around and inhaled it deeply. It tasted like burnt metallic chocolate. I kept it deep in my lungs and felt a wave of insanely warm tingles rush over me before I passed out again. When I came around I sat still for a few minutes. I felt nothing. Then, as soon as I tried to move, I felt the nausea curdling deep inside and ran to get sick for a second time.

We finished off the gear in less than an hour. I felt queasy but high. It was like being heavily stoned on hashish, but with a heavier tingling kick to it. My senses were dulled and internal thoughts really came to the fore. The thoughts were warm and flowed in a sweet and rolling pattern. I felt like a soft mint bouncing down rubber marmalade stairs. Maggie poured us a drink and rolled a spliff to smoke. They had little effect on me. I was warped and warm and was melting into the couch. I just wanted to stay there and mull over the nothingness which wafted through my mind. She was all wired and hyper and had to go and meet some friends down the square. I couldn't move, so I told her to go on and I'd follow her later.

In a typical careless junkie way, she left me there in her apartment. I faded in and out of a slumber. As the fuzziness abated I had a clear idea of where I was again. I went into the toilet and splashed some water on my face. My eyes were dark and beady, but the heroin made me see myself in a very satisfying way. I mouthed some weird sayings to myself and slapped myself across the face a few times to snap myself out of my reverie.

As the buzz wore off I felt more capable of doing something regular. I left the apartment and walked down to the square, looking for more action. I didn't see Maggie again. My brother was down there, chatting to a couple of Scandinavian girls in a bar. I saddled up beside him, ordered a drink and cracked on. No one was the wiser. No one suspected a thing.

A few days later we took a day trip to Tangier. We went as a family, all seven of us on a big tour bus. We left early in the morning and drove to Gibraltar, where we boarded a ferry for the short voyage across the strait to Morocco. It was a mad experience. My dad was being pushed around these cobbled and hilly streets at a frantic pace in the wheelchair. We went from market to shops to restaurants. Outside one set of shops a hawker tried to sell me some pipes for smoking. I asked him for the real deal, some Moroccan hashish.

He beckoned me to follow him, and I grabbed my sister and made her come with me. We raced off down narrow winding streets, far from the tour group. Eventually we got to a small alleyway and the seller came out from a room with a small bag of grass. I argued about the price and tried to get some hashish and not grass. After haggling for a short while I began to fear a little for our safety. I paid the man for the grass and he hurried us back to our group, who were getting back on to the tour bus to return to Spain.

As we approached the port, I became acutely aware of the number of armed soldiers, police and dogs around. This was a heavily patrolled area, seeing as it led from Africa to Europe. I now had a big bag of smelly weed in my pants. When we got off the bus I stood close behind my dad. I insisted that I be the one to push him: there was a separate entrance for him on to the boat, which circumvented the security checks. The nerves disappeared as I sat on the top deck with my family. We ordered some drinks and watched North Africa fade into the background.

That evening I sat and watched the sun set and smoked a big fat joint. It had been a week of new experiences. I had tried heroin. I had smuggled drugs between continents. As the sun dropped down beyond the lowest clouds and vanished for another day, I felt alive. On some level, I knew I was slipping into a dangerous place. But reality was a bitter pill, and drinking and doing drugs numbed things nicely.

When I returned from holidays there was a very official letter from St Sylvester's. A new senior panel was being formed under the guidance of Brian Talty. I had been invited to join. It was a good bit of news. I was happy to be involved and to challenge myself with becoming the number 1 keeper in Malahide. I wanted to prove to myself that I was good. And to prove it to myself, I needed to prove it to others. The opportunity couldn't have come at a better time. I was drifting into the danger zone and this could help drag me right back out of it.

Nobody was happier than my dad. We had something to talk about again. He scrutinized the training, my attitude and the performances I reported back to him. He loved nothing more than sitting with me for half an hour after every training session and going over what had happened. These chats were the springboard to conversations about other things going on in our lives. It was during this time that we really began to forge a relationship as two men, rather than father and son.

The Sylvester's team was dominated by two sets of brothers – the Barneses and the Keoghs. Brian, Martin and Declan Barnes all played for Dublin at one stage or another and were gifted footballers. They had talent, but were not your typical Malahiders. They had a rough edge to them, a tough exterior which reminded me of the Baldoyle teams I grew up playing with. They loved to get stuck in, and Declan in particular was as aggressive as you like.

Anto and Shay Keogh spearheaded the attack. Shay was without doubt the most talented player we had. He could stick a ball over from anywhere and was clinical with a dead ball. I always wondered why he wasn't selected more regularly for Dublin. He had everything you could ask for. Anto Keogh was a brute of a man. He loved to get stuck in and was great at winning the dirty ball.

The rest of the team was peppered with inter-county talent. Brian Silke had played for Galway and was our skipper and full back. He was a quiet man who led with his actions and understated aggression. Keith Galvin, Glenn O'Neill and Niall Guiden all played for Dublin. Timmy 'The Silver Fox' Cummins played for Limerick and interprovincial for Munster. On top of all these we had an array local lads who had played minor and U/21 for Dublin. It was a formidable group.

In goals my rival was a lad by the name of Paul 'Hustler' Hussey, who was the Dublin U/21 keeper at the time. He was a very solid keeper, armed with a monstrous kick-out. In those days there were no kicking tees, and it was actually against the rules to make a divot in the pitch. If the referee saw you digging into the grass before you kicked the ball, he would blow up and give a hop ball. So before every game you had to sneakily make your mounds while the ref wasn't looking.

Hustler could boom the ball sixty yards from the grass. He would take a five-step run-up and plant the ball way off into the horizon. I, on the other hand, was a skinny little runt with a very weak kick-out. To combat this shortcoming, I would place the ball into certain zones between the half backs and midfield which favoured our players. Having come from a soccer background, I preferred retaining possession than hoofing it into a 50/50 situation.

The training was tough and there was a massive emphasis on running and aerobic fitness. We did some fitness tests and I was up there with the top 10 per cent. Even though I was partaking in drugs and smoking and drinking, I was in great shape. We did some body-fat tests, and it turned out that I actually needed to put on some weight – I was borderline anorexic. The weekends of eight hours' dancing at raves had stripped me of any excess blubber.

We had two nights training per week and a match at the weekend.

As luck would have it, Hustler had to play matches for the Dublin U/21 team, so I was given the chance to play for the Sylvester's first team. I never felt out of my depth and enjoyed playing in the challenge games. There was a massive emphasis on work rate and determination, and this translated into the great team spirit between us all.

The new regime meant that I had to curb some Saturday nights. Many of my friends were still going out and getting crazy, but, if I had a match for the seniors on a Sunday morning, I stayed in. Staying in meant heading to another friend's house and having a few cans, a few spliffs and watching *Match of the Day*. It was a simple formula. I studied the fixture list so that I could plan around the big games for getting out and getting on the pills.

There were a few occasions when I went straight from the party to the pitch. One Saturday night involved a massive party at a friend's house. I ended up taking too many pills and was still off my face in the cold light of day in the dressing room. As Talts gave his pre-match speech I was a zillion miles away, dreaming about sweet, fuzzy things and techno ladies. The shouts and roars went up and I knew it was time to get out there and play. As I followed the lads out, Keith Galvin sidled up beside me.

'Get your fucking head together, Lenny,' he said, looking me in the eyeballs, which were popping out of their sockets.

'Yeah . . . yeah, I will.'

We won the game. I played pretty well.

I didn't see any harm in any of this. I was playing club GAA and was doing well. If I wanted to get out and get amongst it, then it was my prerogative. I was as committed as the next man on the team and it wasn't like we were professionals. This was back in the day when it was not frowned upon to have a few pints the night before a game. In fact, if that was your regular ritual, then it was actually encouraged. The benefits of feeling relaxed and normal outweighed the notion that changing your habits would make you perform better.

We were a serious outfit. Talts was a passionate manager and, with Glenn 'Nailor' O'Neill, the Barnes brothers and the Keoghs on the pitch, every game went close to boiling over into an all-out fracas. I loved it. I loved the intensity that we played with. Club GAA was a violent game and required a nasty element to survive. We were not going to get pushed around by anybody, and Talts really brought that fighting spirit to the squad.

By the time I had repeated my Leaving and the summer was upon us, I had established myself as the regular senior keeper. I failed again to gain entry into my first choice of Journalism, but had enough points to head out to UCD to do Arts. So that was what I did. I would live at home and do the commute over to the southside every day. I was excited about life again. I was playing well in goals and was about to begin college. My social life was great and the mental issues I had faced twelve months earlier seemed a long way away.

Or they were buried nice and deep in my subconscious.

I carried on smoking hash most days. I had become very used to it and the daily blast was something I looked forward to. I don't know when I stopped being depressed and had become an addict. The lines for this were very blurred. But I know that every day was a smoky day. My friends all smoked and I wasn't inclined to change the pattern I had gotten myself in to.

At UCD I signed up to study English, Philosophy and Greek & Roman. The great thing about college was that there was no pressure on you to perform. Don't feel like going to your lecture? No problem, roll a number and smoke it with some new friend. Don't feel like studying? Great . . . step right into the busiest bar in Ireland and get drinking. Can't afford to pay for pints? Not an issue, scrape together a fiver, and six cans of Dutch Gold are going into your belly.

At this stage I felt I was turning a corner. UCD opened up possibilities in my imagination. That was all I needed – the potential to be something, to be somebody more than I was right now.

The GAA was playing its part too. My first full year with Sylvester's was the most successful in the club's history. We were drawn against the holders, Kilmacud Crokes, in the first round of the county championship. No one gave us a chance. Crokes were a formidable outfit, but we were ready for them and managed to beat them with an epic performance. Shay Keogh slotted over a winning point from far out on the sideline to win it with time almost up. The win gave us a heap of confidence and we blazed a trail through the Dublin championship. The craic was brilliant within the ranks. We had an amazing combination of hard men, fitness and skill.

The sessions after the championship games were legendary. Malahide Mondays took place in the beer garden of Gibney's and ended up in Tomango's. I loved the messing which went on. In my eyes I was just a teenage boy, playing in a team full of men in their twenties and thirties. There was just one other student in the squad; the rest of them worked and had regular lives. This meant two things. The first was that they were experienced when it came to life. The second was that I was the only one who was broke all the time. I still owe a lot of lads a lot of drinks from those early days.

We ended up in the county final playing against Erin's Isle. Erin's Isle were a brilliant team and had the backbone of the Dublin team playing for them at the time. Charlie Redmond, Mick Deegan and Keith Barr were three top-class players who had just won an All-Ireland with Dublin. They also had a heap of gifted young lads like Niall Crossan and Tony Gorman. They were the complete package, and playing against them really made me want to play better. I found that the bigger the occasion, the more I looked forward to it. While some lads got nervous when they thought of failing on the big stage, I always looked on it as a chance to perform.

It was a great game of football. We played in a packed Parnell Park and the play flowed from end to end. We managed to stifle their attack and, with Timmy Cummins and Shay Keogh in clinical form up front, we ground out a momentous victory against the favourites. It was a great win, a great day and a personal triumph; and yet I didn't properly comprehend it at the time. It was my first full season at senior level GAA. I was nineteen. I was a champion. I thought this would happen every year. Sylvester's haven't won a title since.

We annihilated the livers for three days solid and then had to go and play a league decider out in St Anne's of Bohernabreena in Tallaght. A lot of us were still drunk as we battled with the likes of Joe and Nipper McNally. Joe McNally was a monstrous man, the size of three Brian Silkes. They beat us by a couple of points and we were denied a league and championship double, but the party didn't stop.

My family had come to most of the games and my little sisters became big Sylvester's fans. Dad had collected newspaper clippings from the local newspapers which had reports and pictures from all the games. The success with Syls gave me something to share with my family. I was able to give something back in a way. While part of me was battling with twisted demons, another part of me was a good, wholesome, GAA player who loved to spend time with his family.

In the Leinster Championship we beat Simonstown from Meath and Killarerin from Wexford, to end up playing against Éire Óg from Carlow in the final. While Carlow were not renowned for their inter-county brilliance, Éire Óg had an incredible group of players back then. They were the reigning Leinster Champions and were favourites to beat us.

The training went up several notches as we approached the game. I was still smoking a daily spliff or two, but in the two weeks leading up to the game I didn't drink or go clubbing. It was the least I could do. I didn't look on smoking the wacky tabaccy as any kind of problem. It mellowed me in the evening or during the day. I didn't think it affected my fitness or my sharpness. It was an easy choice for me back then.

The game was played in a packed little stadium, down in Newbridge. My extended family travelled from around Ireland to see the match, and that created a real sense of occasion for me.

Within five minutes Deccy Barnes had been shown a red card. He was obviously targeted because of his short fuse, but he had no excuses when he decked one of their players in front of the ref. It put us on the back foot for the game. We battled and battled, but when our full back Dave Ryan was sent off for a second yellow card midway through the second half, we were in deep trouble. They scored the resulting penalty. I dived right and the ball went straight down the middle.

We never recovered, and they went on to beat us by five points. For the first time I felt the pain of losing a big game with the Sylvester's seniors. I was in tears in the dressing room. A few other lads had red eyes too. But as was the spirit of the men I played with back then, we were not allowed to feel sorry for ourselves. We had made it far beyond our early-season expectations. I remember chatting with Talts a few years later about what went wrong that day. Aside from the sendings-off, he had a theory that we just didn't see ourselves winning the All-Ireland club title. We were happy with being Dublin champions, and that was what let us down. It was not a physical shortcoming, but a mental one.

Early the following season, we used a sports psychologist. This was unheard of at club level, and it was met with some resistance and ridicule. The macho culture was alive and well within our group. Thinking that alterations in perception could improve performance was tantamount to wearing pink frilly dresses and sipping a nice chilled glass of chardonnay. So it didn't last long, and there were plenty of fields to be run around. The training was hard and Talts was relentless in pushing us on as a group.

Meanwhile, college life was ticking along. I was still a virgin. I didn't care too much – I was in no real hurry. It wasn't as though I couldn't get a girl or that I was shy around them; I was simply a little shy sexually. Women like a man to be forward but respectful, charming but a little insistent. I was yet to grasp this. I was still operating in the little-boy league of being funny and flirting. But a woman will not fuck you if you don't make it clear that you want to fuck her. And I was a little afraid of sex. Having been abused messed with my head a bit. And my parents had drilled us with the 'no sex before marriage' routine. Some of it had sunk in.

I signed up to play freshers football for UCD. Because I was playing for St Sylvester's in the Leinster campaign, the management knew who I was, and I was given the number 1 jersey. We had a team with the likes of John Divilly, Michael Savage and Brian Dooher. In the first round we played Queen's in Belfield in horrendous conditions. With a gale-force wind driving rain sideways across the pitch, both teams struggled to get any scores. That was until ten minutes before the end, when a high ball came in; I misjudged it in the wind and spilled to their full forward. As he went to run round me I took him down and conceded a penalty. He stepped up and dispatched the ball to the bottom corner of the net. We lost by two points.

The college exams came and I failed them all miserably. This was no surprise. I had done the minimum of study, and that was nowhere near enough. It meant that I had to repeat my exams in August. Most of my friends were heading to the USA for the summer, but I would be staying behind. I had GAA to play. I had exams to study for. I had responsibilities. I had to face up to them at some stage.

I will forever be in debt to Lisa Campbell, a friend who lent me her course notes. While she had studied and taken notes assiduously throughout the year, I had practically nothing. I looked at previous years' repeat papers and memorized a few answers. Between this and Lisa's notes, I scraped through all my exams with 2 or 3 per cent to spare. It was all I needed. I was in for another year.

The good times would keep on rolling.

4

In my second year in College, I got called up for the Dublin U/21s and was still number 1 for St Sylvester's – but I couldn't get a game with the University team. I travelled to Belfast and Athlone with them to play some games but never got off the bench. 'Do they know who you are?' Talts asked me one day on the way out to Sylvester's training. I was sure they did. Maybe they just didn't like me.

My dad was proud of me. It was a good feeling. MS was dragging him down slowly, but he still came to all my matches and was always ready to encourage me. He loved to talk football, philosophy and women. Sometimes we could argue over ideas for hours. But mostly we would talk football.

I trained with Syls twice a week and had matches with them and challenge games for the Dublin U/21s at the weekend. I was enjoying being back in the sporting groove. To top it all off, I had met a girl with bright pink hair in the College bar one day. We got to drinking and chatting, and before I knew it I woke up in bed beside her. I wasn't sure what had happened.

She told me we had shagged the night before. I was shocked. Wow, what a way to lose your virginity. To top it off she told me she had been a virgin too. We had sex again right away. This time I did remember it.

I was selected to play for the Dublin U/21s against Louth in the first round of the championship. We had a great team, with guys like Ciarán Whelan and Jason Sherlock. My clubmate Keith Galvin was captain. Keith had just won an All-Ireland, playing corner back with the seniors and was a top bloke as well as being a seriously talented footballer.

The game against Louth was a disaster. We prepared in the normal way, had a simple game plan, but were second best all around the park. I didn't have my best game ever and was beaten for a simple goal in the second half. It was a pitiful end to my first competitive start in a Dublin jersey. One loss and the season was over.

I was now studying only English and Philosophy. Both these subjects required a level of thought which I found easier to access when under the influence of hash. The abstract world of existentialism and the poetry of the greats seemed less alien when I was stoned.

I had a general rule never to play a game when stoned or drunk. But training was a different matter altogether. I was stoned at most club training sessions – mildly inebriated, mildly buzzed. I thought I was just as good as when sober. But I am sure now that that was a delusion – I was surely operating at only 70 or 80 per cent. Who knows what I might have achieved had I been sober?

The case against Father Payne was working away in the background all this time. I had to meet with lawyers and talk through various aspects of what had happened. It was never too far from my thoughts. It had become clear that Father Payne's superiors had known what he was doing but had done nothing about it except to move him from parish to parish. The anger I felt about this simmered away. The hash and the booze dulled the edges of my anger and allowed me to exist.

During that second year at College I also got into speed and acid. LSD was the strongest drug I had done. It planted thoughts and visions into my consciousness that were amazing and revolutionary. It was also the drug which brought on the giggles like no other. The simplest act could become the most hilarious.

Sometimes you might forget you were tripping, that's how tripped out you were. Other times you might get lost inside insane thought-worlds, or experience terrifying hallucinations. When I took acid, I made sure I had nothing to do for a few days afterwards. The risk of some short-term madness taking over was too large.

The older lads at Sylvester's would laugh at the head on me sometimes. They called me the New Age Traveller. At this stage I had bleached-blond hair with brown roots growing out underneath. I wore whatever clothes I could find and didn't really worry about looking sharp. I carried a bottle of Optrex Red Eye everywhere I went.

One Saturday evening I was at a party in a friend's house. We were sitting around in a bedroom, smoking hash and drinking cans. At one point there was some messing, and I got shoved off the end of the bed and landed on a pint glass, which broke up into my back. Luckily, the glass missed my spine and kidney by an inch either side; but it went in deep, and I was out of action for almost a month until the wound healed. No one believed my story . . . not in the hospital, my parents or with Sylvester's. The common consensus was that I'd been stabbed.

I drank and smoked more while recuperating, plunged a little deeper into the hole. I enjoyed the lack of training in a way: it meant I could get messed-up guilt-free. Training was the only thing keeping me relatively straight.

By the time my body had mended itself the Dublin U/21 campaign kicked off. Dave Billings, the manager, kept faith with me. We played against Offaly in the Leinster semi-final in Parnell Park and were a few points down with around ten minutes to go. A ball went over the sideline and it looked like one of their players pushed Dave Billings. All hell broke loose. I would normally wait for thirty seconds or so before going to get involved in something like that; this melee lasted long enough for me to run down to the far 45 and start dragging players away. In the aftermath we rallied to win the game. We beat them fair, square and a little bit crooked and we thought that was the end of it.

The Leinster Council had other ideas. There was an inquest into the fight. Some Offaly supporter had videoed everything. Fans with wine bottles had jumped fences to get involved. Players had been kicked in the head on the ground.

We were called in to Parnell Park a week later. Dave Billings sat with us in one of the dressing rooms. He filled us in on the details. Tears welled in his eyes and his voice broke as he laid out what was happening.

'Now, some lads have been suspended for between six months and two years. You'll know who they are as they are not here tonight. We are out of the championship. We are appealing, but there's not much chance of anything changing. It is a disgrace that they can ruin it for all of you like this, but that is what has happened. I want to thank you all for your efforts.'

That was it. Players filed quietly out of the room. I sat there. The over-bright dressing-room lights flickered. I was gutted. It didn't seem fair. We had a team good enough to win the All-Ireland, but now the season – and my under-21 career – was over.

I failed my college exams for the second year in a row. It meant I would be staying in Ireland for the summer and repeating exams in the autumn. I took up a job working on a building site for the summer for the chairman of Sylvester's, Terry Roche. It was a pretty handy job and the pay was great for a young lad.

That summer Dublin were beaten by Meath in the Leinster Senior Championship. Straight after the game, John O'Leary announced he was retiring from the inter-county scene.

John O'Leary had been my hero growing up. When my dad brought us to games back in the late '80s and early '90s, we always stood at the front of the Hill, behind the goal. From there, you could hear the Dublin players shouting and cursing at each other. You could see the steam coming from their jerseys on cold February days during the National League. You could see the power and venom of O'Leary's kicking. He didn't wear gloves, which I always thought was strange. Bruce Grobbelaar wore gloves . . . did O'Leary think he was better than Bruce Grobbelaar?

O'Leary's retirement was great news for me. I had been the U/21 keeper for two years and was playing for the county champions. With the Dublin number 1 now gone, I expected to get drafted on to the panel or be given a few trial games at least.

Meanwhile, Sylvester's went on another storming run through the club championship. We had really matured as a group and were unstoppable all the way to the final, where we met Erin's Isle in a repeat of the 1996 final. I had pulled off some great saves in the run-up to the decider. I was in the best form of my life. This time, though, we were beaten in front of another full house in Parnell Park.

Losing to that Erin's Isle team was no shame, but the dressing room was very quiet afterwards. We had gone from champions to nobodies, and it was the end of the road for some of the more senior lads. I found I drank even harder when I was commiserating than when I was celebrating. I turned up at a friend's house a few days later and projectile-vomited Southern Comfort all over her parents' brand-new couch. She had to call my mother, who dragged me home and put me to bed.

In the middle of the summer I went down to visit my mother's family in Ballygar, Co. Galway. The annual carnival was on and there was a seven-a-side soccer competition which my cousin Tom had entered us into. Tom was a hulk of a man, more suited to rugby than to soccer. My other cousins, Enda and Colm, joined us. Both were around 6' 4" and had played hurling for Roscommon. A couple of other stragglers joined us and we set out to play some soccer. We were big and strong. We had no mobility and no finesse. We had zero flair and no tactical direction. But we were tough, and we kicked lumps out of every team we played against.

In the semi-final we came up against a real soccer team from the locality – Shiven Rovers. They were a slick young outfit. They had shin pads and fancy-coloured boots. They even had matching jerseys! They dominated us in every part of the pitch, but they couldn't beat me. I was in nets and in my prime and the smaller seven-a-side goals meant I was not letting much past. We managed to scramble in the ugliest of goals from a long ball up the pitch and held on for a historic victory for the family.

In the final we were up against Mervue United. Mervue were the champions of the Connacht Senior League. They had some top-quality players. Cousins, aunties, uncles and grandparents all gathered in a small little pitch behind the Square in Ballygar town, to watch us take on the local heroes. The sun beamed high. The wind dropped to nothing.

They played us off the park. We chased them, kicked them and tackled them hard. We hoofed, hacked and harried. I was under intense pressure between the sticks and from a corner they scored with a header that took a deflection. We were in trouble. With a couple of minutes left I shouted at my cousin to cover the goal. I ran out towards the middle of the pitch where we had a throw in. I called for and got the ball and turned and ran at their defence. Their defenders backed off, unsure what to do in the face of a marauding keeper. My family were screaming from the sideline. I got about twenty-five yards from goal and lashed the ball with everything I had. It flew past their keeper and into the bottom corner of the net. The celebrations were ballistic.

The penalty shoot-out was a blur. It was three kicks each before it went to sudden death. We scored our first three. They scored their first two. Their third penalty-taker stepped up and slammed the ball to my right. I threw a fist at it and the ball bounced away. It was over. We were the Ballygar Carnival seven-a-side champions! My team-mates streamed down the pitch and jumped on me. Cousins, uncles, parents and grandparents all streamed on to the pitch. We danced around in sheer glee, then hit the local pub for the presentation and got absolutely baloobas.

I scraped through the repeat exams – a final year in UCD beckoned. The plan was to take this year seriously. I couldn't afford to mess it up. So I went to tutorials. I studied the notes and wrote the papers I was meant to. I handed in my mini-thesis in English and got a first. The title was 'The use of allegory and synecdoche in the poetry of Robert Frost, focusing on "The Ax-Helve"'. I was stoned when I wrote it and stoned when I handed it in.

I was also stoned when the professor of Modern English called me in to congratulate me. We talked about my thesis and about logic and language construction. We waffled about the meanings and under-standings to be taken from poetry. He invited me to come to meet some other students who were thinking at a different level about English and writing in general. I lost track of the conversation at some point – the stoniness took me to a faraway land. But it was a satisfying day for me.

Less satisfying was not getting called up for the Dublin Seniors. I was extremely frustrated with it. I was playing well, I had the pedigree and I was young and talented. I had hoped for a call-up for some trial games, but it didn't happen. I was now too old for the U/21s. As Christmas came and went I began to get disillusioned with life in Dublin. The road ahead was long . . . there was a mountain of study to do and I had to do it. The mountain would have looked a lot smaller if I was on the Dublin senior panel.

The trial of Father Ivan Payne was to take place in January. He was being tried on sample charges, and I wouldn't be named in court, but I felt a large degree of trepidation as the date came closer. I worried that the press could have gotten hold of my name somehow. My parents were the only people I'd told, apart from the police, but I wondered if my siblings had overheard something. I didn't want them to know what had happened. I didn't want any friends or extended family to know either. I didn't want to answer awkward questions or have my family face queries about it. I was ashamed of what had happened. I was ashamed and worried about what people would think.

The week leading up to the trial was a stress-fest. I bought a nice big block of hash and let the stone take away the pain and the memories. When I imagined Father Payne's blinking, twitching, rounded face, I got transported back to a time when I was a victim, a weak and useless little boy. Did I drink to forget? You can bet your bottom dollar I did. Did I do drugs to flake away the pain? Of course I did.

The trial started on a Monday morning in the Four Courts. I went in with my mother as my dad wasn't feeling great at the time. We scooted around the back of the reporters and made our way up to the gallery. From there we could see the barristers and solicitors, journalists and court staff and cops. Plonked in the middle, handcuffed to a uniformed Garda, was Father Ivan Payne, his head bowed. He had aged somewhat, his hair looked whiter now, but there was no mistaking his smooth, tanned skin and twitching eyes. He looked crushed. I stared at him and in a flittering moment of twisted emotion, I almost felt sorry for him. I took pity on his shameful life. There he was, a supposed holy man, being tried in a public court for abusing the innocent. I was filled with a deep sadness. As the session ended and he was led away, I felt deep hatred but also deep loss. How sick and perverted this world was.

The trial was the talk of my friends from the area. It came up over and over again . . . or at least so it seemed to me. I avoided talking about it. I didn't want anyone to know. 'Mad, isn't it,' was my standard reply. Mad that I was the one who blew the whistle on the creepy fucker, I thought to myself. In the end, Payne was sentenced to six years in prison. I had been hoping it might give me some peace. But nothing really changed inside me. I was still angry and bitter.

I was still seeing the girl with the pink hair. I felt I had to tell her about the abuse. It was great to be able to tell someone, but it affected our relationship for a while. A woman's natural instinct is to protect and to care, and that was what she wanted to do for me. It opened up a different side of her female psyche to me. But it was not the side I wanted her to open. I wanted to be a strong, powerful, sexual man.

It was a messed-up time. I was becoming more and more reckless when I was drunk. I wanted to do the most outrageously stupid things. I was prone to back-flip off bar stools, vandalize random objects and put myself in dangerous situations.

I cannot look back and blame Father Payne for everything, but it was a big contributing factor. It made me feel empty and gave me a sensation of hopelessness. Sometimes I just didn't care what happened to me or to those around me. There was a black cloud on the horizon and inside my head I felt at odds with the world. It may not have been apparent from the outside. To the untrained eye I was outgoing and lively. I was good at football. I had a brain and a girlfriend. But in the quiet times, in the down times and whenever I was alone, the dark gremlins would creep around the corner. And for that, I had Father Payne to thank.

One evening I was at a party in my sister's flat in Fairview. I arrived late and was pretty hammered, having been drinking with my girlfriend for the afternoon and evening. The party was in full swing and I necked a pill and began to melt into the couch. As the pill kicked in I got a quare feeling of restlessness. So I decided to try and surprise the party by going outside and appearing through the living-room window, which was open. The only problem was that the window was on the third floor of an old Georgian house.

I went around the side of the house and looked up towards the window. There were two gutters I could climb. At the top, I would need to leap across a three- or four-foot gap, grab the sill and hoist myself up.

I began climbing. As I shimmied up, I went past a second-floor window of the adjoining house. A couple were rolling around in bed, under the covers. I stopped and looked in and then kind of came to my senses and kept climbing.

As I got to the top I realized that I had no hope of getting across the gap to the ledge. I looked down at the ground . . . it seemed a long way away. The pill was kicking in strong and my eyes were having trouble focusing. I panicked a little. Shimmying down, I picked up too much speed and lost my grip on the piping. I fell the last twelve feet or so and landed in a crumple on the concrete.

I lay on the ground for a minute or so and then gingerly picked myself up. Nothing seemed broken – but then I felt this almighty pain at the base of my right heel. I hobbled back into the party, said nothing and carried on.

My heel was heavily bruised and I could barely walk for a few weeks. I had to stop training with the club again, and this allowed me some time to relax and just do nothing. I got chatting with a friend in the pub one night. Joxer was a musician and I was a writer. We would talk about philosophy, Bob Dylan and football. He was driving a van to earn a living at the time and we got to talking about travelling. The idea of going to Australia came up. Maybe we could head over for a year and get away from the shite here in Dublin.

I liked the sound of it. I still had thoughts of playing for the Dubs, but it seemed further off than ever right now. I was out injured and way down the pecking order. There had been trial games and challenge matches but I had received no call-up. The court case had drained me and I was feeling quite glum about my prospects in Ireland. I had a chat with my girlfriend about it. She seemed keen and talked to a friend of hers about going over too. We made a vague plan to leave after Christmas. I would get my degree, save some money and get the fuck out of Dodge.

I would have to break the news to my family gently. My brother was living in Spain and had plans to move to the US after he graduated university, but my parents and sisters were all very settled in Dublin, and I was close to them. Nights in the house were always filled with laughter and banter. I knew that if I went overseas I would be gone for a year at least . . . and I had a feeling it would be much longer. It was a tough conversation to have. I didn't want them to think I was rejecting them. The simple story was that I needed something completely new and fresh. Otherwise I was on a path to some serious mental problems. I loved them all dearly and loved being around them . . . but a man has got to go and be a man sometimes.

My dad was extremely supportive. He understood that I needed to grow up and be on my own. My sisters and my mother gave me their blessing too. It was a relief for the wholesome young GAA man inside me: now I had permission to go and sample some true freedom.

I prepared for final exams by studying the questions asked in previous years. The professors and tutors also dropped multiple hints as to what type of questions might be asked. I gambled a bit in my preparations, but the gamble paid off and I graduated with honours in English and Philosophy from the University College of Dublin.

I got another job working on the building sites, trying to save money for travelling. I was working with lunatics but I enjoyed it. Meanwhile, I was ticking away with Sylvester's, though the wheels had come off a little there, and we were not the force we had been in the two years previous. I mentioned to the management that I was thinking of heading to Australia. Terry Roche sat me down and had a heart-to-heart with me. He asked me to write down any job I wanted and he would help organize something for me if I stayed. The only thing I could think of was being a journalist. He told me to leave it with him, but to seriously consider staying.

At the end of the summer I swapped the building sites for a job as night porter in a hotel out in Howth. Being a night porter meant arriving at 11 p.m. and looking after the residents' bar if there were guests drinking late. If there had been a function that evening I would clean the toilets and reorganize the tables for whatever was on the next day. After this I could sit back and relax and have a quiet pint or two in the corner – far away from the security cameras. In the morning I would prepare the breakfasts for any guests leaving early.

Arriving to work at 11 p.m. meant there was no chance of me turning up completely straight. I had a few cans or spliffs before coming in to work. And the fun didn't stop there. I would be behind reception for a good hour or two until the upstairs bar closed. One evening I was manning the station and got chatting to a couple of

lads who were obviously on drugs of some sort. It turned out they
had lots of cocaine and were more than happy to share it with me.
They gave me the bag and I chopped out a giant line behind the
reception desk. As I was doing so, the general manager – I'll call him
Mr Keegan – came out from the residents' bar. I covered the cocaine
with the book I was reading. The two boys looked over a little nervously as Mr Keegan came in behind the reception, pretending to be
looking for something. He began to make idle chit-chat while scouring the reception.

'And who are these lads?' he asked in a whisper.

'Just waiting for a taxi, Mr Keegan . . . all good.'

'OK now, I need the function room reset for that wedding
tomorrow.'

He blabbed on for a little, before making his exit. I looked over at
the lads and they broke up laughing.

'Fuck it!' I said as I pulled back the book and hoovered up the
coke. We had a good laugh as I handed them back the bag. Resetting
the trestle tables that night took less time than usual.

Not all my drug experiences ended up as pleasantly. One evening
I got a call for room service. I poured two pints of Heineken and
brought them up to the room. It was three or four in the morning
and all was quiet in the hotel. I knocked on the door and said, 'Room
Service.' A male voice told me to come in. As I entered I smelled the
familiar scent of hashish. The room contained two single beds and
there were two burly-looking skinheads smoking a spliff.

'Put them down over there,' one man instructed me in a thick
Northern Irish accent.

'Do you smoke?' the other asked me.

'I do,' I replied.

'Sure sit down and roll us a spliff sure.'

So I did. I turned on the walkie-talkie and rolled a joint, which I
sparked up.

'Do you do coke too?' one asked.

'Ah sure I do,' I answered, and before I knew it there were three fat
lines in front of me. I snorted one quickly and they got to talking.

They began to ask about the prices of drugs in Dublin. They talked about quantities and were intimating that they were down to do a big deal of sorts. They ridiculed me about a few different things, and I felt a bit uneasy. One of the men sat up on the bed and moved a little closer to me. I took a look at the tattoos on his forearms and noticed that they were Union Jacks with bulldogs and some kind of weapons and thorns mixed together. I got the heebie-jeebies and tried to make my excuses.

'Where are you goin' hey, sure there's nothing to be doin'?' they started heckling. My mind began swirling and I got the sweats from the coke and the spliff kicking in at once. As I opened the door I heard them utter some words which sounded like, 'Say anything and we'll come and kill ye, you little fucker.'

I let the door slam shut behind me and hurried down the hall. I went straight to the hotel kitchen and over to the chef's knives, which were stuck to some magnets at the side of the fridges. I picked the largest one I could find and then slid down behind the meat freezers. I sat there. I sat there and waited. The whirr of the fridges filled the aural void. A clock ticked above the entry/exit doors. Everything was dark and still.

I took out a piece of paper I had in my pocket and began to scribble a note. I wrote that I had been threatened by men in Room 119. I wrote that they were in the UDA. I told my mother and girlfriend I loved them and crumpled up the paper and placed it in my pocket. I was frightened. I thought they might be coming down after me at any second. I contemplated calling the cops or someone from the hotel. I thought about calling my family. But in the end I did nothing.

I did nothing except sit in the kitchen for three hours until the sun came up. I sat there with the knife close by my side and watched the clock count down until the receptionist came in at 7 a.m. I went down to reception a half-hour beforehand, and the panic and fear I had felt abated. Nothing had happened. No one had come for me. I had freaked the fuck out and had gone into a crazy demented state of paranoid delusion.

The drugs, I thought to myself, the drugs really do mess me up sometimes.

On a different evening I was alone behind reception. The hotel was completely locked up and only four rooms were occupied. These were my favourite nights. It meant having a few pints, watching some late-night TV, and a good snooze until half an hour before reception opened. The phone rang, and a lady in Room 113 wanted two gin and tonics. I made the drinks and headed up the stairs, knocked on the door and announced, 'Room Service.' The lady answered, 'Come in,' and I opened the door.

I walked in with the drinks and looked at the lady. She was lying, naked, on the bed, with a white sheet covering her nether regions. I asked where did she want the drinks and she replied, 'Over here, beside the bed.' I carried the tray over and placed the drinks on the bedside table, trying to avert my eyes from her boobs. She was a lady in her late fifties, I'd have guessed. Blonde hair cut short. She was obviously quite drunk. She moved her knee up at an angle and turned on her side to face me.

'Why don't you join me for a drink?' she asked suggestively, her eyes lowered like some kind of seductress.

'I can't I'm afraid, I have work to do,' I lied.

I was tempted by the madness of it all, but something about the situation screamed danger. On top of that I still had a girlfriend. And she was in her fifties or sixties . . . I returned to reception and the external phone rang. It was a young man who was trying to track his mother. He described this lady to a 'T' and was genuinely worried. She had stayed here before when she went on one of her binges. I told him I couldn't reveal the identity of anyone to anybody but the police. He wouldn't take no for an answer, and twenty minutes later he was at the front of the hotel, banging to be let in.

Eventually I had to call the cops on this guy. They came and explained the same story to him. She was a grown woman who had the right to do whatever she wanted. She was doing what she wanted all right, drinking G&Ts and hitting on the young night porter!

After a few months of saving money, I was ready to book flights to Australia. I had hoped my girlfriend would come with Joxer and me, but eventually she decided she was going to stay in Dublin and do a postgraduate course. I was shocked. I thought we were going to travel together and be a couple. That was not going to happen now.

So me and the bould Joxer went and booked our flights, stopping off in Bangkok for four nights, before landing in Sydney. I was all over the place emotionally. I was extremely excited to be heading to a new country . . . a new life. I was nervous to be leaving home for the first time. I was sad to be leaving my family and friends behind. I was gutted that my girlfriend had stayed behind. I had fallen for her. But she chose the career path over the 'let's just go and see what happens' path. We made plans to keep in touch, and agreed that she would follow when she was finished. But I knew things would never be the same.

She came with my family and dropped me and Joxer to the airport. There were hugs and tears in the departures lounge, but once we made our way past security and beyond the waving hands and wet eyes, we started hooting and high-fiving each other. We headed straight to duty free – where, funnily enough, we met my former Dublin minor manager, Alan Larkin. He was delighted to see me and wished me well. I took this as a good omen and a sign from the GAA: go do what you have to do, young man; we'll be waiting for you when you return.

I was ready to see what the big bad world had to offer.

5

Bangkok, January 1999

Night had fallen in Bangkok. Through the hotel window I heard distant dulled beeps and shouts from thirty floors below.

I looked again at the night sky and the skyscrapers which dotted the horizon. This earth was a magnificent, tumultuous place, I thought. I put down my beer, picked up my notebook and wrote the words '*not banging much in Bangkok*'. I underlined the two bangs. Bang bang.

I stood up and walked over to the window, flicked open the safety catches. The warm night air licked in around the air-conditioned hotel air. It was filled with sweat, spices and fumes. It carried smog and wet, perfumed heat. The sounds of honking cars, vrooming engines and shouting hordes were much closer now. They passed through my ears, my eyes and nose. They swarmed my senses.

I climbed up on to the window ledge and I felt that whirling, fluttery feeling in my belly. I gulped back the last of the beer. I held the side of the window and looked down to the cars, the concrete and the people below. Then I started to inch my way out along the narrow ledge. My toes dangled freely over the edge. I moved to where I could no longer safely be grabbed by anyone.

My eyes scanned the city horizon and the busy streets below. Lights flickered and shadows moved. It was serenity itself and I felt calm inside. I thought about my family so far away . . . I was going to miss them. My sad heart thumped heavily inside me. I thought of my sisters laughing in an empty kitchen and the squinting frown of the paedophile, Ivan Payne. There was a vast black distance being laid out in front of me . . . It was good to be going far away, I needed life to change. I wondered if it would matter if I fell. Would I really care? I swayed a little and clamped my hands backwards to stop myself falling. I was calm, but my mind was racing.

I stared out at the blinking night-time world. I was free. For the first time in my life I was completely free to do whatever the fuck I wanted. And I was standing on a window ledge thirty floors up, tee-tering on the brink of death. One gust of wind and the ultimate memory obliteration would be mine.

I heard a shout from behind me. I turned and saw Joxer's head poking out the window. I had left him down in the hotel bar when I came back up to get some smokes.

'What the fuck are you doing out here, man? Come in, you fuck-ing idiot.'

I looked at him sheepishly. I grimaced. I knew he was right. I began to inch my way over, little by little, until I could grab his arm and could grip the inside of the sliding window. He hoisted me in and I stood on the soft carpet floor again.

'That's some fucking attention-grabbing bollix . . . what the fuck are you playin' at?'

'I don't know,' I answered. 'I don't know.'

'Are you OK, man? Seriously?' he asked again.

'Yeah, I think so . . . I don't know what happened.'

He looked at me for a short while and just left it at that. He didn't push it and never mentioned it again. It wasn't as though I was acting depressed – I was just a little crazy.

We went back down to the hotel bar, where we had met some South African women. These women came to Bangkok to buy cheap clothes and resell them in Africa. Joxer had told them we were musi-cians, he being the guitar-playing singer and I the drummer. They were suitably impressed. They took us under their wing and brought us to a famous live music bar on Patpong Road. We were given the best seats in the house and the manager came and introduced himself.

When the main band came back from their break, the manager of the club joined them and took the microphone. He was a small Thai man who spoke in broken English.

'Lady and Genta man,' he announced 'We awe so happy tonight to annouw the wewwwy spewcia guest.'

The crowd all cheered and gave applause.

'Would you pewee wewcome to de stage, all the way fom Iweland . . . Mista Joxaaa and Mista John!'

The crowd of 300 or so erupted in applause. I instinctively stood up and milked it, but Joxer was having none of it. He was a real singer and guitarist, but I was a complete blagger. Nevertheless, I saddled up there and took my place behind two giant conga drums and started thumping them. Nobody seemed to care that my rhythm was terrible – apart from the band. They knew straight away and gave me the strangest of looks while I was up there. When I finished, the crowd went wild and gave me a rapturous ovation.

My adrenalin kicked in and I unleashed myself on Bangkok. I ended the night at some strip joint, drinking with a creepy English lad called Richie. He looked like a wrinkled version of the Milky Bar Kid. Joxer and the women had long since gone home, but I was on a mission. My eyes were like water-filled balloons. The women were incredibly beautiful. They were sent to your table to talk to you and get you to buy drinks. They called you handsome and would touch you gently on the arms. It didn't feel that sleazy . . . in fact I thought they were the sweetest and cutest girls ever. But I was wet behind the ears and had a belly full of drink in me.

On my way to the toilet, a couple of girls came up and danced around me; one grinded into me from the front and the other from behind. Two more came over, laughing and dancing around me. I was the king of the world right then. Tacky pop music blared over the speakers. A disco ball reflected purple, red and silver flashes. I strobe-danced in a glittering empire of lusty delights. I laughed in slow motion triumphantly. As I revelled in my greatness I saw something flick towards the ground to my right. A second glance and I saw my passport land. I blinked again, looked up and the girls had disappeared. My bum bag had been emptied.

I was a goofy kid back then. I'd put everything I had into a bum bag and strapped it to my belly. By the time I realized they were robbing and not idolizing me, I was one credit card and $100 lighter. It wasn't the worst result in the world. They saw me coming about five miles away and I probably deserved it for being such a twat earlier in the day. Maybe there was some kind of obtuse karmic connection – put yourself in a position where you could die unnecessarily and you will be robbed . . .

We flew to Sydney a few days later. We were staying with a friend of mine from college called Gary. Gary was gay, and no sooner had we landed than he had us down in a trannie bar on Oxford Street. It was another eye-opening night. We went back to a party hosted by a tall and handsome transsexual called Lynda. Lynda gave us a tour of her place; the bedroom featured mirrors on all the walls and the ceiling. There were handcuffs on the table-side locker and the print of choice was leopard.

We sat around, drinking goon and smoking some potent Australian grass. Goon was cheap wine you bought in a cardboard cask. I looked over at Lynda. She was wearing a really tight miniskirt, had huge protruding cleavage and looked like a high-class hooker. It was crazy. I felt compelled to look at her cock area and saw no bulge or bump at all. I thought it might have been tucked backwards under her ass in some kind of special holder. My curiosity got the better of me and when she looked over I had to ask.

'Eh, Lynda, where do you put it?' I inquired.

'Where do I put what, honey?' she asked back lasciviously, her eyes fluttering.

'Where do you put your cock?'

She looked at me with a pout of her lips and a drop of her shoulders.

'Why don't you open your mouth and I'll show you.'

Everybody howled with laughter and I genuinely blushed. Joxer bowled over in a cackle of deep stomach chortles. I had no comeback and it shut me up pretty quickly.

Sydney had morning clubs, evening clubs, nightclubs and recovery clubs. Everywhere was a buoyant mix of outrageous queens, tough-nut bikies, cool euro clubbers and regular degenerates. And there were drugs, lots and lots of drugs.

One night Gary brought us to a club called Helmut. The club had a giant metal door and some really tough-looking doormen. They checked us out, asked a few questions and let us in. The music was pumping trance and the dance floor was packed. Leather-clad men with assless pants were being dragged around by giant trannies. Random men would smack them and yank the chains attached to their dog collars. Camp topless boys dressed as fairies flung their arms in the air, wobbling on tall, purple stilettos. Glittering pink lights shimmered and flashed against darkened mirrors. The smell of amyl nitrate permeated the air.

Gary asked me to follow him to the bar. En route he took a right into the toilets. I looked inside and couldn't believe what I was seeing. There were about ten men in there; some were naked; some were half clothed and others on their knees. They were wanking, sucking and gripping each other. There were cocks everywhere. Gary started laughing. 'Watch this,' he whispered to me as I stood there in shock. He walked over and slapped the ass of one lad who was getting head.

At that point, Joxer and I fled.

A few days later I met a guy who had some connections in the GAA world in Sydney. He told me there was some handy work on building sites available with the occasional game of Junior B standard football thrown in. I followed up, and within a week I was dossing around as a chippy's labourer and training two nights a week in Bondi Junction. The pay was cash in hand and my boss would literally come to training and stuff a bundle of notes into my hand.

One night we went to meet some friends in an Irish pub called the Cock and Bull. We may as well have been in Carrick-on-Shannon. There was Irish music, Irish women, Irish dancing, Irish Guinness, Irish GAA jerseys and Irish messing. I felt cheated. I was working with Irish, playing GAA with Irish and now drinking in an Irish pub. What the fuck had I travelled 17,000 kilometres for? I vowed never to enter that pub again and to jack in my job and the training.

Part of me knew it was a bad idea. The GAA had always looked after me. Whenever I was playing and training hard, life was relatively good. The thing was that, so soon after leaving Ireland, I needed a break. I needed to forget. I wanted some new experiences. Playing in goals in Sydney for a ragball team was not part of the agenda. At some stage I would come back to the sport I loved so much, but now was not the time. It was time to do some living.

I got a few nights a week working as a dish pig, a few weeks' work making wheelie bins. Then we decided that it would be worth our while getting out of Sydney. Joxer fancied hitting the open road and seeing some of the vast country of Australia. I liked the idea. We began hatching plans.

We bought ourselves a Kombi van for $1,000 and planned to head up the coast. We picked up a friend called Kaitlyn who would share the costs with us as we travelled. Kaitlyn was a backpacker who worked as an S&M mistress to fund her travels. She had a long, pale face, big grey eyes and the softest Scottish accent. I was fascinated with her work and asked her all about it.

'It's not sex, Lenny,' she told me in her gentle Edinburgh brogue. 'I mean, if some guy wants to pay me $50 to piss on him, then why shouldn't I? I mean, you'd do it if it was the other way round, right?'

'You have me there,' I answered.

I became a single man again in Sydney. I tried calling my girlfriend once a week and getting into an internet café occasionally, but it was too hard. This was before the time of Skype, Facebook and smartphones. We were drifting apart. When she told me she was going to Japan and had met someone else, I was relieved more than anything else. It freed me up to roam and pillage.

Finally hitting the open road was bliss – just me, Joxer and our Scottish S&M mistress. We smoked a little grass and listened to Creedence, Bob Marley and Bob Dylan. Life was free and easy. We stopped off in the evenings and would cook up beans and pot noodles on our little camper stove. It was simple and we got to stop in some amazing remote locations. At night the three of us crammed into the back of the van, where we slept on a double mattress. Kaitlyn was sandwiched in the middle of the two of us but, aside from a little spooning, there was nothing untoward.

At the end of one night in Byron Bay, Kaitlyn was a little hammered. We were on our way back to sleep in the van when she turned to me.

'Lenny . . . why don't we stay somewhere else tonight?'

I looked at her with my eyebrows up and my hips swivelling. Joxer was already asleep in the back of the van.

'Come on . . . let's just stay in a hotel for the night and fuck!'

I was drunk, single and needed the experience. She put a hotel room on her credit card – $100 it cost her. It was a hefty sum in back-packing world.

We rocked into Brisbane a few weeks later and parked the van up in a hostel. Kaitlyn decided to keep travelling with some Italian guys she'd met. We said our goodbyes, and I went out looking for work as Joxer and I were now officially broke. When I returned I found a letter with my name on it inside the van. I scampered off to read it in private. Inside was a pair of slightly soiled panties and a note saying 'In memory of our $100 night . . . xxx.'

Joxer and a few other lads we had met were very curious about the letter. They kept pressing me and questioning me. I was smug and evasive in answering them. After a while though, they began to let it slip.

'Nice pair of dirty knickers in there, Lenny, was there?'

I looked at them and it slowly dawned on me. It was a scam. They fell around laughing. They had stitched me up. I made a mental note to tell Joxer less about my sexual experiences in the future.

I was a long way from home, physically and mentally – but I was following the progress of the Dubs. They made it as far as the Leinster final that summer, where they were beaten by eventual All-Ireland Champions Meath. Lots of guys I had played with at minor and U/21 were involved: Ciarán Whelan, Jason Sherlock, Ian Robertson, Paddy Christie, Keith Galvin, Mick O'Keeffe. Part of me dreamed of being involved in front of the big crowds and the TV cameras. Part of me knew that I wasn't far away in terms of ability. Seeing all these lads made it mean that there was hope for me yet.

But while they were slogging it out and training hard to perform, I was smoking grass and driving up the East Coast of Australia in a van. While they were lifting weights, I was drinking beers, snorting speed and shagging S&M mistresses. I was a long way away physically, but even more so emotionally. So while the thought of getting back to the top was there in my mind, I knew I had to enjoy myself while I was away.

In Brisbane we got jobs in an Irish bar. When off duty, we partied hard. I met an Aussie girl there and went up to North Queensland with her for a while. We sailed the Whitsunday Islands, but employment was scarce. In the end we hitched back to Sydney for the Millennium New Year party. It took us three days to travel 2,000 kilometres. We slept rough one night on a bench beside a field full of thousands of cane toads. At night the sky filled with swarms of migrating bats. We made it to Sydney in time for the fireworks and got straight into the pills. At this stage a big group of my school and college friends had arrived in Sydney. I found a job working in a bar on Oxford Street and life began to get real messy.

There was a lot of speed floating around in those days. Speed was the perfect drug for me at the time – it kept you awake and let you drink without getting too drunk. It also made me deranged enough to allow myself to shag women other than my girlfriend. I wasn't proud of myself, but I was young, horny – and women . . . well, women wanted to shag me. I was an amoral, drugged-up, drunken womanizer.

Around this time I got a call from home that my granny had passed away. When I heard the news I took to the streets and walked and cried for hours on my own. She was my godmother and someone who I loved dearly. I ended up in a dingy bar at the back of Kings Cross and sat drinking a few beers, looking deep into the past. I wanted to be home to share the pain with my flesh and blood. I wanted to be back there to try and cheer people up. I wanted to be there to be involved in all that was going on.

Instead I was drinking crap beer in a hovel in a land far away. I was full of self-pity and self-loathing. I questioned all the decisions I had made to be where I was right then. In Ireland, I had been close to playing for the team of my boyhood dreams. Was I capable of achieving anything any more? Was I the kind of tenacious and determined character who never gave up? Had I the guts to keep trying in the face of all adversity?

It didn't seem to me that I had any of the necessary mental strength. I felt weak and useless. I felt as low as I ever had.

A few days later another call came from Ireland. It was Terry Roche, the Sylvester's chairman. He was touching base, wondering what I was up to. By that point I had been away for over a year. He wanted me to know that I was still in their thoughts and plans. I thanked him and went to clear my head. Life in Ireland was beckoning me back. It meant security, stability and love. It meant there was still the chance of excelling and some day getting back into the reckoning for the Dubs. It was tempting. The angel on my shoulder told me to consider it wisely.

Instead, I just carried on doing what I was doing. The addict in me didn't want to give up what I was doing. I was allowing myself to drift far away from what I knew I should be doing. In fact I was forcing myself to. The devil inside did not want a pure and happy life; he wanted a fucked-up, sordid and twisted affair. He wanted sex, drugs and rock and roll, and that was a lot easier to get in inner-city Sydney than in suburban North County Dublin.

So this pattern of debauchery continued for the majority of the year. I put the thoughts of Ireland, the GAA and family firmly to the back of my head and vowed to return to them at some stage. I was going to carry on, helter-skelter. I had a cool job running a bar in the heart of Sydney's party district. I had a big extended group of friends and I had women who loved the man I was trying to become. Life became a blur of late nights, early mornings and sweaty mayhem.

The following New Year's Eve we went to a late-night hospitality workers' party in Q-Bar on Oxford Street. My girlfriend and all my work mates were there. My boss was a woman who was a year or so older than me. We really enjoyed each other's company. Nothing had happened between us, but there was an obvious attraction there. On this night she asked me to store a bag of her belongings in my place, as I lived just around the corner from the club. I nipped back and, as I dropped the bag on the ground, I saw a pair of her knickers in there. I got some twisted ideas.

I returned to the club, got a drink and joined the group around the dance floor. I stooped low into the ear of my boss and told her I was wearing a pair of her panties. Above the pumping music she leaned in closer and shouted, 'What did you say?'

'I'm wearing your panties,' I screamed back at her, the disco lights flashing and the crowds cheering in the background. I was coming up on a pill and felt wobbly and euphoric.

She looked at me incredulously.

'Come on, I'll show you!'

The club had photo booths and we went inside one, drew back the curtains and sat down, sharing the single seat. My hands shook as I undid the top of my pants to reveal the lace of her black panties. Her eyes narrowed like a cat's, she pulled me in and we kissed passionately. At that very second the curtain flew back and I turned to see my girlfriend standing there.

'You facking bastard!' she screeched and slapped me across the face, then pulled the curtain shut. Before I could do anything, the curtain flew back across. Another venomous hand flew in and slapped me across the face a second time. The curtain slid closed again. I was now completely up on the pill I had taken and I just looked back at my boss, exhaled deeply and began to laugh. What a messed-up world I inhabited. I really was a slimy degenerate. I went out to chase after my girlfriend, but was told to let her go by her friends.

My mind was spinning and the drugs were kicking in hard. Thoughts swirled and blanked. There was little I could do now besides click the giant 'Fuck It' button.

I ordered shots, got more pills and went on the rampage. I went from club to party to woman to party to drugs to work to woman to work.

Five days later I returned home to my apartment. My girlfriend had moved out. I was a shivering, shattered mess, running on the fumes of emptiness. I gave notice to the landlord and moved into an old converted coffee shop with some friends. I started seeing my boss, having break-up sex with my ex and shagging another couple of girls. But I was a complete ghost of myself.

After a lot of soul-searching I decided it was time to go home. Australia had broken me. The wild city living, the drink, the drugs and the women had pushed me to the brink.

I left a few days after Mardi Gras, which is a gay festival in Sydney. Oxford Street was mayhem. Our bar was rammed. I wore black-and-white striped pants and a pink singlet which was ripped down the middle. My hair was peroxide-dyed in the style of a reverse mullet: short everywhere except over the ears. I had a miniature glitter disco ball hanging from my nipple piercing. I was off my face and spent the evening running around, doing lines and dancing on bar counters. The night passed in a blur of flashing lights, shattered smiles and intoxicated black. It was a fitting end to my time in Australia.

6

I arrived back in Dublin at the end of the Irish spring. I had been gone almost two and a half years and I was completely empty. My brain was like two eggs over easy. My body had the flesh of a bulimic teen. I was as fit as a puddle.

I had missed the *Evening Herald* sports reports, my mother's wholesome cooking and giggles with my sisters. I had missed the soft drizzly rain, the thoughts of who would win an All Star and the roar of the crowd on the Hill. The idea of getting back to playing a high level of sport was never far from my mind, but the harsh reality was something I would now have to deal with.

In my time away I had played just one game of football. I had spent a few weeks training when I first arrived in Sydney, but after that I had done nothing but drink, smoke and do drugs.

My family were happy to have me home. I was happy to see them too. My dad was still full of optimism for my chances in the sporting world. Every day he spoke about what I should and could be doing. While his physical health had deteriorated somewhat, he was still able to get out and about, and his mind was as sharp as ever. He encouraged me to get back into playing something as soon as possible.

I had missed him. His encouragement and belief had always helped push me on. He had always helped me believe I could do better. The Dubs and Sylvesters were still training and playing football week in week out. I was the one who had left. I was the one who had tapped out. I realized I was not the centre of the universe.

The road back began with a trip out to Sylvester's on a cloudy Saturday morning for training. Things had changed. Barney Rock, the former Dublin player, was now manager. The squad had almost halved in size. Most of the older lads were gone. The training was haphazard and disorganized. As I jogged around, filling the lads in on some of the gory details of my time away, I felt very out of touch.

My mind wandered back to sunny beaches, sexy disco dancers and surging drugs. As I wheezed around the bumpy pitch I felt a heavy dread. I wasn't sure I could take it. I had been taking drugs and partying for over two years solid. I was completely out of kilter.

I picked up some bar work in the bar of a swanky hotel called The Morrison. Keith Richards from the Rolling Stones was a regular and my favourite of the celebs who turned up there. We got on well. He had a natural charisma, he loved the craic and always tipped well. The hours were late and long but I needed the money. It was hard to make training and play matches. I was battling to get some regularity in my life. But working in a bar and drinking on my days off was not conducive to any kind of decent lifestyle.

Meanwhile the Dublin keeper Davey Byrne got injured and a young U/21 keeper called Stephen Cluxton came in for him. Had I stayed in Dublin, I thought, that could have been me. I felt bitter, but vowed to do my best to get to the top.

Sylvester's had lost their division 1 status while I was away and were struggling to be competitive. As uninspired as I was, I needed to make an effort. I saw an ad for a nine-to-five job as a Customer Services Officer with Ulster Bank. It would mean I could train and have weekends free like the rest of the normal world. I went for some interviews and tests and managed to convince them I could do the job.

The job was in the Malahide branch of Ulster Bank. I moved in with an old friend Stevie in Portmarnock. There were four or five friends living here at any one time. It was homely mayhem. I could catch a bus and be in work ten minutes later. But working in the bank was a complete culture shock. I was responsible for people's money and it was mind-numbing work. The lack of gratification was offset by the regularity of a good weekly wage and weekends off. I was not here to work my way up the corporate ladder. I was here to try and get normal. But it was like wrapping a frog in cling film.

I would have a couple of cans with the lads some weeknights. On others I would open a bottle of wine, smoke a spliff and paint or write in my room. I had a split personality which was in a state of constant flux. The thoughtful artist and writer battled with the vapid womanizing jock. Both were fuelled by intoxicants. I struggled to reconcile the two people I was. Getting a little inebriated and painting or writing brought meaning to my life. It made me happy. But I was never completely satisfied.

In Oz I had given up smoking grass. It was too potent and caused me such severe paranoia that I imagined people were constructing convoluted and complicated conversations just to get at me. So it was nice to get back to the mellow buzz of hashish. Once Friday came, though, I needed to get smashed. Part of me was still living with a deep, unresolved pain, and getting fucked up was my form of denial. I often called in sick on Mondays, physically and emotionally depleted from the madness of the weekend.

On my birthday a big group of us went into town. I bought a bag of pills and was scoffing them for fun. We were in Capital Bar, on George's Street. I was off my head, running around, dancing, drinking cocktails and being a wobbly-jawed nuisance. I was on the dance floor, swinging around some girls. I took a shine to one and moved in a little closer. The strobes flashed, the bass bins boomed and legs and arms were flying. I was a dream monkey charting a voyage to liquid infinity.

Next thing I knew, two burly-looking lads were in front of me, pointing and shouting. My eyes rolled and I struggled to understand them. One had a beer bottle in his hand. He swung and cracked it off my forehead. I fell back in a daze, blood coming from the wound. A security guard jumped in the way, but this scumbag leaped over and jammed the broken bottle into the side of my neck. I collapsed backwards and blood squirted from the second wound. Security and management dragged me away, back to where I thought my friends were. Others grappled with these guys and dragged them and some of their group out the side entrance. Blood pumped from my head and neck. I was in shock but charging on the pills I had consumed.

I bolted out the front door and stormed across George's Street. My adrenalin had skyrocketed and the speed, coke and MDMA were rattling through my system. I began doing Jackie Chan-style kicks and punches at no one in particular. The security guards looked over at me, shaking their heads. I sprinted back across the road. Blood was dripping down my skull and from my neck. I was too hyped up to care. The blood felt like hot melting skittles plopping down my face. I liked it.

'Where the fuck are they?' I shouted, doing a quick karate chop at no one. I couldn't contain my body movements.

'If I was you I'd go back inside now,' one of the doormen answered.

'Fuck that, where the fuck are those cowardly cunts?' I demanded. I felt I could take them all out.

At that point, one of them looked over and saw me.

'There he fuckin' is,' I heard him shouting. Ten ugly fat-headed dirtbags turned and stared, then began to run around the corner towards me.

The security guard leaned in with a very worthwhile suggestion.

'If I was you, I would start running.'

I turned on my heels and began to sprint up George's Street. I had a clear run in front of me. Behind me this group of fat overweight fucks hurled bloodthirsty roars at me.

I had a ten-metre start, and these lads were not in good running shape. After fifty metres only one guy was still within a few metres of me. I turned to him and laughed like Nelson from *The Simpsons* – 'HA HA' – and accelerated across the road. I sprinted hard down a side street and did not look back. I ran for my life all the way up towards Christchurch, before slowing down and hailing the first empty taxi I could see. I was careful not to let the blood from my neck soil the taxi seat. My jaws were chattering and I was flipping out of my mind.

The driver dropped me at my house in Portmarnock. I jumped out and began knocking at the door. I was hyped up and the adrenalin was still surging through me. I was banging on the windows and through the letter box. It was 3 a.m. and at least one of the lads should have been at home. I checked my phone to see where they were. I called them.

'We're at home,' they told me.

'You're fucking not,' I answered. 'Come to the front door.'

Nobody came.

'Which house are you at, Lenny?'

Only then I came to my relative senses. I was outside a house I used to live in. This house was now inhabited by three girls. There was a blood-stained lunatic screaming, banging and shouting madness through their letter box. For the second time in an hour I turned on my heels and ran.

I took a week off work after that. I got a doctor's note citing post-traumatic stress. It was vaguely true. Ulster Bank decided to move me to the Swords branch. This entailed a longer bus ride, but was otherwise the same monotonous gig. My routine didn't change much. I looked at the new branch as a new place to take advantage of. The bank always had relief staff ready to come in, so I never felt even a smidgen of guilt.

In the midst of all this I was managing to put in some solid performances for Sylvester's. Out of nowhere I was called up for the Dublin Juniors and selected to play on a team captained by Tommy Carr against Meath. It was a complete bolt from the blue. It was a big honour and I wanted to take my chance. It meant I was somewhere in the reckoning.

We played Meath on a spring evening in Parnell Park. Our team hadn't played together before – I met most of the lads for the first time in the dressing room beforehand – and it showed in a listless display. I had a solid game, but we were beaten all over the park. Tommy Carr lost it at half-time. I remember looking at the blood vessels popping out at the side of his temples and wondered, would one of them explode? He was filled with a violent anger at the abject display he had seen in the first thirty-five minutes.

'You are fucking playing in a fucking DUBLIN shirt,' he screamed like a banshee in heat, kicking over the physio's table. He had a very high-pitched voice for such a tough man. 'Play like it fucking means something to ye!'

It meant fuck all, evidently, and we were beaten tamely by five points. It was the end of my brief flirtation with the Dublin set-up. I was disappointed, to say the least. I hadn't played badly myself, and I wanted to be in the reckoning for the Seniors. But it was another one-game championship for a Dublin team with me in goal.

We had a huge party in the house one weekend and I was a broken man by the end of it. Monday morning came and I got myself together to go to work. I walked down to the bus stop. I said to myself that if the bus was late I would quit right there and then. I was in an absolute bundle; the inside of my mouth was eaten away from the pills, my head was puffy and throbbing and I was frail and paranoid. I stood for ten minutes and no bus came. I was about to walk away when I saw it trundle around the corner. I knew the driver and he pulled up and opened the door for me. I looked at him for a moment and then shook my head. He laughed, closed the door and kept on going.

I shuffled down to the seafront and found a phone box. A light mist was drizzling in from the east. I could see the waves breaking slowly on Portmarnock Strand like hypnotic arms of nature. I dialled the number for Ulster Bank Swords and asked to speak with Mary, the manager.

'Hi, Mary, It's John . . . look I won't be coming in today, I just eh . . . I just eh . . . I just can't come in . . . ever again.'

'Why, what happened?' She sounded very worried.

'I don't know, I'm depressed, I think. I just can't face going in to work there any more. I'm really sorry.'

'I'm really sorry to hear that, John. You just get yourself better.'

In fairness to Mary, she called the next day and, a few days later, again. She had kept my job available in case I changed my mind. But I was done with the banking world. No matter what I did, I just couldn't stay away from my filthy addictions.

Stevie had shown me an ad in the *Herald* looking for a bartender in a cocktail bar in Greece. I applied and got the job.

Telling the family and my club mates this time round was a little more difficult. It seemed like I was running away. It had been good to be back around my family. They were sad that I was leaving again, and my dad especially thought I was wasting my time, my life. In a way I was. But in Dublin I was struggling on many levels. The GAA wasn't satisfying me as I was out in the cold with the Seniors. Sylvester's were struggling badly. I had no job, no career and no girlfriend to keep me grounded. My addictions were getting the better of me, and the edges were beginning to fray in Ireland. I needed some new bridges to burn. I needed to escape again. So it was off to Greece with me.

I landed on the island of Kephalonia and was met by my new bosses, Rob and Tanya. The airport was a one carousel, one customs officer affair. A smell of jasmine and oranges wafted through the air. They brought me to my new home, a derelict five-room guesthouse which stood on a crossroads. There was a shop and a farmhouse beside me. Cypress, pine and olive trees stretched as far as my eye could see. From my balcony I could see the blue waters of the Mediterranean. There was no traffic, no noise and no people.

I was the only person staying in the guesthouse. I had a small stove, a bed and a bathroom. I bought a few beers and smokes in the shop and sat in the evening warmth. I set up my easel and began to paint a little picture of the landscape around me. All I could hear were crickets, the wind and some nesting hens in the farm below. The heat was perfect. I was far from the maddening world.

Work began a few days later. I was given a scooter and learned the ropes of the island. The weather was glorious, with deep blue skies and a stark, epic coastline. Skala Town had a long, smooth-stoned beach and would come alive in the summer. I dyed my hair with peroxide and hit the beach. For the first week I swam, worked and drank while painting in the evening in my Hotel California. Soon I found a more modern apartment in beautiful farmland at the bottom of a hill, just outside the town. I fell in love with the island.

As the month rolled by, so did the risks I began taking. I was drinking most days before work. I would have a few drinks during work and I would then have a heap of drinks after work. On my days off I would drink and drink and drink. Through it all I was whizzing around on my scooter with no helmet and usually shirtless. Work was booze and social life was booze. There was no in-between. I drank beer in the afternoons, vodka in the evenings and Scotch at night. I was smoking heavily and eating lightly. The alcoholic in me had a whole new lease on life.

One evening I met a cute girl with blonde dreadlocks. After getting hammered in the little local nightclub, I tried to bring her to a remote beach where we could get down and sandy. The last thing I remembered was losing control of my scooter and her flying over the top of me. I woke up the next morning in bed. I looked across and saw her naked beside me. I thought that maybe I had dreamed the accident. I tried to get up, and the bed sheet came with me. I was covered in blood. I could barely move my shoulder. The girl woke up and filled me in. I had lost control and flew into a ditch. She had landed on me and rolled into some bushes. I passed out, but when some locals came to try and help me, I wanted to fight them. So they patiently let me calm down and brought me home.

I had to take a week off work. I needed stitches for a cut to my eye, and my arm was in a sling. When the local copper saw me, he shook his head. He had spoken to me a few times about drink driving. Not in the 'I will arrest you' kind of way, more in a 'You will die' kind of tone. I had almost killed myself twice already.

On my week off due to injury, I went to check emails in the internet café. I saw that the new Dublin senior goalkeeper, Stephen Cluxton, had been sent off in the defeat against Armagh. I stared at the screen for a long time. I was in a physical heap here on a remote Greek island; in a parallel universe, I could have been there, playing in Croker. I felt sorry for myself. I went down to a local bar and began drinking Harvey Wallbangers and Rusty Nails long into the night. I was full of regret and self-pity.

The summer crashed on. My boss, Rob, took the scooter away from me for my own safety. I would walk home from the bars and sometimes never make it; instead I would wake up in fields. My painting had stopped and I simply drank and worked and shagged. The womanizing drunk was crushing the romantic artist. The hard-training jock was nowhere to be seen.

As the season slowed down, there were fewer and fewer tourists and it was time for me to head on my way. I left the island in a shroud of gloom, regret and sadness. I had loved my time here. I had been a drifting, drunken lover-man and I had lived the alcoholic life. I saw visions of a potential future flashing before my eyes.

I took a ferry to Athens and drank ouzo for two days straight. I was wild with drink as I shuffled around the capital. I was stumbling drunk as I stood in the Parthenon and laughed at the idiot tourists snapping their photographs.

And so it ended. I returned once more to Dublin. I was wrinkled from the sun, the drink and the smoking. I was skinny as only a drinker can be. I had that sinewy strength still, but I had done no training, aside from the swimming and sunbathing. There had been no football for six months. It was a complete comedown to be back in Dublin. Summer was over. I was back, living in my parents' house. It was tough to deal with. My dad was glad to have me back again, but he knew I was a long way away from him. He was keen to see if I was back to play football, study or work . . . maybe all three. My mother and siblings were glad to have me back, but I was not the energetic force I should have been for them.

I was depressed. I had been drinking and drugging heavily for years. Sober reality was something I couldn't handle. My mood had darkened to the point where I needed to move and travel in order to stay even remotely sane. I was not ready to face up to Dublin and all that it represented. I hadn't made my peace with the past yet. A small part of me yearned for who I used to be . . . but I didn't know how to be him any more. I was changing and I needed to change some more before I would be OK.

I had some money left in the bank. It was enough to get me away somewhere. I went into town with my sister one day and went to an internet café. I sat browsing the google box, considering my options. I picked three places I thought I would enjoy . . . France, Sweden and India. I tapped my sister and asked her to pick a number. The number she picked corresponded with India. I opened a page and booked a flight to Delhi for the end of the following week. I had my foot firmly on the accelerator and didn't want to stop.

I was flying on a wing and a prayer.

7

Sitting in a small café where I had just eaten breakfast, I smoked a few local cigarettes and stared out over the vast valley. In the distance the snow-capped peaks of the Himalayas rose high and heavenly. An eagle hunted far above in the cloudless sky. I scribbled a few post-breakfast thoughts, paid my bill and began walking back towards the hostel where I was staying.

I had made my way north from Delhi to McLeod Ganj, a suburb of Dharamsala in northern India. It was home to the Dalai Lama and the exiled Tibetan government, and to an abundance of spiritual retreats and centres. There was a deep feeling of serenity and history palpable in the air. Backpackers from all around the world congregated here, looking for that alternative experience. I wasn't sure what I was looking for, but I thought I'd know it when I found it.

A little Indian man passed by me as I walked.

'Hash, weed, speed, cocaine?' he whispered to me. I ignored him and kept walking. Seen it, done it, fell asleep in the T-shirt.

'Opium?' he asked in a louder voice as he squirrelled away.

'Opium?' I asked, turning to face him. He saw the lights flicker on in my mind. That was all he needed.

'Come come, follow me.'

Before I knew it I was walking to the outskirts of a tiny village with a hep in my step. I followed the little man to a house which was perched on the side of a cliff. He banged on the large metal door a few times and, after someone checked the eye slit, the door opened and we were allowed in.

It took my eyes about twenty seconds to adjust to the darkness. There was a big old kitchen to the left with a long wooden table covered in some pots, pans and bags of spice. The little man beckoned me to follow him into another room to the right. He pointed towards a couch against the wall and I sat down. In front of me was a large double bed. On the bed were a woman dressed in full colourful sari and a small boy cuddling up to her. I greeted them – '*Namaste*' – but they ignored me. Their eyes were fixed on the TV in the corner. The manic music of some Bollywood blockbuster blared around the room.

The little man pulled up a cushion from the couch and yanked out two massive bags from inside. One was packed full of grass and hashish and the other had many little bags in it. The woman brought tea.

I took a small bag of grass and a block of hash, which cost a few rupees. He then took a big packet of tinfoil, opened it and revealed the sticky black goo of opium. I took an amount roughly the size of a Kit-Kat finger. We sat and talked numbers for a few minutes while I rolled a spliff. As we smoked and drank the tea we negotiated the best price for both of us. He gave me a 'discount' and I paid him US $20. It seemed like good value to me. He told me if I brought any more people to him that he would give me free drugs.

I was already in love with this place.

I said my thanks and goodbyes and made my way back into the bright blue day. Before long, paranoia crept into my head. Being caught with three types of narcotics was not something I had planned for my time in India. The cops would be very expensive to buy off. I walked at a brisk pace with my head down and made it back to the hostel with no problems.

My hostel room was twice the size of a single bed. There was a window with iron bars, a small writing desk and a chair. The concrete walls and floor were plain, grey and solid. I had a shared bathroom and my own key to come and go as I pleased. It was good enough for me. For $2 a night I wasn't expecting the Hilton.

I checked my watch – it was close to midday. I was ready for my first dabble into the world of opium. I quickly rolled a spliff to help me through the process. I lit up and inhaled the sweet taste of *charas* – the Indian name for hashish. I had some vague ideas about how to take the opium and so I began experimenting. I should really have asked my dealer, but I didn't want to seem like a complete novice.

I made a pot of hot tea in the communal kitchen and brought it back to the room. I slowly dissolved a small amount of the opium into it. It tasted very weak and I didn't notice much of a difference in how I was feeling. So I made myself a little bowl from a Coke can. I crushed it down in the middle and used my Swiss army knife to make some little holes on a flat piece of it. I placed some of the opium on this, lit it and began to inhale. I began to get a little more light-headed, but it was nothing like the buzz and high I was expecting.

I then took a small piece of the gooey opium and placed it right on the tip of the knife. I held the lighter underneath it, but not close enough so it would directly burn it. This caused the opium to emit a small amount of smoke, which I inhaled. This began to hit the spot. My mind seemed to get very light and my senses went into a heightened mode of alertness. I felt a warm, soft euphoria around my neck and brain. My skin went all tingly and fuzzy and I felt a gentle energy ripping around my blood, increasing in intensity. I repeated this process a few times. My mind wandered into a sweet and fanciful place of nothing. Slowly my brain kicked in again and again, with throbs of ideas and thoughts, and then nothing again.

I stayed there in that state for a long time. Hours must have passed as I had finished off almost half the opium. I was engulfed in a giddy euphoria.

I took out my copy of *Mein Kampf* and began to read.

Mein Kampf was written by Adolf Hitler when he was in prison in the 1920s. I had bought the book from a street dealer in Delhi as I had always wanted to read it. What better way to get an insight into the mind of this evil genius? I wanted to know what underpinned his assault on civilization.

As I read I scribbled notes which outlined logical flaws and erratic thinking. I postulated and formulated. The opium and *charas* helped me digest his writings at a frantic rate. In my heightened state I thought I had a clearer picture of what had truly motivated this man. I felt extremely smart. My mind was accelerating through the ideas and words that I was reading. After a while, though, I could focus only on the evil this man had committed. I thought of all the people he had had killed in the name of his ideas. I thought of his annihilation of races of people. I thought of all the nice Israeli girls I had met in India.

I panicked.

I tucked the book under my arm and rushed out through the hostel grounds and on to the street. Night had fallen and groups of men were huddled around fires burning in old oil containers along the narrow cobbled paths. It was winter and McLeod Ganj was at 2,000 metres of altitude, so it got cold at night. The air was sharp and dry. A few stray dogs barked and scrambled down a lane to my left. I was frantic in my thoughts. I needed to cleanse myself from this evil, immediately.

I spotted a group of men who were huddled around a fire on the opposite side of the street. I walked across the cobbled stones to them and showed them the book. They stared at my manic eyeballs. They looked puzzled. I started to shout about how evil Hitler was. I pointed at the book and shouted at these homeless Indian men: 'Pure evil!' My eyes were bulging and my throat was bone dry. I went to throw the book into the fire. The men tried to stop me and pulled the book back out. 'No, Baba . . . no no no . . .' they said. But I wasn't having any of it. I shouldered one of them out of the way and grappled with another. I grabbed the man's hand who tried to retrieve the book. I applied some heavy pressure to his wrists. His hands opened and the book dropped back into the flames.

I stepped away from the group and my heart rate settled down again. The men had moved away and were talking among themselves and shaking their heads. I laughed out loud to myself. A maniacal laugh erupted from deep within. The yellow flames warmed my face and in the flickering half-light I saw fear in the eyes of these poor Indians. I saw their fear and I saw the words of an evil madman burning before my eyes. Hitler's words and thoughts burned high into the Himalayan night.

I turned away and hurried back to the hostel.

My mind was addled and I was really flustered. I needed a drink to take the edge off this feeling. I walked to the shared toilets and washed my hands and face. I decided to head to a local bar where they served Godfather beers in 500ml bottles – at 7.5 per cent they could really knock your head off. I began working on knocking my head off. The drugs had made me anxious and I needed to steady myself.

I sat down close to a group of Westerners and got talking to them. My powers of conversation had improved somewhat since the book burning. One girl was really cute – blonde hair, brown eyes and that big, straight-toothed, American smile. She was playing footsie with me under the table and glancing in my direction with a quick flick of her eyes. I had never been one for footsie, but my wired-up opium mind found it exciting and risqué. The booze was beginning to kick in too, and I had forgotten how deranged my thoughts had been an hour or so before.

It turned out that one of the last trance parties of the season was happening that night, in a café on the side of a local mountain. We drank on for a few more hours and then took a *tuk-tuk* to a point beyond which we needed to walk. We clambered up the side of the mountain with a local Indian guy, who showed us the way. He warned us to be careful as it was a steep drop to death if you slipped. I was full of drink and wired with various drugs, and his words of warning just added to the fun of it all.

We got to the party in one piece, and the scene really was something to behold: a rickety little structure, built of bamboo and tree trunks, perched on the side of the mountain, with a terrace which doubled as a dance floor. The sky was lit up with bright, blinking stars. Young hippy chicks with dreadlocks danced with their eyes closed. Old crusty wizards with long white beards moved to the deep melodic trance being pumped out by the DJ. Young Indians and backpackers mingled and laughed.

We bumped into a lad from Cork who seemed to know the Americans. He offered me an acid trip, which I readily accepted. As I went to place the little square of paper on my tongue, I dropped it on the ground. It floated left and right and evaded my flailing attempts to catch it. It landed somewhere in the muddy grass beneath me. I crawled along on the ground and tried to find the tiny square of hallucinogenic fun, but it was no use. I was a little crushed by this and needed to get high again. I didn't want to share the opium, so I made a brief exit from the party. I stumbled out through some bushes and along a little path. I needed a quiet spot where I wouldn't be disturbed.

I found a little clearing but tripped over some shrubs and collapsed on top of some short, stubby branches. As I placed my hand down to lift myself up, the ground gave way – and it was only then that my senses adjusted and I realized where I was: on the edge of a cliff. My balls shrank back up into my stomach. I held my breath and shimmied back on my belly a little way, scraping my stomach on the bushes. One more metre and I would have fallen to my death down an abyss, with no one knowing who or where I was. One more metre . . .

I retreated until I was able to get to my feet. I looked around and spied a big sturdy tree I could prop myself against. I eased myself down slowly and sat with my back against the trunk. I slouched low and took out my penknife, lighter and the opium. I tried to light up but my hands were shaking too much. I took a few deep breaths and looked up at the night sky. I was a long way from everywhere.

I tried to light up again and this time I was successful. The wave of relief was instantaneous and sweet. I stayed there a while and smoked enough to feel that euphoric lift engulf me again. I looked at the stars above and thanked Krishna that I hadn't plummeted to a horrible death below.

I made my way back to the party and settled down in a corner beside my new friends. We drank and smoked some *charas*, and I told them of my close encounter with the edge of the cliff. Gradually I felt the edge of my senses eroding away and I lost the ability to speak. My mind clouded, my eyes got heavy and I passed into a comatose sleep on a rusty metal chair.

I was woken by the cute American girl. She was rocking my head gently, prodding me in the side. It seemed like she was talking to me from a zillion miles away. They were leaving. It was dawn. An old wizard smiled at me with his eyes closed, sitting across from me on some grass. My face and shoulder were caked in dry blood.

I got up and followed the Yanks. It was cold and I was shivering hard. I was a goat, in body and mind – a drunken, depraved goat. The sun was breaking over the Himalayas to the east and to most people this beautiful sight would have warmed the heart and the mind. But I was in the horrors and cursed the brightness.

We walked back to our village in relative silence. As I launched random tirades against anyone and everyone, the others walked ahead of me, unsure of what had happened to me. The girl had gone from flirting with me to fleeing from me. I let my bitter and twisted humour off its leash and there was no place for them to join in.

As we got back to the village I turned to say goodbye. 'I hope I never see you again,' I blasted and turned and walked away, not looking back. I told myself it was a joke and fuck them if they couldn't take it. I staggered home and felt miserable, wired and dead.

I emptied the last of the drugs on to the table in my room. There was enough for a few spliffs and a few bowls of opium. I lit a smoke, swigged some warm beer and finished off the drugs. For a few short moments I felt good. I felt that soothing high but then, just as quick, I became numb and dull. I took out a pen and tried to write. I needed to say something about this. I tried to articulate what was going on. But my words were garbled and my thoughts slurred. I thought about that cute American girl, but all I heard were my parting words echoing through my mind.

My mind drifted back to perverted thoughts. I fantasized about her being here with me, smoking these drugs, feeling high and remote and together in an isolated downbeat ball. I thought about her lips and her sweet-scented female skin. I looked around my room at the bare concrete walls, the cold, stone, grey floor and at the single picture of some Hindu god on the back of the wooden door. The god sat, cross-legged, with its eyes closed. It had six arms and pale-green skin. A warm yellow sun rose behind its head.

I passed out. When I woke I was feeling depressed and dirty. I went for a walk in the mountains to clear my head. I found myself ascending a path through some light highland forest. Giant fir trees swayed in the breeze. Beyond, in the distance, echoes of people laughing drifted up from the town below. I lit up the remains of a spliff and kept moving.

I came across a monastery where they did ten-day silent retreats. It seemed like the perfect place to be silent for a while. I thought that it might do my mind some good. I wandered in and asked a monk about joining. He told me that there was a ten-day wait for the next one. I thanked him, walked away and spent a few hours exploring the Indian forest; sitting beside little mountain streams and quietly enjoying the shrubs and the flowers.

Ten days was too long to wait, and I decided to leave McLeod Ganj. I needed a different experience. In the words of Bob Marley: 'If you're not living right, then you must travel wide.' I headed by bus south-east along the flank of the Himalayas to a town called Rishikesh. The bus drivers in India drive like men possessed. They overtake at breakneck speeds around blind corners. They overtake even when they can see vehicles overtaking in the other direction. I found the journeys easier if I closed my eyes and said a few quiet words to some higher power.

The Beatles had spent some time in Rishikesh in 1968. They were interested in transcendental meditation and had stayed here to learn techniques from the Maharishi. I thought I could tap into some of that residual energy somehow. It was a dry town, and that suited me – my mind was dark and I was feeling weird. I smoked *charas* on the banks of the Ganges and I swam in its putrid water.

Unlike in Australia, where I always had friends around, and Greece, where I was working with people, in India I was completely alone. I sat there in the hazy sunshine and thought about home. I said silent prayers for my family, hoping they were doing OK. I felt guilt for being away. Part of me knew that they needed me, but another part of me couldn't bear to be in Ireland.

I thought about the Dubs. It had been almost six years since I was involved with the U/21s. It seemed so distant now. I had brought myself into a completely different world. Lots of my old teammates were training and making sacrifices to try to win the All-Ireland. Six years is a long time. I was resigning myself to the fact that maybe it was all over for me.

Did I miss the GAA? Did I miss the banter in the dressing rooms? Of course. Did I miss the craic you had with big groups of lads out slogging it together? Yes, I did. Did I feel like I had something left to offer? Yes.

More than anything else, I missed the challenge of trying to make it as the best in my position. I missed the possibilities that lay in every trial game, every scout watching and every manager taking notes.

I allowed the sunshine to heat me before I picked up my belongings and wandered back to the hostel. I walked past a group of Indians begging, but I ignored them as I had done most days since I had been there. On this day one of them approached me. He was angry.

'Why do you pass us every day and not help anyone? All we want is just a few rupees,' he asked.

I told him I was not rich and didn't give money to everyone.

'But do you know we are not beggars because we are stupid or lazy? I am a doctor! My friends are lawyers. We are all educated. But here in Mother India if you do not know the right people then you can never get ahead. And every day you walk by and look at us as though we are nobodies. Do you know what that is like?'

I had no idea. All I knew was that speaking to this man was making me feel immensely sad. It made me feel like a miserable human being.

I told him I was sorry and I offered to give him a few rupees. But he refused them. He just wanted me to feel it and to know what was going on.

In his eyes I saw a hopelessness, the kind of look which you cannot fake. What kind of person had I become? Who was I that I could not share a few cents with the poor and the helpless?

As I walked along I spotted a small barber shop. On an impulse I went in and asked the head barber to give me a '1' blade all over. He complied and when he had finished I asked him to take the cut-throat to it. A little audience of curious Indians had gathered around to watch this Westerner shave his head. I stared into my reflection in the mirror in front of me. I looked like an East European junkie. My eyes were sunken and red. My skin was pale grey and I had lost a lot of facial flesh. I slapped my hand on my head and felt that sticky smooth texture of a freshly shaved human cranium. I loved it.

I turned 27 in Rishikesh. On my birthday I walked to a small spot along the Ganges where there was a little beach area. The sun rose high and I began to relax. I smoked some *charas* and I wrote poems in my journal. I went for a swim in the foul water of the Ganges. My head cleared and my thoughts evaporated.

An Indian man walked by with his son. He stopped to talk with me. He knew of Ireland and he said he saw a spirit in me. He told me I was a teacher who would help many people someday. He told me of the ancient gods who gave them the Ganges. The sun baked down upon us. My gloom lifted. I shared my *charas* with him. He was eating some kind of leaf which he shared with me.

He took out a musical instrument and played me some songs. I read him some poems, sitting in the sand on the banks of this sacred river. We could barely understand each other, but we shared a moment when the past disappeared and the future never was. I was at peace with this random man and his son. We were all at peace together.

I decided to push on for Goa – a two-day journey on overnight trains. The trains in India were a fascinating experiment in culture. First class was where the Westerners went. They booked ahead and normally got a sleeper carriage. Second class was where the Indians with a ticket would go. You might also find some Westerners here who hadn't been organized enough to book first class. Then there was third class. Third class was for those who didn't buy a ticket.

In Mumbai I arrived late at the station, and I hadn't booked a berth for the overnight leg to Goa. By the time I got to the platform, all the first- and second-class berths were taken. I stood and looked at the third-class carriages. They were packed, and the latecomers were trying to get their hands on something they could hold on to. My options were a night in Mumbai or a step into the depths of the unknown.

I stepped forward, squeezed into the wall of humanity and took a firm grip on a metal rung. I passed my backpack over heads and it disappeared into the train. The train sounded its horn and began to rumble slowly out of the station. Conductors were blowing whistles and banging on the sides of the carriages. I squeezed my feet on to the edge of the doorway and was literally hanging on for dear life.

Dusk was settling as we left Mumbai. After ten or fifteen minutes people had somehow squashed deeper into the carriage and I was left with a seat on the edge of the doorway. I held on to the rungs with both arms but was more relaxed now. The slums seemed to go on for ever. We passed mile after mile after mile of shanty town – poverty on an unimaginable scale.

Men and women came and squatted close to the tracks, pissing and shitting. Dogs came to sniff, lick and piss on the human excrement. The sun turned a burning orange, cutting a hazy shine through the grey, smoggy air.

I was the only non-Indian in the carriage. A group of young guys decided to befriend me and pulled me into their group. They were crammed in the link between two carriages. They were drinking some kind of Indian moonshine, which they offered to me. I tried a little and it blew my head off. It brought back flashbacks of insanely drunk *poitín* mornings in Dublin many years before. One of the guys was some kind of bodybuilder and he got it into his head that we should fight. I was not up for that. He could have ripped me limb from limb, judging by the size of him. I squeezed backwards through the cramped carriage corridor: I didn't want to die that day.

I located my backpack and found myself a spot at the other end of the carriage to rest. I passed out on the ground and curled up between my backpack and an old Indian man. He spooned me a little, but I was too tired to care. He was warm for a spindly old fella. In the early morning I came to, feeling pretty sick. I made a quick dash for the toilet to heave my guts up. I opened the door to see that the toilet was a hole in the ground. In front and to the side of the hole were two hot steaming human shits, freshly dropped. As I puked I felt sicker from the smell and the sight of the human faeces. I felt even sicker after getting sick.

The train was a lot emptier now as many people had gotten off at various stops overnight. I met some Punjabi boys who showed me how they could head-butt metal doors and not feel pain. They carried long daggers, and the eldest of them told me he was ready to use it if necessary. I believed him. The train rolled along slower now and I took up a position in a doorway and watched coastal India roll by. I lit a cigarette and bought some *chai* from a vendor and contemplated life. There was a humid touch to the breeze now, and the dominant tree was now the palm, not the fir. I could smell the sea in the air.

Arriving in Goa was like getting to heaven. The sun roasted high in the sky. I made my way to a beach called Palolem. I walked along the soft sand and finally picked a hostel with cabins facing the water. I had a room with a view of the sea, a hammock and a bed. It was run by a nice family and I felt really happy. In forty-eight hours I had gone from a cold prison-cell-style room in the chilly north to a warm beachside hut in the south.

My days began with banana and honey pancakes and peppermint tea. I watched the early-morning sun as I munched my first meal of the day. I found some cool cafés and bars further down the beach, where I could write in the afternoons. I found the local *charas* dealer and before long was smoking some nice reefer. I went down to one of the bars to watch English soccer. I made friends with the barman, a local guy called Pazzi. Before half-time we were snorting ketamine behind the bar. This became a daily pattern.

Ketamine is a tranquillizer that often acts as a hallucinogen. It relaxes the muscles and your mind flows in a wild and zany stream. It can be a short and incredibly powerful blast if taken in the right quantities, at the right time. The drawback is that you can sometimes find yourself in a place called 'the K-Hole'. The K-Hole is a dark, paranoid vacuum. You may find yourself surfacing some time later, many miles from where you lost consciousness, surrounded by people you do not recognize.

I knew I was slipping away into some kind of insanity, but I was almost powerless to stop it. I existed in a hazy, hallucinogenic, Indian blur. Sometimes, the things I perceived related to football: the studs of boots, the latex of my keeper gloves, the shout of a full back roaring for the ball, balls flying in my direction, the eyes of the crowds, the red fire on the blue crest of Dublin . . .

One day, I began an experiment: I thought it would be a good idea to dabble with a new identity. I decided to start telling people that my name was Sebastian and then make up whatever came into my head as we spoke. I recorded everything in my diary. One night I met a Finnish girl called Sofia. She was tall and blonde, had high cheekbones and pale-blue eyes. I drank with her and her friends and we had a cosy evening meal. For some reason I told her and her friends my real name. I told them about my experiment and they laughed at how weird I was. The next day we played cricket on the beach as the afternoon sun faded. I smoked *charas* and they sipped beers. I stayed off the ketamine after meeting Sofia and her friends and I dragged my mad mind back from the brink.

One evening we went to a trance party in an open-air bar which overlooked the beach. I managed to get my hands on some pills which I thought were ecstasy. It turned out that they were laced with all kinds of other drugs, and as I came up on them my mind began to fall apart. I lost the plot completely. I forgot who the Finnish girls were. I wandered away from them and got lost in the party. By the time I was back to some kind of semi-normal state, the girls had long gone home. I stayed dancing in the corner of the dance floor until I was almost sober. I went home, curled up and tried to sleep the pain away.

I spent the next day on my own in a deep state of depression. After my pathetic display of drug-induced weakness, I was sure I had ruined my chances with Sofia. I sat watching the sun go down and supped a few quiet beers and smoked a little *charas*. The after-effects of the drugs had me slightly numbed and mindless. I stared away into the distance. Along the beach I saw the vision of a girl approaching in a light pink sarong and with a yellow flower in her hair. As she came closer I recognized the blonde hair, the tanned sallow skin and the big friendly smile.

'How are you, crazy man? Do you remember who I am today?' She kissed me on the cheek, pausing for a few seconds with her arms around my neck, her body bent over to meet me.

'Uhhhh . . . ha ha ha . . . uhhhhhmm . . .' I laughed nervously. She laughed. I laughed. We both laughed. My insanity was no more. I was forgiven.

'I don't think you need to do so many drugs, John Boy,' she told me. 'You are crazy enough without them.'

I laughed, we talked more and she ordered a beer. We stayed there for the evening, sipping beers and smoking *charas*. As night descended we moved up to my little hut to get her some warmer clothes. The warmer clothes never materialized. We stumbled over to my single bed, where we ravished each other for some time, shaking the foundations of my humble abode. In the afterglow of our physical love I opened the door and we lay in silence together. We watched the waves lap in and heard the sounds of the Indian Ocean around our ears.

My mind and body were quiet for the first time in a long time.

As luck would have it, Sofia and her friends were travelling on. We spent a few more days together and then we had to say our goodbyes. I was sad she was leaving, but happy to have found someone I could connect with.

The day she left I went to a local bar and drank heavily. I was on a roll and met a gorgeous Israeli girl. She had deep brown eyes, a curvy figure and auburn hair. I was instantly smitten by her confident and sweet nature. We arranged to meet the next day for drinks. But the next day I broke out in a weird facial rash. So I stood her up. I couldn't go out in public as I looked like a diseased backpacker . . . which I suppose I was. So I spent a few long days in my room, reading and smoking my brains out. I avoided the thought of her and of life itself. I fell into a sad state of self-pity.

I knew I was wasting away here. I was a twenty-seven-year-old man in his physical prime, drifting away in paradise. I was lost. My writing was abysmal – either simplistic or insane. There seemed to be no middle ground. I was reading authors like Wolfe, Kerouac and Kesey. I loved how they wrote, but struggled to write like them. I knew they all experimented heavily with drugs when they wrote. I wanted to have that too. But I was writing like an eight-year-old who kept a secret diary. I was running out of patience with myself.

What did I want in life? I decided to write a clear and simple list: the first three things that came into my head when I asked myself: 'What would make me happy?'

(1) Write a novel
(2) Get close to my dad and spend quality time with him
(3) Play GAA for the Dubs

That was it. There was no mention of drugs or women or drinking. There were no thoughts of more travel. These were the three things that would make me who I wanted to be. Until now my plan had been to head to Italy and to work in the mountains for a snow season. Now I knew was the time to face the music in Ireland. I felt energized and excited.

I started training. Every day I ran and sprinted along the beach. After breakfast I jogged along the edge of the water. I increased the distance and tempo as the days went by. I started pushing myself in my sit-ups and push-ups. I practised diving in the ocean, flipping left and right and improving my agility. I was still in relatively good shape. I didn't carry much body fat, and after a tough first week I felt strength coming back into my body. I avoided Pazzi and his stash of ketamine. I avoided drinking. I still smoked *charas* all day, but that was not a problem for me then.

I followed the same route every morning when I went running, and every morning I saw the same yoga girl, by a big cluster of smooth rocks. I looked and smiled in her general direction, but she ignored me. She focused on her breaths and poses. Her sun-bleached hair blew in the wind, flickering against the taut line of her collarbone. Her body moved slowly from stretch to stretch, whirring in a state of radiant mindfulness.

Every day I pushed myself harder as I ran past her. I did more and more ridiculous exercises in her peripheral vision. Still she ignored me. I made up some yoga-style stretches and would peer towards her as I did them. She stared ahead, impervious. I was motivated. I was trying to impress this yoga girl with my agility and suppleness. But I failed to ever gain her attention. Every day she was in the same spot, lost in her yoga world. She stared past me into the gentle waters of the Indian Ocean. Without ever saying a word to me, Yoga Girl helped to push me on. She helped me get in shape for my return to Ireland, and to football.

I had come to India to find myself. When I did, I didn't really like who I was. Left to my own devices I slipped away into intoxicated, carefree delight. Meaning was lost and I became a real drifter. All the magic faded and the heavy indulgence meant I became a mess. But it was here that I finally figured out what I wanted in life. I was ready to rekindle the love of my family, the joy of GAA and the wholesome madness of Ireland.

I spent my last few weeks in Goa writing, training and mellowing. I was getting fit and could feel the life surging through me. Every day I woke up and looked out at the Indian Ocean from the hammock on my balcony. I imagined myself back in Ireland, catching high balls and pulling off spectacular saves. I knew that I was ready. My imagination was back home. Now I would follow it.

8

Dublin, January 2005

I walked along the coast road on a bitterly cold Friday night. The wind cut in hard, pinching my eyes, flinging fat drops of rain against my face. I shuddered, pulled up my hood and began to jog. I was on my way to the Bayside Inn, a refuge on this most miserable of evenings.

As I passed an old telephone box I had an idea. I went inside and sparked up the remains of a joint I had half smoked. There was nothing better than Afghan gold to take the edge off the misery of the weather. The old familiar kick of hashish filled my brain and veins. Splattered and battered, the plastic door rattled and shuddered. I stood here, safe from the elements, smoking the last of the spliff.

Far from the warmth and sultry delights of Goa I was now. I surveyed the raging storm outside. The wind howled up under the gap at the bottom of the door. There was nothing for it but to return into the fury of the Irish winter. I hurried out and began to jog again towards the shops. I reached the entrance to the pub, dried my face and rubbed my eyes. I opened the big wooden doors and entered the old world. The pub was a time machine, stuck in the mid-'90s. Faces I knew turned to stare at the latest straggler to wander in. I went up to the bar and ordered a pint. Standing beside me were a few lads I hadn't seen since I left school. We chatted for a few minutes and they joined me in our corner of the pub. Nothing had changed in the inn; still the same tacky brass fittings, wooden tables and deep maroon carpet.

We chewed the fat about life and what had happened since school. I told them I had been in Australia, Greece and India. I told them I was back and that I was going to play for the Dubs. That was pretty much the only thing I had on my mind. I couldn't think of anything else to tell them. They looked at each other and smiled back at me. My eyeballs were Christmas red and hanging out of my head. My tan had faded and the Irish winter had stripped my flesh of colour. I was pale and sheepish, having been out on pills the night before. My face was sucked in and I had chewed the insides of my cheeks. I look bunched.

They tried not to laugh in my face, but I could see they thought I was having a laugh. They knew I had played at a high level many years ago, but that was, well, many years ago. These lads followed the Dubs. They knew the scene. For me to tell them I was going to play for the Dubs . . . They knew I took drugs. They knew I drank and was a stoner. They knew I had been away for a long time. I remember that look they all gave one another. It was a look that said, 'Maybe he *did* take too much acid back in the day.'

I was back about six weeks from India and had already fallen back into bad old habits. Broke after my travels, I had swung a job as a manager in a new bar in Howth. I started the job a week or so after coming home and I found it tough going. It was a new venture, and it was a high-pressure environment. The hours were late and long, and I was mentally shattered at the end of the working week. I knew the working hours would hinder my progress in the GAA world, but I was hamstrung by the need to earn money. Aside from labouring, the only substantial experience I had was working behind the bar.

I had good intentions, but as the weeks went on I found myself drinking hard on my days off. Inevitably I found that after a few drinks I would want to get mashed up on something harder. The beast would take over and the old demon of recklessness would rear its ugly head. It was frustrating, but I was dealing with life in a familiar, standard way. I was making questionable decisions – job type, drinking habits and commitment to training. But I still held a belief that good things lay in store. I thought I just needed to get through the first few months of readjusting to Irish life.

So I stuck it out. The job paid pretty well. I moved into an apartment in Howth with a work colleague. We had a balcony that opened out over the harbour, with a view of Ireland's Eye and far beyond to the Irish Sea. My morning coffee was supped while penning prose and staring into the vast grey horizon, over the yachts, the trawlers and the scampering human forms.

I was back playing with St Sylvester's. For all the bad living I was doing, I still had my natural fitness, and I told myself that I could manage it. I was training one or two nights a week, and as summer approached I made plans to up the dedication. I had reclaimed my no. 1 spot with the seniors and it felt good just to be back, playing some kind of team sport. It was all part of the plan I made on the beach in Goa: Write a book, get close to my dad and play for the Dubs. Reclaiming the Sylvester's keeper spot was the first step on the road to the Dubs.

I was spending some quality time with my dad, too. He came to visit me in the apartment one evening. My mother dropped him up and I ordered fish and chips from the local chipper. We sat there, admiring the view over the harbour while chewing the fat. I put on an old spaghetti western in the background. We ate our fish and chips doused in gallons of salt and vinegar in a contented state.

He told me tales of when he was young and growing up in the inner city of Dublin. It was a time when bikes and trams were the way you got around, when boys ran around playing conkers in short trousers. He told me stories of thieving he used to witness down in the docks along East Wall. Men with horses and carts would saddle up behind an unloading boat and help themselves to the cargo in heists so simplistic they sounded poetic and beautiful. He told me stories of dancing in ballrooms around the city as a young man. I shared some stories of my own. This was what I had come back for.

We never broached the subject of drinking and drugs. He never knew the extent of my problems. He always told me that I didn't need drink. I had confidence, a sense of humour and could talk to women; what did I need drink for? He never drank himself and was a Pioneer most of his adult life. He chose this path as his own father, who died before I was born, had been an alcoholic. It was in the family, this addictive gene. I felt I could relate more to it now. I had more perspective on where I ended up when I succumbed to my temptations. It was something I really had to watch out for now.

One quiet Wednesday evening, while on my break at the bar, I was playing a game of battle chess on the computer in the back office. As the computer launched into a little animated sequence the owner of the bar opened the door and came in. He stared at me, then at the computer screen and then back at me.

'Checkmate?' he quipped.

'I'm just having a break,' I told him, but I knew what he was thinking. He was thinking I was a piss taker. We also argued over the door policy and staff issues. There was only going to be one winner. I was pretty sure I would not be getting my three-month trial contract renewed.

So I began to look for a new job. I saw an advert on jobs.ie for a bar manager. The conditions, location and all the rest looked great. I was really keen and clicked to find out more. When I read who the employer was, I realized I was reading an ad for my own position! When I called my manager and asked him about it, he said he knew nothing about it. But I feared the man did protest too much.

My contract was not renewed, and I decided to go on a meltdown session. I called the Man and arranged for some coke and yokes. I went on a rampage and bumped into an old female work friend on the dance floor in The Kitchen. We exchanged drugs and laughs and got off our bean together. We spent hours together, drinking and smoking and carrying on. We left here and got a lock-in at the old Viper Rooms along the quays.

As the night rattled into the morning we wanted to keep the party going. We went to the Chancery Inn, an early house on the quays. The bouncers let us in and we took up a spot in the corner and gobbled some more pills. People's faces slanted and curved, their skin a radiant grey. Eyeballs blinked slowly and, when they opened, the eyes would swell out larger and larger. Men with beady heads, snarly faces and orange teeth were climbing the walls.

We went on to my friend's place, and before long were in her bed, kissing and rolling around. At some point she whispered in my ear, 'Will I get out the whip, cuffs and the butt plug?'

I froze. Everything in my mind shot down at once. Normal me said yes, but what I actually said was, 'Eh, no.'

She was a little taken aback. I could only assume that I had been telling her I was into everything while I was coming up on the drugs. But I was in shutdown mode now.

'OK then,' she said slowly. 'How about some oils and a massage?'

My mind thumped in on top of itself. A cute girl wanted us to rub oils on each other in a drugged-up mush. Correct answer: 'Yes.' John says, 'That's not my speciality.'

She paused again, obviously trying to figure this out.

'OK then, what's your speciality?' she asked curiously.

I lay back in a regressive fear. I recoiled into myself. My brain was flashing blanks and screaming nothing at me. It went into the foetal position. I went mute, gulped and almost cried.

'I don't have a speciality,' I whispered.

She lay back, pursed her lips and pulled up the duvet. I lay there, looking at the ceiling. It was shimmering in a translucent glow. The light fitting moved as though made of water. I was relieved in a way. I didn't know what my mouth was saying, but I was happy to just lie there and stare at the ceiling. I passed out after a while, and when we woke I made my excuses. She said she might be around town again that night and would text me.

I never received a text.

I went on into town, hit the ATM and carried on drinking in the Sackville Lounge. When I got home a few days later I slept for two days straight. I was woken by a phone call from Sylvester's. It was time to come back to reality and go training. There was a league match coming up that weekend. It would be good if I showed up for one training session at least. I agreed. It was miserable winter training: knee deep in mud, running around pitches, jumping through ladders and cones under failing yellow floodlights. I struggled. My lungs were burning and my muscles weak from the toxic abuse. I got through it, but it was tough to stay motivated.

A few days later one of my sisters let me borrow her scooter. She didn't need it and it was mine for a few months. Soon I was to be seen flying around the streets of Dublin on a pale-green 1970s Vespa. It was great to have a little bit of freedom. I began to enjoy training again. I would clamp my oversized kitbag between my legs, hop on the bike and blaze a trail out the back roads from Howth to Malahide. I froze my proverbial tits off, but it took a lot of my stress away.

I got a job in the IFSC working as a barman. There were easy hours, new friends and lots of women. My fellow barmen had changed my name on the till to *Kingdong*, much to the amusement of businessmen who needed a receipt for expenses. I enjoyed the work and they were flexible enough to allow me the time off I needed to train and play matches.

I got into a good routine. I was working, carousing, and spending time with my family. Winter became spring became summer. I was spending more time with my dad. His MS was getting progressively more debilitating, but he still managed to make it to most of the games I played. The weather was fine for large parts of the summer and it made life incredibly pleasant. I started to feel like I was on track again.

I met a pretty Catalan girl in the bar one day. We went for a drink after work and ended up in bed. We were a crazy fit. She was a wild and emotional basket case. It was an experience in itself just being with her. She pushed my buttons towards extreme emotion. Be that as it may, we soon moved in together in the city.

Raging arguments aside, living with a woman was good for me. The regular meals, sex and company helped stabilize me to a degree. I was taking the GAA seriously again. We had a new management team at Sylvester's in Dave 'Super' Ryan and John Sexton. I had played with Super when we won a championship and it brought things full circle for me again. He allowed us keepers to do exclusively keeper training, and I began to feel better about my game. I was performing well and the team were shaping up to become a force in the club scene.

The Dublin management team had changed again. After a disappointing summer of 2005, Tommy Lyons had stepped down and Pillar Caffrey had come into power. I didn't know too much about him, but he had brought his club, Na Fianna, to an All-Ireland club final. Dave Billings and Brian Talty had been brought into the team of selectors, and that could only be good news for me. Billings had been the manager when I was on the Dublin U/21s, and I liked the way he did his business.

He really knew how to instil confidence in people. Although the two U/21 campaigns I had been involved in were failures, I still came away feeling like I had something left to offer. After the second campaign, when we were ejected from the championship following the brawl against Offaly, Billings took the time to call me up and give me a breakdown of how I had performed. He praised my ability to read the game and my decision-making under pressure. He told me I had performed at a level which he expected to see from an inter-county senior.

Brian Talty had been the manager when I first played senior GAA for Sylvester's. He was a great manager and gave us tactics, training and toughness. He brought us on as a group, and Sylvester's won our first and only Dublin Club Championship under his guidance. He was a serious operator and had a training regime laid out twelve months in advance. He was responsible for giving me a chance at the top level in club football, and that helped bring me on as a player. For those reasons I was immensely loyal to him.

He was also the kind of man who would pick me up three or four times a week to go training or playing matches. He passed my house on the Baldoyle Road and would pull over, put the hazards on, walk across the road, ring the doorbell and wait patiently for me. He was also a very passionate man, and sometimes, when he didn't like the way training was going, he would storm off in a rage. I would then be left behind in Malahide, scrounging for a lift.

I'd spent three good years with Talts. From giving me advice on women, life and football to training me to an incredible level of fitness: he was a great role model. Now, with him and Dave Billings involved in the Dublin senior set-up, my chances of being involved increased.

Still, my focus and discipline weren't the sharpest. As the evenings grew short again, I took my foot off the pedal with training. There was an occasional league game but nothing to worry about. I was busy with work and enjoying life the rest of the time. Christmas came and went and I really hammered it hard. My girlfriend had returned to Barcelona for a month so I gave my liver, lungs and brain cells an awful going over. I was weak as a kitten at the end of it all. And then, one quiet January evening, my phone rang.

'Lenny? Howiyah, Sham?'

'Talts? Well, what's the craic? Who gave you this number?!'

'Ah now, Sham, you know me . . . Tell me this, Lenny . . . are ya interested in playing a trial game this Saturday morning?'

'For the Dubs?'

'Who the feck else, Lenny?'

'Of course I'm interested.'

'Right so, Sham, we'll see ya at 9.15 in Whitehall Colmcilles. Don't be late.'

I fist-pumped the air, then punched the couch over and over. I danced around the house, screaming at the top of my lungs. I thanked Jesus, Jehovah, Allah and any other gods I could think of. Finally, the call had come in. This was what I had been waiting for. This was what I had dreamed of, back on the beaches of Goa. I had the chance to make an impression.

I was excited but nervous. I had done zero training for a month or so. In the mornings I had a wheezy, chesty cough which took twenty minutes to clear. My muscles were like skinny fishes. I got down on the ground and did thirty press-ups there and then.

I called my dad to tell him the good news. I then drove out to the house and sat around and told the rest of the family. Everyone was extremely excited. They knew how much this meant to me. Dad was stoical and tried to put a serious face on, but I could see the glint in his eye. He mentioned composure, how I should roar like a bull and be completely prepared. He was buzzing on the inside. It meant so much to me, but it meant a lot to him too.

I drove out to Whitehall bright and early on the Saturday morning in my newly acquired eighteen-year-old VW Golf. It was a cold, dry, grey day. There wasn't much traffic on the roads. I turned up a Ministry of Sound CD full whack to get my brain pumped. I found the pitch on time and pulled into the car park. I was going through a lot of positive self talk. I was talking myself up and up. I convinced myself it was just another game of football, but that I was going to smash it. As I turned off the ignition and looked out at the gathering bodies, a sharp shiver of nerves flew up through my testicles and settled in the gut of my stomach.

I hopped out of the car and walked across the car park with a self-conscious stride. I spied Talts and Billings standing beside each other outside the dressing rooms.

'Well there, Mr Leonard!' Dave saluted. Talts had a friendly hello for me too.

I blasted a garrulous hello back at them, trying to mask the nerves with ostentatious confidence. I noticed Pillar and a few of the other selectors in the background, scrutinizing the interaction. These men had believed in me once and there was no reason why they wouldn't again. I walked over to the team sheets and my name was first on the list for the blues. I didn't recognize many of the other names on the blue team or the opposing reds.

In the dressing room the mood was quiet and nervous. Not many people knew each other. Ski Wade came in and gave a pep talk. I introduced myself to the full back line and went over what calls I would make for what. There were a lot of nervous young faces in the dressing room. I was at least five years older than the average lad in there, and so I made it my business to try and make them feel better. It was my responsibility to act, as well as look like, an experienced and seasoned player.

The pitch was soft and slightly bald, which slowed the pace of the game right down. There were a lot of individuals trying to impress, and invariably players took too much out of the ball. This meant very poor support play and sacrificial runs being made. In turn this made it hard for the forwards to get any breaks through on goal. The end result was that I had fuck-all to do, apart from kicking the ball out.

My kicks weren't great, but I caught all the shots that dropped short, distributed safely and kept a clean sheet. I made sure they heard me on the sidelines. I screamed my lungs out at the young corner backs. Organizing and encouraging was what I needed to do. It was what they would notice on the sideline.

'That's it, Deego, keep it tight.'

'Who's running back, lads?'

'Get fucking tight to him.'

'Get a block in, Murrier!'

As I walked off the pitch back towards the dressing rooms, Talts approached me. 'Well, Sham, how did ya go?'

'Ahh, all right, I suppose . . . didn't get much to do. I haven't been training much so . . .'

'I know, Sham. Can you make training on Tuesday night?'

'Yeah!'

'Out the Old Airport Road, 6.30 p.m. for 7 p.m. start . . . all right?'

'Fucking right it's all right!'

My stomach began to churn. As I entered the dressing room I felt immense power inside me. Pillar came in to us and had a few quick words. He thanked us all for coming out and said that they would be in touch with lads during the week. That was it. I was now on the training panel for the Dubs. I was buzzing like a bluebottle. I was grinning and mumbling and I felt waves of happiness surging through me. I had been building up to this moment for over twenty years. And on this grey January day in Whitehall Colmcilles in North County Dublin my dream was being realized.

I drove straight home to tell my dad. I was singing at top voice, winking at strangers and tapping my hands on the steering wheel. When I got to the family home my dad was still in bed. He was spending longer hours in between the sheets these days. Some days it was late afternoon before he was able to get up. He had been battling MS for over forty years now and the disease was wearing him down.

I went into his room and lay down on the bed opposite him.

'Well, son, how did it go?' he asked in a whisper with his eyes half closed.

'Not bad, Dad, not bad . . . I got drafted into the proper squad.'

His eyes opened and a glint of light burst from them. We had dreamed these days together. We had dreamed this possibility together.

'Ah that's great, son, that's great,' he whispered hoarsely. 'Now make sure you give it everything, all right?'

'All right Dad, I will . . .'

His eyes closed again, very slowly, like a cartoon character's eyes. He lay still on the bed and I lay with him for a while. After a few minutes his eyes opened again. He looked at me with a narrow intensity. I braced myself for some nugget of wisdom he might impart.

'Son?'

'Yes, Dad.'

'Can you get me a drink of juice there?'

I got him a drink of cranberry juice from the bedside locker. He guzzled it down. He was parched and tired. His eyes shut again. I gave him a kiss on his forehead and left him to rest. I was worried about him. He was getting older and weaker, but there was not much to be done about it. He was still able to chat with me for a few hours when I visited in the evenings. That was all I could hope for. They were moments of clarity in the chaos of my life until at that time.

As I drove home, my mind was electric with the thoughts of training with the Dubs. I had been on the minor and U/21 squads, but this was different. This was the big time. This was the team I grew up watching and aspiring to be part of. It had been a long time coming, but I had earned it. The vision had never left my mind: the vision of playing for Dublin. It had always been there, waiting for me to be ready to step up. Now I was ready.

Tuesday, 24 January 2006

I checked my gear bag one last time. I had everything.

I checked the directions to the training pitch one last time. I knew them.

I checked how I looked in the mirror one last time. My hair was styled in the slightly messy style that was popular. I thought I looked good. I thought I would fit in. I looked like a young footballer. I got in my car and hit the road. I wanted to be early, but not too early. I wanted to seem eager but not wet behind the ears. I wanted to impress.

I pulled in to the car park, closed my eyes and drew in a few massive breaths. I calmed my mind and slowly started talking to myself. 'OK, man, this is it, this is what you've been waiting for . . . you're the man right, you're the fucking man . . . let's go show these what you're made of . . . let's go fucking do it . . . COME ON, MAN . . . this is FUCKING IT!!!!' I opened my eyes and punched the steering wheel. I was ready.

I opened the car door and took in the dry, cool air. It was dark and the floodlights cast a white electric glow over the scene. A plane flew low overhead. Cars drove in quickly and bounced over the speed bumps. As I got closer to the dressing rooms I made out a few figures in the bright lights – I saw the navy Dublin colours and some Arnotts logos and knew I was in the right place.

'Howiyahz!' I said to two men I didn't recognize standing outside the dressing rooms.

'Howiyah, Lenny,' they answered in unison. 'Head on in and get changed.'

I opened the door, walked in and felt a little giddy. On the left-hand side of the corridor there was a table filled with fruit, energy drinks and bottled water. On the right-hand side were three small dressing rooms, built to hold maybe ten or twelve people each. I glanced in the first and it seemed a little too full and busy. I walked to the second and it looked like the first. I got to the third room and there were only a couple of lads in there. I made my way in and sat down in the corner.

I didn't recognize either of the lads in the room, but one of them managed to lift his head and mumble a hello. They didn't have official Dublin bags so I knew they were not long on the squad. They looked a lot more nervous than me and I found some comfort in that. I opened my gear bag, stripped down and started getting ready. As I pulled up my socks Ray Cosgrove entered the room. I had played minor and U/21 with Cossi and he greeted me in his usual cheery manner

'Ah, Len, how are ya doin'?'

'Howayah, Cossi! How are things?'

'Jesus we're fucked now, ha?'

We had a good laugh and the confidence grew in me. Jason Sherlock then came in and sat down beside me. Jayo was the star of our minor team, U/21 team and a legend of the game in Dublin. I had known him for many years through college and the GAA scene in Dublin. He epitomized Dublin and was someone I always got on well with.

'Howiyah, Lenny.'

'Howiyah, Jayo, how's things?'

'Pumped up and ready to go for another year of it,' he answered dryly. He and Cossi laughed at this. Winter training was not the highlight of the year for these men.

I felt like I belonged here. I was involved and accepted from the get-go. I saw the other new lads in the background going quieter and quieter. I was lucky that I had a connection with these behemoths of the game. A few more faces came in that I recognized, and the banter kicked up a notch. I was here. This was no flashback, no drug-induced hallucination.

I put on my beanie and walked out of the dressing room, kicking lumps of muck as I went down the corridor. I passed Pillar and Talts and a few others. I nodded a hello in the manliest manner possible. I wanted to appear friendly, but tough. They said a quick hello and no more. I exited the dressing rooms and jogged over the tarmac to the pitches, where a few lads were kicking balls around. I saw Paul Clarke and Ski Wade setting up cones and pointing at spots in the distance. I made my way over to the goal, and a few lads began taking shots. The only one of the other keepers I recognized was Stephen Cluxton – I'd seen him on TV.

I just got straight into doing what I loved most – jumping around a muddy goal, trying to pull off spectacular saves. The shots came in thick and fast, and I felt good. There was nothing new here. These guys didn't seem to kick any harder or more accurately than what I had experienced elsewhere.

The session began with a whistle being blown and the old familiar 'Right, lads, bring it in . . .' being called. We were told to put our arms around each other, to huddle together in unity against the cold. There was no welcome, no ceremony, just business as usual. There was no thought that lads needed to be treated with cotton wool. You'd either got it or you didn't.

Paul Clarke described what would be involved in the session. 'Right, lads, we are going to train for fifty-five minutes tonight. We're gonna do a good warm-up first. We'll then go into three separate groups, working on different skills. Ski Wade and Duffer will work over here on a defensive drill, Talts will take a handling drill over here, and I will be working on a kick-passing and running drill. Keepers will work with us tonight. Then we'll do a warm-down and in for a shower. There'll be a few words from Pillar afterwards so don't rush off. Grub is down in Kealy's. Any questions? No? Good, Henno, take them on a half-pace run around the two far pitches and back. In twos, lads. Let's go!'

I slotted into the middle and jogged along. Lads were laughing and joking and the mood was good. There was a whirr of noise which crackled against the still of the dry, cold night. The ground was slightly frozen. I felt pride running along with this group of men on the outskirts of Dublin. The collective steam and breaths of forty lads formed a misty cloud that followed us around.

Every part of the session was planned meticulously. Each drill had a point and purpose. After each drill there was a short active recovery. There were no medium- or long-distance runs. Running was incorporated into tackling drills, kicking drills and blocking drills.

Then I got my first glimpse of the different level I was now operating at. We were in the middle of a simple kicking drill. You kicked the ball thirty yards into the chest of the man opposite you. You then sprinted to the end of the opposite line. I mis-hit a kick and the ball sailed five metres to the left of my target.

'Ahhhh, bollix!' I shouted, letting it be known I wasn't happy.

A whistle blew. Clarkey took centre stage and started shouting.

'Right, lads, I don't want to fucking hear that. I don't want anyone fucking and blinding when they make a mistake. Do you want the opposition to know you fucked up? Don't fucking react even if you do mis-hit a pass! They don't know you didn't mean to kick it there. Deal with it in your head and make the next one better. I don't want to hear it!'

It stayed with me. It was a simple concept, but it helped my mind deal with the inevitability of making an occasional error.

After one running drill we recovered in groups of three. I was in with Paul Casey and Bryan Cullen, doing a hand-passing drill where you pass the ball as quickly as possible to each other. I took it all in: the shallow breaths, the steam pouring from the bodies, the distant shouts from players, the shouts of Casey and Cully – 'Yes Lenny, Yes

Lenny, Yes Lenny' – as the balls flew around. The deep, dark sky lorded ominously above, as the scream of a jet ripped ferociously through the sky. I felt alive.

Our group moved to the tackling drill. In this drill you passed the ball to a man in the middle, received a return pass, took a shoulder from the man in the middle and passed the ball on. Our man in the middle was Ciarán Duff, a legend of the Dublin teams from the '80s. A man who I grew up watching and mimicking was passing me the ball and about to give me a shoulder. I had watched this bearded warrior from afar in my youth. Now I got to hit him close up.

I caught the ball, passed it to Duffer and he passed it back. As I ran to take the shoulder from him, I braced myself. I thundered into him but was met with an overwhelming force. It was like running into a wall. I gasped like a little boy and coughed up the ball, winded and rattled.

'Come on, for fuck's sake,' someone shouted.

I didn't know who it was. I dropped to pick up the ball but kind of scooted it along. My back crumpled and my lungs emptied. I ended up giving it a wobbly, weak kick along the ground to the next player and jogged to the end of the line.

'What the fuck is that, Lenny? Pick the fucking ball up, for fuck's sake!'

I didn't even look around but held my hand up as I crouched low to get my breath back.

Welcome to the real world.

9

In March 2006, life was peachy. I was part of the team of my child-hood dreams. I had a nice girlfriend, a car, a decent job where I was appreciated. I was hitting the gym and eating well. I was spending quality time with my family. Sometimes I'd have a few nice sociable drinks with good friends, but my addictive madness had been quelled. I was being challenged and satisfied on many levels. The anger, sad-ness and depression of the past decade had faded away. I was feeling as good as could be.

Clucko had a knock in the run-up to our first league game, against Tyrone, so Paul Copeland, the established number 2 keeper, got in the team and I was picked in the match-day squad for the first time. To be involved in team meetings where we planned to stick it to the defending All-Ireland champions gave me butterflies in my stomach. Like everybody else, I had read reports of games in the newspapers for years. Now I was on the inside. Now I was listening to the ideas which drove top-level GAA teams on. Now I was part of the story. On the Tuesday and Thursday before the game we went over exact instructions of what to expect and what we would dish out. We intended to lay down a marker, to impose ourselves. Winning that physical and mental battle was more important than the scoreboard. To be in that Dublin dressing room meant more to me than anything else I had known up until that time.

In the run-up to the game, Pillar had a go at Coper in front of a few of us. After an A v. B game where one too many kicks had gone astray, Pillar approached the keepers and let fly.

'Coper, what the fuck is going on with you? I need you to switch on. This is a big fucking weekend, all right? Get your act together!'

The Tyrone game became the famous 'Battle of Omagh', with a number of melees and four sendings-off. In the aftermath, Coper got another earful from Pillar for running seventy yards to get involved in one of the skirmishes. Coper seemed to be under pressure, and this gave me hope. I wanted him to fail, and I felt no shame in that.

After the Tyrone game I returned to being third-choice keeper and was out of the match-day squad for the visit of Monaghan to Parnell Park a week later. There was a break for a few weeks, and when the campaign resumed against Offaly on 4 March I was still out in the cold. But I had been training like a maniac and really felt I was close to being selected as number 2.

The announcement of the squad for the League match against Cork came on the Tuesday beforehand. With all three keepers fit and available, I was given the nod as the sub. I was chuffed. The balance was shifting.

A few days later I received a call from my mother: Dad was not well. He had taken a bad turn. My boss covered for me and I sped out from the city centre in my Golf. I arrived home a few minutes before the ambulance. Dad was in bed, covered in a mountain of blankets and duvets. He was breathing very deeply and slowly. His chest wheezed heavily. He managed to open his eyes a slither. I held his hand and told him everything was going to be OK.

The last few weeks had been tough on him. When I called around to sit with him, he had trouble speaking. He couldn't hear properly and he could not stop hiccuping – he hiccuped non-stop for weeks. It was driving him demented. He sat slumped in his wheelchair in the sitting room in sweltering conditions: the central heating was on full blast with the fire going too.

He had trouble sleeping and, when he did sleep, he had dark and disturbing nightmares. He was losing his voice and his hearing. His bodily functions were breaking down.

'I've had enough, son,' he whispered hoarsely, his left arm propped under the greying beard that covered his chin.

He sat with his face tilted sideways, plopped heavily on the palm of his hand, his elbow propped on the side of his wheelchair. It looked as though he was in extreme discomfort, but it was the best he could manage these days.

'I've had *enough*, son,' he whispered again. 'I can't speak any more, I can't hear . . .'

The words came as though squeezed from a granite throat. Tears were welling in his eyes, and in mine too. I tried to make light of it.

'Ah sure what would you want to be saying now anyway, Dad, ha?'

He stared at me for a long time. He tried to utter something but it didn't come out. I stared back at him and let him take his time. He licked his chapped lips and tried again.

'I'd want to say . . . I love you,' he whispered, the tears filling his tired old eyes.

I stood up and hugged him and told him I loved him too. They were the last words we ever spoke to each other. As I type these words now, I am very grateful for that.

The ambulance arrived and they took him away. I jumped in the back with him and held his hand. We sped along, with sirens blaring. My mother followed behind, ignoring all manner of traffic lights and breaking speed limits. They had an oxygen mask over his mouth and his eyes were slightly open. I kept chatting to him. I held his hand and looked into his eyes. I think he knew who I was. I think he knew what was going on. I tried to be as chirpy as possible.

When we got to Beaumont Hospital he was put in a ward and stabilized. Some of my siblings arrived and we settled around his bed. His condition was serious but stable. I was surprised at how few sheets and blankets they gave him. I was worried about all manner of things. But I had to go training. I headed off and left him in capable hands. I knew there was no way he would want me to miss a training session just because he was sick.

Training was a blur and I shovelled through it as best I could. I had only been with the Dubs a few weeks and didn't want to miss anything, didn't want to be seen to be an 'excuses' guy. I kept my problems to myself. I always remembered a speech Brian Talty gave us many years ago when I was playing under him at St Sylvester's. It had been a pretty torrid training session. Afterwards he gathered us into the dressing room.

'What the fuck is wrong with the lot of ye?' he screamed, his eyeballs bulging from their sockets. 'You're all fuckin' pricking around like a shower of shites who couldn't give a damn about winning this game.'

He strode around the centre of the dressing room, eyeing up every player there.

'Well, what the fuck are we up here for? Why the fuck are we bustin' our guts for the last twelve months, if this is how we train now?'

Spittle flew around the room. His shoulders pulled back, his fists clenched and he was screaming. He took a bin and kicked it down the middle of the dressing room. Steam hissed from the players as our bodies cooled down in the ice-cold, stone-grey dressing room.

'Any excuses, lads? Any fucking excuses?' he shouted around the room, eyeballing each and every one of us again. 'Well, if ye have any fucking excuses there is a bin right fucking here and fucking throw them in there. I don't give a fuck if it's your missus, your work, your teacher or fucking any other fucking thing . . . if any of ye walk out of here with some excuse for the shite that we are playing right now then we might as well fucking give in.'

He paused and let the words sink in. The blood was pumping through his temples.

'There are no fucking excuses. It is us and only us. Now, has anyone any excuse they'd like to throw in this fucking bin?'

No one said anything, and after a minute or so eyeballing everyone Talts stormed out of the dressing room, almost smashing the door off its hinges. The whole team sat in silence. Normally there would be one or two sniggers and a few wisecracks, but that night no one said anything. Everyone showered and went home.

We went on to win the Dublin Club Championship for the first and only time in our history that year.

I remembered that. No excuses.

After training, I hurried back to the hospital. My dad had been moved to a private ward. My girlfriend had joined my family, and we all sat in the room with him. I expected him to have improved by the time I got back, but his breathing was even more laboured and he was deep in heavy sleep. We sat around the bed and chatted in hushed tones and waited for news. Hours passed and the clock was hitting midnight.

A doctor came and spoke to us as a group. She told us that his condition was extremely critical. We asked what that meant and she told us he wouldn't make it through the night. He had an infection and it was spreading quickly. There was nothing more they could do. We were to say our goodbyes. The doctor apologized, then turned and walked away, her heels clicking loudly on the smooth, polished floor.

We all went into a state of shock. I had come home to spend time with this man and now he was about to die. We all took turns to be alone with him. When I closed the door and sat down, I was overcome with a knowledge of death, mixed with love and fear. It felt like I was about to burst inside. The man who had guided me through everything was about to die. I made him some promises. I told him I would achieve great things. I told him I would give the Dubs every effort imaginable. I told him I would look after the family. I hoped he heard what I was saying.

When we had all said our own goodbyes we sat around in a group. We sat there quietly, his breathing becoming quieter and quieter. It was late, after two in the morning. He began to stir a little – his eyes creeping open, his mouth opening ever so slightly. He spoke in a jumbled, alien voice. His throat was raspy. His mouth was dry. My sister gave him a little drink.

We all huddled around him, urging him to speak. He tried again, but we could make out only jumbled sounds. We were frantic, desperate in our need to know. He took another rest and we gave him another drink. We asked him to try to spell out the words. The sounds came from the underground, as though coughed quietly through a muddy hanky.

Slowly and carefully we picked out some letters.

H - O - L

We argued among ourselves a little, trying to piece it together. He gurgled, softly whispered and coughed.

A - N - D

We took it to be 'hold hands'. He gurgled a little more and we took this to be yes. We all joined hands. We sat there, waiting. He tried to speak more, but the strain was too much. We settled and waited. He tried again but it was too hard. We let him be and sat again in the depths of a peaceful silence.

We sat like that for hours. His breaths were deep and slow. He seemed at ease. We relaxed in a trancelike state around him. We whispered to him and he breathed. We whispered and he breathed. The dark of night began to give way to the soft early dawn. A tiny sliver of light crept in through the venetian blinds.

As day dawned his breaths slowed right down. They became deeper and deeper, longer and longer, slower and slower. We all held hands a little tighter. I heard my sisters saying sweet words to him. It was as though I was in a dream. I heard my mother uttering last goodbyes in hushed, gentle tones. My vision blurred, my eyes filled and my mind throbbed. He seemed to sigh too deeply. Once, twice, three times. There was defiance in his lungs. The last sigh exhaled so deeply. He gave one more short inhalation and then the longest, most powerful exhalation I have ever heard. It was over. He lay there, still. I began to cry, my sisters began to wail and my mother sobbed and hugged him. We passed some time like this, huddled around his lifeless form.

My aunt arrived in the morning and helped us to reassemble ourselves. We opened a window to let Dad's spirit out, in keeping with some old tradition. The doctors came and we went through some formalities. I helped to lift him up and place him on a stretcher for his autopsy. I was amazed at how skinny and light his body was.

My thoughts tumbled and I forgot all meaning. Millions of subatomic particles imploded. Billions of un-thought ideas fell asunder. A crescendo of echoing distortion filled the void. The pounding call sang mayhem. The pounding call sang mayhem. The pounding call sang mayhem.

On the outside, my eyes, rivet-pulled together, stared ahead. I heard an echo lulling behind my ears

> Drink my boyo, drink
> It's the brave face for them all
> Drink my boyo, drink
> Fear not that you shall fall

Something snapped inside me. It broke far under my conscious self and ripped through the fabric of my life. It sucked in and skewered every part of me. I bounced headlong in fast-forward animation. Footsteps, boozer, pints, lager, ale, shorts, whiskey, shots, lager, shuddering, singing, ranting, arguing, drinking, smashing, shouting, screaming, raging. Nothing made sense. Nothing mattered. I died a little.

I came around the next morning on my old friend Dessie's couch. I had no memory of getting there. An empty bottle of whiskey was beside my head. I had unravelled. I had vague flashbacks of people crying, pushing me and shouting. I had pressed the 'Fuck It' button. It was the only thing that made sense.

Our house opened for the wake a few days later. Late in the evening Pillar and Talts called down and paid their respects. I was humbled that they took the time to visit. Pillar told me he would mention my dad in the dressing room before our league game against Cork that weekend. I welled up but kept the tears back. I was a fragile egg right then. I was meant to be down there in Cork, but would be burying my father instead.

We went west to Galway, where we laid my dad to rest in a small plot in my mother's home town of Ballygar. In the graveyard, the mossy-topped headstones stood tall, saturated in the drizzle that licked down from the ubiquitous grey clouds. We carried Dad's coffin to the hole in the ground where we would place his bodily remains. My sister sang 'Raglan Road' as we lowered him down. Some old women chattered ignorantly against the quiet of us all. Their voices carried on the wind. I glared at them. Then it seemed they vanished. Strangers shook my hand and said kind words. Cars dropped us, picked us up, moved us and left us. A yellow fire burned inside my eyelids . . . it smelled like peat, once formed in these desolate fields.

I hit the bottle with my cousins. We traded stories of youth and of legends in a small pub, supping pint after pint and chaser chasing chaser. We drank to the memory of our dead ancestors. We sat on high stools for a few days and shared the pain together. I drank hard, and the blur of emotion and booze rendered me numb, mute and full of pity. Days flurried past in a time-lapsed flickering effect.

I got back to Dublin in time for training on the Tuesday after. I had only missed one match and one training session. I was happy about that much at least. I felt detached; my normal self had vacated the premises. I avoided eye contact and went about my business as quietly as possible. I didn't want pity. I just wanted to get on with it.

Some lads came up and offered quiet condolences – Mossy Quinn, Jayo and Whealo all made it their business to come over and say something. It told me a lot about the character of these men. It meant a lot to me. It took bravery to say a little word, and it helped me feel part of something. I answered them all as tersely as possible to prevent a complete breakdown.

The other lads knew and were a little quieter around me. They gave that sad glance of respect that happens after death. It was a pursing of the lips, a grimace and a nod, all at once. It happened in a split second and was gone.

I felt humbled, and I felt lucky to be in this dressing room; without training, I would have fallen apart. I was lucky that my dad waited to die until I was in this place. If I wasn't here I would not have coped. I would have spiralled into insanity. I had told my dad on his deathbed that I would give everything I had to be successful here. I aimed to be true to that.

I went upstairs to the gym to do a quick warm-up. Every chin-up, every squat and every bench press burned my muscles. I was going to appreciate every second of this chance I had. As I jogged past the management on my way to the field I gave a nod of recognition. They said a friendly hello, I cracked a joke and I got on to the pitch.

I took my place on the far side of the goal and started kicking balls back to Vaughny, Keaney and Mossy. I stood in nets and flung my body around and saved some shots. The dusty ground comforted me as I landed and rolled. I felt the most absurd and alienated feeling wash over me. I was empty but I needed to be here. This was my only out, this journey with the Dubs. This was all I had now, and I clung on to it for dear life.

I immersed myself in training. I bought into the ideas preached by management. I trained in the gym twice a week and with the keepers three times a week. I was militant in my dedication. I allowed myself zero wriggle-room. The weight of my dad's death hung heavily on me, taking away joy, extracting the happiness.

If I was not working I was training. If I was not training I was resting. If I was not resting I was playing. There was no time for anything else. There was no time for my girlfriend. She began to feel excluded. We were living in a swanky new apartment in Smithfield, but I was rarely home to enjoy it with her. She was frustrated and wanted more. But I had lost my dad and found the Dubs. Where could she or a social life fit into this new existence I was in? She came into the bedroom one evening and told me she was going back to Barcelona the following day. She left and I sat there, wondering if I could have done something differently.

I had signed a year-long lease, but my landlady was kind enough to release me from it after three months. She was a Kerry woman and she knew the story only too well.

'Yerra, ye wouldn't be the first couple to split up over the GAA and ye won't be the lasht . . . I might need you for tickets in September so you may do me a favour then.'

The GAA saved the day again.

Luckily my old friend Stevie had a room available in his house in Portmarnock. I moved in. It was great to be back living here. I had a big double room and the house was massive. It was bachelor-style living. Football, poker and pizza were the order of the day. It was the perfect tonic.

My family were all struggling, too. My brother had returned to the States but my sisters and mother were all still living in Dublin, and I tried to step up to the plate for them. I made it my business to speak to them as often as possible. I called out to the house and we sat and were sad together. Our family had had the guts ripped out of it.

Our dad was the lynchpin to us all. He had made us all tick together and could fix the problems we never saw.

I felt it was my duty to offer something to my sisters and mother that bore some resemblance to what my dad had offered. I tried my best. But I was busy and dealing with my own depression and mental mayhem. I was as positive as I could be, kept the girls involved in my own journey and tried to encourage them all in whatever they were doing. But there was nothing to make things better.

I began painting again to ease my troubled mind. I set up an easel in my room and painted abstract compositions of colour and shape. I read old books, studied poker and wrote stories and poems. I knew the acid test lay in the weeks and months ahead. There would be questions asked and I wasn't sure what way I would answer them.

Throughout my life the GAA had always been here for me. Not as some abstract entity, but as a real and helpful group of people who cared. In the dark times you find out what that community spirit means. I thought about the service for my dad's removal; the lads from St Sylvester's who came up to the front of the church and gave that manly handshake/one-armed hug. I was dribbling jittery tears down my face. They gave me strength in a way you seldom experience as a man. It was something I wouldn't forget.

I was going to take the deep pain and turn it into energy for the All-Ireland crusade. We were all here for one reason and one reason only – to bring Sam Maguire home to the banks of the Liffey. Five times a week, fifty men got together to plot and plan, to train and practise, to improve and learn. We were united by that drive to be the champions of Ireland.

At the end of that first training session back after Dad's funeral, Pillar went through some of the highlights from the weekend's game against Cork. There was a little video showing various aspects of our play which needed attention. Ray Boyne had the stats and they were analysed and digested. We all stared and listened.

'Right, lads,' said Pillar. 'You can head off now, but I want you all to think about one thing when you leave here tonight. I want you all to remember that you are the privileged few. You could walk into bars the length and breadth of Ireland tonight and hear the nearly men on high stools, telling all around them what they could have been, they should have been or they might have been. Don't let this opportunity pass you by. Never forget the chance and opportunity you have by being with this group of men you see here around you. Make sure you don't look back with regrets.'

I would have no regrets.

10

April 2006

It was a frosty night at the Clanna Gael pitches in Ringsend. The field was alive with the sound of cackles, shouts and the thud of colliding bodies. Footballs flew high into the night sky above the glare of the floodlights. They vanished like ghosts, and then reappeared. Players tackled furiously to my left, battering the man on the ball into submission. It was like a military training camp: sparse, serious and smelling of industry.

I dived low to my right, caught the ball and threw it back to Stephen Cluxton in one movement. I jumped up, moved quickly to my left, got set and caught a shot from Keeper Coach Gary Matthews. I turned to my left, got set and sprang low to save a shot from Paul Copeland. I hopped up, turned back to face Clucko and repeated. I was moving well, pushing it hard. I employed cyborg concentration, aiming for perfection. I had spring and aggression. I wanted to stand out.

Gary broke down the goalkeeper's game completely, stripping it back to the fundamentals. We worked on position – good feet and good hands. I soaked it all in and worked on moving as fast as I could without getting sloppy. We repeated the simple things over and over. Quick feet, get set and collect the ball. It was all about positioning and how to get there quickly.

I was training with two of the best keepers in Ireland, and I was holding my own. I was pushing Coper for his sub keeper spot. Coper had won an All-Ireland at U/21 level and was a solid keeper. But I thought I could take his place. He seemed very relaxed when he trained. It wasn't that he didn't train hard, but I thought I had an edge, and that I would prove it before the championship came.

Clucko, well, Clucko was another matter altogether. He was a machine.

At the end of our keeper session we were called to do some running with the rest of the squad. It was active recovery, short and sharp running – lengths of 120 metres down to 50 metres. I was a few yards off the pace for most of the longer races, but was closer over the shorter ones. I was not really bothered. I wouldn't be judged for my speed over long distances. I struggled badly in the backwards running, getting hammered by 20 metres over an 80-metre distance.

After training I got a lift home from Ski Wade as my car was being serviced. I asked him how I could get better at running backwards. In the safety of the lift home I thought it was OK to ask questions I would never ask in public. Big mistake.

'Tell me, Ski, how do I get better at running backwards? I was getting battered out there tonight.'

Ski was a tough-looking man, with a skin head and rough, grizzled features. He looked at me strangely, as if I had just asked him out on a date. His face scrunched up and a scowl ran along his forehead. He let the car sit in parking with the engine running.

'How do you get better at running backwards, Lenny?' he answered.

'Yeah, how do you get better at running backwards?' I replied, realizing I was falling out of favour quickly.

'Ya fuckin' practise runnin' backwards, Lenny, that's how you get better at it,' he lashed, shaking his head and reversing out of the car park. Obviously.

I never asked Ski any more questions after that.

I loved the keeper training. Each session started with us doing a basic warm-up with the rest of the squad. This sometimes depended on Clucko's mood. If he went straight to the goals, we would too. Normally, though, we all mucked in and warmed up as a group. Afterwards the three keepers and Gary went to our corner of the pitch and got training. In winter we wrapped up well: tracksuits, tops, thermals, beanies and three-quarter-length bottoms. Everything you needed was taken care of. Gary brought us new gloves every month and there was no excuse for not being able to train well.

I loved the attention to detail. All our boots and kit were supplied by sponsors. We all had squad numbers, and every bit of gear, from socks to gumshields, was supplied in good time. In my first year my squad number was 43. My tops came with 'JL' or '43' on them. It was professional and, for me, a source of serious pride. When I saw my first Dublin kitbag with my name on the side I was humbled. It felt great to see it in writing. It meant I existed. It meant there was something to show for it all.

We got a good slagging from time to time off the outfield players: 'How was your session, lads? Tough playing donkey over there in the corner, was it?' While they ran and tackled and chased and harried, we appeared to stand in the corner of the pitch and throw the ball at each other. We stuck together, though. The Goalkeepers' Union is one which transcends all sports. We are the base of the spine. Without us, nothing works.

I have done all types of training – running, gym, GAA, rugby and soccer. The only thing tougher than goalkeeper training is boxing. There is a certain intensity and madness: you need to throw yourself through the air and on to solid ground for an hour or more at a time. You need aerobic and anaerobic fitness, agility, stamina, strength, flexibility and excellent hand–eye coordination. The manic levels you train at surpass the levels required by outfield players. Any goalkeeper will tell you that!

I obsessed over my training, analysing every tiny aspect of it: my diet, my gym work, my levels of energy, my mindset and my attitude. My addictive personality craved more and more of everything. I had become a gym junkie. Dumb-bells and ice baths replaced alcohol and drugs. I pumped my body full of good carbohydrates, protein and creatine. I began to show muscle change and topped 90 kilos for the first time ever.

Training broke down into squad work and gym work. Each month Clarkey gave us a plastic laminate sheet with a timetable mapped out for us. All matches and training sessions, including their locations, were on it. It made it simple to plan your time.

On some gym days I went down to the local GAA fields in Portmarnock and practised my kicking. It was an area in which I needed to improve. I wanted the longest kick-out in the squad.

And, to adopt the words of Ski Wade, I fuckin' practised to get better at it.

I borrowed a bag of balls and got to work. I began at the 14-yard line and slotted the balls gently over. I then moved out to the 21-yard line and did the same. After warming up I went to the 45-metre line and started hitting them with a little more power. Then I ventured as far as the halfway line. As the weeks went by, I got greater accuracy and distance. If I could slot over a 45 from the right of the goal, then I would be able to pick out Ciarán Whelan when kicking the ball out in a match.

I varied my run-up and my follow-through. I tinkered with the amount of power and the amount of slice. I experimented with my body position and shoulder swing. I tried slicing down through the ball *à la* Cluxton, and the big hoof *à la* Padraic Kelly of Offaly. In the gym I was building up the power in my legs. I thought of them as golf clubs. I had been using a five iron to tee off with. I needed to be able to switch to a driver when needed.

On these days in the long, empty fields of North County Dublin, I transported myself into a different world. As I stretched and limbered my kicking muscles, I let my mind drift. In this new world I was in a packed Parnell Park. I was playing league games and tipping shots around the post. In this world I was thumping the balls sixty yards down the field. Geezer and Whealo soared like winged gazelles to pluck my kick-outs from the sky-blue air.

In this world I imagined taking to the field in Croke Park. Where was Clucko? Sometimes, in my mind, he got suspended, other times injured or sick. Sometimes I started the games, sometimes I came on as a substitute. Without fail I heard Des Cahill commentating in my head . . . 'The ball is kicked out by Leonard . . . long, high and accurate into the arms of Shane Ryan . . .'

I heard the roar of the crowd and the chants of the Hill. I could smell the grass and see the eyes of the enemy. I heard the crowd chanting my name: 'There's only one Johnny Leonard, one Johnny Leonard . . .' In this world I was ready. I had played the games a thousand times before. I was a winner, a champion and a hero.

Then I would come back to reality and look around the vast, empty sprawl of grasslands I stood in. I would stretch my hamstrings a little while longer. My mind was ready, at least.

Being involved with the Dubs was the best drug ever, and the addict in me wanted all I could get. I never lacked confidence, but my dad had taught me that there was always someone out there who was better than you. His motivation was to get me to try harder, but in me this idea fed a slight inferiority complex. There was always a niggling doubt that maybe I just wasn't good enough. And now I found myself battling to be a substitute keeper. Seldom seen and seldom heard, the sub keeper ploughs a lonely furrow. You train as hard as anyone, but you rarely get on the pitch. I was locked in a battle to be the nowhere man.

We finished the league in mid-table, avoiding both the playoffs and relegation. There was a seven-week break until the Championship kicked off, away to Longford. I had been sub for three of the league games, and as the training intensified through April and May, I considered myself to be in the ascendency versus Coper.

At the start of May, Pillar announced that we had a few weeks to stake our claims for Championship places. The squad would be trimmed down from the extended group of over forty to a tighter group of thirty. Our progress in training would be measured. Our performance in squad matches and challenge matches would be scrutinized. We would be allowed to play for our club teams, and our form there would be assessed.

I clicked up a few notches in everything I did. I tried to lead and be seen to be enjoying the challenge. In club matches and squad matches and keeper training sessions, I was loud and focused. I played solidly in challenge games against Monaghan and Antrim. Coper played solidly in his halves too. We were both giving it our best.

At some point Gary informed us that all three keepers would be kept on for the Championship squad. While this news removed some of the pressure, it meant the battle to be the outright number two wasn't over, and could go on all summer. As the weeks went on, the intensity in everything we did ramped up. It was going to be close. Coper had the experience and the power of possession. I was playing as well as I ever had and was breathing hard down his neck.

The longest training session of the year was the Tuesday before our first Championship game – the night the team would be announced for the match. After each training session, five large ice baths were prepared. Two minutes in the ice, then two in a hot shower. I found being submerged in the ice gave me a moment to meditate into a calmer state. I pictured being selected as sub keeper. As the ice clinked against my shoulders, I imagined that number 16 jersey on my back.

Afterwards we went to the gym for the team meeting. Pillar started on a long-winded talk about effort, squad membership and all that kind of stuff . . . I was nervous. This single moment would decide the rest of my year. Was I in or was I out? He waffled on and on. I tried to stay calm, but I was dragged into a warped vortex.

He started to name the team. I heard him mention Clucko and then everything went a bit fuzzy. There was no meaning, only symbols and suggestions. Ronald McDonald, was it? I could understand nothing. Everything echoed and bounced. Kurt Cobain and Alan Brogan were starting. I thought I heard him give a surprise start to Billy Bob Thornton at corner forward. Hurry the fuck up, Pillar . . . my mind was collapsing on top of itself.

'And the subs,' he announced, glancing around the room. He stopped and laid eyes on me. 'Number sixteen is Johnny Leonard, Nunber seventeen . . .'

I closed my eyes and gave thanks. I felt my whole being surge with happiness and pride. A whole new world had opened up. Six months ago I was in a drug-fucked mess. Now I was on the panel for a Championship game. As we left the meeting I got a few slaps on the back and a few nods of recognition. It was all I needed.

I made my way to my mother's house and shared the news. It was a great tonic for us all. My family needed some kind of relief from the sadness that was hanging over us. It brought some spark and pride back into our lives. We all spoke about my dad that night, about how happy and interested he would have been.

Our opening match in the Leinster Championship was away to Longford. We arrived in St David's at 10 a.m. on the Saturday and got into a light training session – nothing more than a limber-up and a get-together. I could see that Coper was hurting. He was a lot less enthusiastic than usual. It was a dog-eat-dog situation, and I felt nothing for his plight.

The tactics had been spoken about on the Tuesday and Thursday. Players had shared their experiences of playing in Pearse Park, Longford, and against the particular opponents we would be facing. We had studied video. We had talked about simple tactics and our five key principles of play. These were the building blocks of our game. They never changed, and we spoke about them in every team talk, before games, at training, over dinner and at half-time of matches. There was nothing complicated about them, which meant even the more cognitively challenged among us could remember them.

Rule 1: The Three-Second Rule – Let it go

Try to release the ball within three seconds. We were blessed with some incredibly quick and athletic players. Moving the ball quickly worked to our advantage. This was vital for playing against both blanket defence and traditional styles. If you moved it quickly, then their defence had less time to regroup. If you moved it long and quickly, then you could counteract the teams who sat deep and defended in numbers. It involved incredible fitness, to maintain support for the player in possession, and accuracy, to ensure you didn't just kick away aimless balls. For a player to be able to release it, he needs options. Players needed to be intelligent as well as hard working. They must think ahead and see what was going to happen and be there to support.

Rule 2: The Tackle – It's 1 v. 1 plus 15 v. 15

Tackling was something that was worked on assiduously in the camp, with Ski Wade leading the drills. Each player was responsible for tackling one player only. That player might be the man you began the game marking, or it might be the man who was closest to you at the breakdown. Players were expected to communicate clearly to ensure all men were accounted for at all times. This approach to the tackle was related to our overall strategy as a defensive unit, whereby – in contrast to teams with swarming defensive styles – each man always marked a single man. The idea was that we should never be vulnerable to overlap situations in dangerous parts of the field.

Rule 3: Kick-out Positions – Before, During and After

These were the basic zones in which we lined up when a kick-out was taking place. The half backs and half forwards all understood where they should be in order to create space for our midfielders to win the ball. For example, our right half back could tuck in deep or wide to the wing to create space for Shane Ryan to make a long run to win a shorter kick-out. Or, if the kick was going to Ciarán Whelan, then the half back positioned himself on the side of his opponent which would be closest to the breaking ball.

Rule 4: Our Re-Starts – Quick Quick Quick

All our re-starts were as quick as possible. This linked with the philosophy behind our three-second rule. If we moved it quick, then teams would not be able to live with us.

Rule 5: Blocking – You Hit the Ball

There was a huge emphasis on blocking. Apart from points on the board, it was the statistic we valued most. The team with the most blocks in a game normally wins it. It was a measure of defensive skill, hard work and determination. The aim was not simply to get in the way: the defender should attack and hit the ball.

These five principles were relentlessly drilled into us at every team meeting. If we stuck to them and applied them with the highest level of commitment possible, then we normally won.

The Saturday before the day of the Championship match was also the opportunity for a speech from one of the selectors. The day before the Longford match, Dave Billings took centre stage and spoke about unity. He showed us the back of a US dollar bill and talked about the Eye of Providence. Like the pyramid depicted on the $1 bill, we were all individuals who were part of the whole. The obscure references would have confused a lot of the footballing brains in the room, but I think I knew what he was getting at! After Dave was finished we watched a short video, made by film-maker Dave Berry, featuring Dublin fans and chants, and players scoring and clashing with opponents – all set to pumping, inspirational music. We walked away, feeling bulletproof.

At least I did.

On match day we met in Parnell Park and waited for the Garda escort to bring us to Longford. I got on the bus and sat down on a seat by myself in the middle. I had a couple of papers and my iPod. As we set off westwards, most of us popped in the headphones and stared ahead. A few lads dozed off, others read. The younger, brasher lads down the back chattered and giggled.

I was too old to go and sit straight down the back, although if a clubmate of mine sat down there, I might have followed him (unfortunately, I was the only Sylvester's man on the panel). The closer to the back you were, the more craic you'd have. But to be able to have that craic depended on having a certain status within the group. The back of the bus was no place for the introverts. You needed complete confidence in where you stood in the pecking order if you were minded to venture down there. It was a place for the young and the strong, those who understood the group dynamic subconsciously.

I read the papers and stared out the window at the green fields and the deep-blue summer sky. There was an incredible string of traffic en route to Longford, and we needed the Garda escort to make sure we got there on time. As we drove past the long lines, the Dublin fans beeped their horns and waved their flags. There was a real carnival atmosphere and it added a lovely backdrop to the journey.

At one point, as a Garda motorbike was signalling the oncoming traffic to allow our coach to drive up the centre of the road, a driver misread the signal. The car veered on to our side of the road, hurtled towards the ditch, then flipped, flew in the air and landed on its roof in a field. By the time our bus drove past, smoke was billowing from the engine as the wheels spun round and round, with the car nestled deep in the long, green grass. It was a surreal sight – the lines of traffic choking the sides of the road, the flashing lights of the Garda escort, the vast blueness of the open sky and the smoke puffing its way towards the heavens.

By the time we reached Longford I felt mentally relaxed but physically stiff. The town was buzzing, the buildings draped in bunting, the streets heavily populated with yapping dogs and children eating oversized sandwiches. We entered the stadium, dropped our bags in the dressing room and took a stroll on to the pitch in our tracksuits.

The locals and Dubs were slowly making their way in. The tang of cider and porter wafted lazily through the country air.

There was still almost an hour and a half until throw in. We were bang on schedule. From the arrival time in Parnell Park that morning, right through the game and until we returned later that evening, everything had been accurately timetabled in five- and ten-minute segments. Nothing was left to chance and there was no confusion about where or when anything was happening.

Clucko and I were the first two changed and on to the pitch for our warm-up. Gary called the shots and we worked through a rigorous routine which got our feet, hands and body warmed up. Quick hands, quick feet, high balls, low balls and fully extending dives. We finished with a little, thirty-yard, 'pinging' kick drill. This was when you sliced down hard through the ball and kept the trajectory low. The warm-up was planned and timed to have Clucko ready for peaking as the game kicked off.

The buzz was building in the stadium. The high sunshine was bringing the best out of people. Dubs fans were already giving a good lash of 'Molly Malone'. The Longford locals were yippin' and hooin' as if the *céilí mór* was kicking off. They didn't seem to have a song, per se – just sporadic outbursts involving the words 'Longford' and 'Boyos'.

We returned to the dressing room to get our match jerseys and organize any last bits of strapping or gear that were needed. The defenders and forwards were taken into the empty shower area for last-minute instructions from Ski. Then we all gathered in the main dressing room for Pillar's pre-match speech. He talked passionately about the journey we were on and what it should mean for us all to be there. As was his way of doing things, he then sent the subs and trainers out, saving his last few words for the fifteen lads who were starting.

The stadium was heaving now and full of noise and clamour. From inside the dressing room I could make out the sound of lads' voices, rising and falling, rising and falling. Finally there was a great hurrah, the door burst open and the team romped out and on to the pitch. We clapped them on, shouting words of encouragement.

As we made our last few adjustments, Clarkey pulled me aside and asked me to put on the '*Maor Uisce*' bib. When the ball was out of play it would be my job to dish out water and pass on instructions from Pillar. I would be getting my first taste of Championship football, but not quite how I dreamed it would be. Adam Sandler's character in *The Waterboy* popped into my mind and stayed there.

With fifteen minutes until throw in, the little stadium had filled up completely. Clucko and I kicked balls out to the midfielders so they could get their eye in. I thumped them high and long and I felt as good in my kicking then as I ever had. As throw in approached I asked Clucko, did he need anything else, and he said no. I shook his hand, wished him the best and jogged back to the dugout.

Clarkey sent me up the line with a rack of plastic bottles – three of water and three of energy drinks. As I jogged along I heard the crowd giggling and shouting friendly abuse at me.

'Gerrup ya bollix, Lenny, you're only the waterboy!'

'Ah gizza drop a' water there, Lenny, will ya?'

'Any gargle in dem bottles wha?'

I gave a few lads a wave and, in scenes reminiscent of the male models having a petrol fight in *Zoolander*, I squirted a good lashing of water at some of them. I was going to enjoy the moment.

Because of the heat I was busy sprinting on and off the pitch, supplying the lads with liquid refreshment. The Longford defenders didn't say a word. They were seriously focused. No one reacted to my terrible jokes about the water being filled with – *wink, wink* – 'the good stuff'.

It was a scrappy and tough game. We never looked our free-flowing best, but we managed to grind them down and squeeze out a narrow win. It was a good test for us. It wasn't pretty. It wasn't fluid. But it was a win . . .

On the way back to Dublin we stopped at a small hotel across from a picturesque lake for our post-match meal. The management gave us the go-ahead to have a few pints. After eating we took a stroll across the road to sit at some picnic tables. The evening sun was dropping low beyond a forest on the far side of the lake. We were supping pint bottles of Bulmer's with pint glasses of ice. The swallows flew low, catching midges on their wings. Two fishermen rowed a boat to the middle of the water. The sun shone down on us. Ice crinkled music-ally against the glasses. There was chatting and joking about the game.

Behind us we heard a roar go up. Our table turned to see the milk-white naked body of Mark Vaughan running past us. Everyone raised a cheer as Vaughny sprinted by and up on to the rickety wooden dock. The decibel levels rose a little more as he reached the end of the dock and leaped high into the air.

His big, snowy body paused momentarily in the air, suspended as though lost in time. The orange shine of his pubic hair glistened in the sunlight. The jowls of his face wobbled in ultra-slow HD, frozen in a silhouette against the sun. Then time accelerated quickly again and he landed with a massive fat splash in the dank, dark waters of the lake. We all laughed our heads off, watching his pasty body splash around. Luckily no women or children bore witness to the alabaster shimmer of his naked torso.

There were three weeks before our next game, and we assumed this meant we could hit the town and have a few drinks back in Dub-lin. But before we left the bus Pillar announced there was a recovery and training session in DCU at 9 a.m. the following morning. I had a serious hankering to hit the piss hard, but I would have to curtail myself. I wouldn't be able to stop if I got going properly.

Ringing in sick for the Dubs wasn't an option.

11

On the Tuesday before our next match in the Leinster Championship, I drove to St David's, parked the car, hopped out and breathed in the sweet, summer air. The sun was still high in the blue sky. A lonely cloud hung down to the west. The distant low sound of laughter rippled from the dressing rooms to my right. A lawnmower rumbled away in some distant garden. I looked out at the pitch and saw that familiar sight of Clarkey and Ski setting up the cones for tonight's session.

I walked into the dressing room and sat down in my usual spot, between Vaughny and Keaney. Vaughny, to my right, was a conveyor belt of words. He talked incessantly. Keaney and Dec O'Mahoney, to my left, were a little more reserved. I put my bag down and began unpacking.

My gear bag was jammed full: two pairs of boots, two pairs of socks, sport-type underpants, jockstrap, box to protect the family jewels, UnderArmour leggings, shorts and compression tops to help keep the muscles warm, two pairs of heavily padded goalkeeper shorts to cushion the hips when you land on the ground, three-quarter-length tracksuit bottoms, two training tops, a T-shirt, a rain jacket, a beanie, a towel and shower gel.

My gear was always clean and my boots polished. Earlier in the year I turned up for a challenge game against Monaghan with some muck on my boots from a game I had played for the club the day before. When Jayo saw the dirt on them he wasn't long giving me an earful.

'What the fuck is that, Lenny? That's some way to prepare for a match for your county.'

He was genuinely disgusted. He shook his head and walked away. It never happened again.

Unpacking the bag and getting the gear on could take ten or

fifteen minutes. It was a nice slow ritual. Mossy and Geezer sat across from me and were always good for some banter. Vaughny was waffling on about some shenanigans he and some friends had been up to. Pillar poked his head through the plastic strips that acted as a door and looked at us with a quizzical, amused expression.

'What's that, Mark?' he asked Vaughny.

'Oh, nothing, Pillar,' answered Vaughny, grinning maniacally like a naughty little schoolboy.

I shook my head and laughed and took my Blue Book from the side pocket of my bag. The Blue Book was a diary customized for the Dublin senior inter-county football team. It contained quotes, timetables, ideas and plans. You brought it to every training session in the side pocket of your gear bag. Inside the front cover was a quote from George Patton, a five-star US general during the Second World War.

I flicked open the front cover and stared long and hard at the quotation on the inside. It was part of our pre-training ritual to recite this quote in pairs. It was left up to the players to take responsibility to find a teammate with whom to recite Patton's words. I looked around for someone who was almost changed and ready to recite . . . Dec O'Mahoney. Dec was a man's man, a quiet man; the kind of silent monster you wanted standing behind you in the heat of battle. I gave him the eye and we nudged closer to each other. We began to mumble the quote.

'Today you must do more than is required of you. Never think that you have done enough or that your job is finished. There's always something that can be done – something that can ensure victory. You can't let others be responsible for getting you started. You must be a self-starter. You must possess that spark of individual initiative that sets the leader apart from the rest. Self-motivation is the key to being one step ahead of everyone else and standing head and shoulders above the crowd. Once you get going, don't stop. Always be on the lookout for the chance to do something better. Never stop trying. Fill yourself with the warrior spirit – and send that warrior into action.'

Our voices droned together as we speed-read in the lowest tone possible. When I first heard of this ritual I had a little chuckle to myself. I thought it was a joke. Were we really meant to read a quotation to each other before every training session? Being a man of words myself, I quite liked the idea. But there was a cringe factor which surfaced when you read it with a tough, hardy midfielder like Dec O'Mahoney. And there were those who gave it short shrift because of how embarrassing it was. It made lads feel uncomfortable.

Not that making us uncomfortable was something that management were afraid of. In the early season we had a team bonding night at the Olympia, watching *Alone It Stands*, a play about the day in 1978 when Munster beat the almightly All Blacks in a game of rugby. Afterwards we went to a bar called The Front Lounge, where we had an area reserved. The Front Lounge was a gay bar. I had been there in my college years, and saw men kissing each other for the first time. When I went for a piss in the toilet, a man beside me started masturbating while watching me. It was rather funny to be there with the cream of Dublin's GAA.

Our area was at the front of the bar. We stood there in a fenced-off area and guzzled back the pints. Some of the younger lads weren't quite sure what to make of it. There was a little confusion, but much mirth. The regular clientele were having a great time ogling the young, athletic meat which had landed in. I chatted with some of the management about the choice of bar.

'We wanted something that would get you out of your comfort zone,' I was told.

The Blue Book for this season had been presented at a ceremony after our Saturday morning training session. This happened the week after the squad had been cut to thirty, just before the Championship kicked off. In the gym, beneath the basketball hoops and with the morning sun streaming in through the triple-glazed Perspex windows, Pillar gave a rousing speech. He spoke of special places, special people and the desire to be a success. He spoke of the transient nature of the game, of sacrifice and of commitment. He called each one of us by name and hand delivered the sacred tome to us.

He then pulled out his copy of the Blue Book and held it aloft. In here, he told us, was the simple code for us to follow. In here were the words written by players gathered in the room. These words dictated how we should behave to be the standard-bearers for Dublin GAA.

Reading the Patton quotation before every training session was cheesy, but we did it. We did it because we were soldiers and we wanted to win. We did it because we wanted to please the management. We did it to be part of the collective.

Pillar's opening gambit at some team meetings might be: 'How many of you read the quotation before you went training today?'

A few hands would go up – sometimes less than half the room.

'This is what I'm talking about, lads. This is not fucking good enough. It is the inches that will win this for us . . . the fucking inches!'

You were either on the bus or not. There could be no middle ground. Sometimes I cringed when I thought about having to read it with one of the lads, and there were times when I conveniently forgot. Most of the lads just read it and got on with it. But there were others who scoffed at the very thought of it.

There was a huge emphasis on the mental side of things. After every training session there was a team meeting. We might analyse opposition, review performance or talk tactics. We might discuss discipline, mindset or mentality. There were quotations dotted around the dressing rooms on large, laminated placards. They reinforced the ethos and mindset we were trying to embody. One week there was a quote from the US Navy Seals: 'Pain is weakness leaving the body.'

It all added up. We were together for the guts of five hours, three times a week: warm-up, group sessions, warm-down, ice baths, squad meeting and meal included. This did not include two gym sessions a week. This did not include club and county matches. The net result was, you spent up to thirty hours a week training to be with this group. It was commitment at a heavy physical and deep emotional level. We did it for love, not money – and almost a third of us never got any game time.

Behind the goal every Tuesday and Thursday I saw the familiar sight of Dublin Gerry. Dublin Gerry was a constant at every training session, every match and every Dublin GAA occasion. He popped up, no matter where or when the Dubs were out. He was a diehard character, a man with the chin of Clark Gable and the voice of Moore Street. He stood behind the goal and retrieved balls for us. When a ball went high over the nets behind the goal, he burrowed his way under the hedges and retrieved it.

He turned up every week. He was a constant source of chatter at the side of the goal, and no matter who we were playing, he would have some nugget of wisdom about them. He would be telling you a story as you lined up a kick-out, or as you prepared to try to save a piledriver from Vaughny or a neatly placed shot from Mossy. He loved being here. He loved it as much as we did – maybe more. It was in his heart and in his soul.

Two weeks before our next Championship match, we were called into our huddle before the session began. Clarkey took us through what was happening for the week ahead, what the training would be like. Then Pillar spoke a few words. He wanted to add a new element to our pre-match ritual. Each of us was to grab a teammate by the shoulder as we jogged around the pitch during the training warm-up. We would be doing the same thing before our next Championship game: after the pre-match team photograph in the centre of the Croke Park pitch, we would jog down slowly to the Hill in this manner, presenting a united front. We were to soak up the atmosphere of Croker. We were to encourage the Hill and the noise. The idea was to absorb that energy, noise and fervour collectively for a short few seconds.

When we eventually axed this ritual two summers later, Davey Henry remarked succinctly: 'It was a bit gay anyway, lads, wasn't it?'

It was. But it worked in its own way, too.

Our next opponents were Laois, who were managed by Kerry legend Mick O'Dwyer at the time. O'Dwyer had galvanized them as a group. They won the Leinster title in 2003 and had reached the final in both '04 and '05, losing by a single score in both games. They had pedigree, but we had done our homework on them. They were a steady team with a few big names. But they were physically quite light and we were fearless about playing them. We analysed them, but the overarching message from management was to play the five principles. That was all. We would win if we stuck to them. For the most part I liked it, this primary focus on ourselves and our way of doing things.

On the Thursday after training the focus was on the media. One of the problems Dublin players faced was the amount of exposure we faced. By the very nature of being from the most populous county in the country, the team was given a disproportionate amount of coverage.

Management's line was: 'If it came from outside the group, it did not matter.' We weren't supposed to read the newspapers. This allowed players to keep their minds and attitudes in the right condition. The hype which surrounded the Dublin GAA team was an external force which did not need any stoking from the group itself. Pillar got stick for being so terse and bland in his dealings with the media. He did not want to give any other county any ammunition whatsoever.

Senior lads like Jayo, Whealo and Clucko stood up and spoke about their experiences with the media. There was no benefit to listening to what was being said or written. They were simply selling stories to the masses. We were to ignore them, whether they were good or bad. Taking impressions from anyone outside the group of fifty was not part of the equation. The philosopher in me broke it down to a simple conditional syllogism.

Major premise: If a Dublin player pays attention to media commentary during the Championship season, he is placing himself at risk of believing the hype and allowing it to affect his performance

Minor premise: Dublin players do not pay attention to media commentary

Conclusion: Dublin players are not at risk of believing the hype and having it affect performances.

The media and pundits routinely claimed that the Dubs got carried away by their own hype. Maybe the fans did. Maybe the media commentators themselves did. But hype did not exist inside our camp. We were training hard, working hard and running hard. We were working on our mentality and doing video work on our opponents. We were a football team working our socks off to be champions – nothing more, nothing less. The vast majority of the Dublin squad were extremely humble GAA men. There was belief and confidence there, but we were never arrogant or bombastic about it.

I read article after article reporting on our Achilles heel: The Hype. The irony was that 'The Hype' existed only in the minds of certain journalists. TV pundits and commentators, too, drawled on about this idea – not mentioning any names, especially not someone like Colm O'Rourke.

The day of the Laois match – Sunday, 8 June – was another glorious summer's day. The sun shone and the wind was minimal. It was a fine feeling to be involved in my first Championship game in Croke Park. I knew my family were close by in the Hogan Stand and that some of my friends were on the Hill. Even though 60,000 people were here watching, the magic of a community-based game was that almost every one of them was supporting a player or players they had a real connection to.

We met in Parnell Park before midday. I got in to see the physios for a quick rub-down and to get my fingers strapped. Clucko was already out on the pitch limbering up slowly. Myself and Gary joined him, and went through our usual rigorous warm-up. It was a warm summer's day and the sweat was bucketing down before long. The rest of the squad did a light jog and went through some slow drills. We returned to the dressing room, where I changed out of my sweaty top and put on some runners. I grabbed a bit of fruit and a jam sandwich from the supplies table before heading outside and on to the bus.

Our kit man Tony Boylan put in a CD and turned it up. The Killers came on: 'All These Things That I've Done'.

In front of the bus three Gardai on motorbikes pulled up. One spoke briefly with Pillar, who gave him a firm handshake before slowly stepping up on to the bus. The world slowed down, and I could hear my breath exhaling, molecule by molecule. I was there. I was on a Dublin Senior inter-county squad, being driven by Garda escort into the fortress of Croke Park. It was my first time.

The sirens wailed in the background as though I was listening to them underwater. Our bus pulled out of Parnell Park and on to the streets of Dublin. There were flags draped from windows fluttering gently in the light breeze. My eyes blinked heavily, a pressure building on them as they closed. Traffic paused as we fast-forwarded by.

Emotions were bursting inside me. Croke Park loomed ahead. There was white noise in my mind. My breaths were deeper now, my eyelids tougher to open. I knew I was where I had always wanted to be. As we turned in under the giant Cusack Stand, the Garda escort slowly whirled away. Now it was real. Now I existed. I felt the love of Dublin. I felt the power of being a Dub. I felt the responsibility that was on my shoulders.

The doors of the bus opened. Time suddenly caught up, as though I had been in some parallel world. Words, beeps, honks, shouts, roars, echoes, laughs and engines all caught up at once. It was business time. I caught Talts' eye as I picked up my gear bag.

'All right Lenny, let's fucking tune in now, Sham.'

Myself and Clucko went through another warm-up in the training area under the stadium. We worked on loosening up again, but also on sharpening the speed of our reactions. The drills were a little quicker. I took a back seat as Gary really ramped up the intensity for the last few minutes. But I was still ready for the call to come: *Lenny, get togged, Clucko has pulled a groin*. I was ready.

Back in the dressing room, the defenders were called into a small room which served as a tactical hub. Ski Wade went through our plan for defending through the game. Ski was an intense character. He spoke as though he was about to punch you in the face. Somehow this added to his effectiveness in reiterating how we were going to play as a defensive unit. When he was done with us we were sent out, and the forwards were called in for their own last-minute words.

Back in the dressing room I grabbed a few jaffa cakes and a Powerade. The noise of the stadium seeped down through the concrete. It was more than just sound . . . it was the promise of what was coming. It was a deep and ancient rumble. Paul Casey paced around the room. He was loud and was shouting last-minute instructions at no one in particular. Clarkey went through his routine of shaking hands with every player. The subs sat to the left, steely-eyed and calm. Cully and Whealo sat with their eyes closed. The forwards, to my right, chattered and giggled like a group of naughty elves.

Pillar called us in to the training area for last words and instructions. He spoke about desire and hunger and emphasized the need to stick to the five principles. As ever, he then instructed everyone to leave the room, save for himself and the first fifteen. We waited in the corridor outside, bouncing footballs and stretching neck muscles. The TV cameras pointed down towards us. Match day officials banged on the door to hurry them up inside. Eventually the door opened and we applauded the team on to the pitch. The stadium erupted and we paused in the centre of the pitch for the photo. Afterwards we grouped together and jogged slowly, arms on shoulders, from the halfway line right up to the Hill. The volume ratcheted up as we advanced forward, self-consciously, like a pack of wolves. Love and hatred flew at us from all directions. It was a powerful force.

We destroyed Laois all over the park. They had no answer to our quick, aggressive play. We turned on the tap and emptied the tank. It was great to witness the lads playing so well. Jogging up and down the sideline was an electrifying experience. The Hill was in great voice. Only once did Laois muster a smidgen of a fightback, which spurred on that most unimaginative of chants from their fans: 'Laois, Laois, Laois, Laois, Laois,' shouted quickly and with no melody. They had been really tough opposition for the previous few years, so giving them a battering gave us real belief. It also put them back in their box, which was always nice when an opposing team seemed to be on the rise.

After the game the dressing room was chirpy without being elated. The quick word from Pillar was: a job well done. I felt relief after finishing my first Championship shift in Croke Park. My family and friends had all been there to see me jog along that sideline. It had been a long road to get here. I was now twenty-nine and knew I wouldn't have long around this squad. I had wasted so many years with drunken, drugged-up debauchery that these moments seemed infinitely precious to me. As I peeled off the medical tape from my wrists and thumbs, I thought about my dad. For years, he had brought me to watch the very team I was now part of. He would have been proud. It would have meant more to him than anyone else I knew.

After the match the team bus brought us out through the stadium on to Jones's Road, then Clonliffe Road and up to the crowds along the Drumcondra Road. Groups of fans stopped and cheered. Outside Quinn's and Fagan's, fans were packed along the footpaths. The sirens from the Garda escort alerted the supporters and they were in full voice as we drove by. The sunburned pink faces of the Dubs contrasted beautifully with their sky-blue Dublin shirts. Young lads, drunk as monkeys, ran around topless clutching flagons of cider. There was merriment and devilment in the air. I felt powerful and serenely contented to be on the bus.

We arrived at DCU, where the first team did a warm-down, had a swim and did some ice baths. The rest of the squad did a light training session. We started with a cycle, then a jog and then hit some weights. There was a good, relaxed air about the place. Fifteen lads milled around the gym in cheeky humour, lifting weights and having the craic. I did a few bicep curls and bench presses, ensuring as buffed-up a look as possible. There would be dancing and revelry no doubt tonight.

Afterwards we made our way down to one of the canteen halls in the College for the post-match meal. I grabbed some food and sat down the back, where we watched *The Sunday Game* on the TVs. It was a first chance to chat properly with the lads who had played in the match. It was all pretty low-key and relaxed. The lads had been instructed to be as verbal as possible with the opposition when we got the upper hand. If they made a mistake we were to remind them of it. If we scored a point against our marker then they were not to forget it. We were to be in their face, and aggressively so. It was a tactic which had been used against us over the previous few seasons.

Towards the end of the meal a familiar-looking head poked around the doorway and got the nod of approval from Pillar. With that the leader of our country, Bertie Ahern, made his way to the top table, where he sat with management. His handler filled a plate with meats, veg and spuds and brought it over to him. I had a good chuckle to myself at the absurdity of it. Where else in the world would the Prime Minister go for a meal with the local amateur football team?

After he finished his meal Bertie was given the floor. He stood up and addressed us.

'Well, lads,' he began in his high, nasal drawl, 'I, eh, I eh, just wanted to say, eh, eh, eh, thank you for today and congratulations on a fine victory. It is important you lads know what it means to the people of Dublin, that you go out there and represent us like you do. It means so much both, eh eh, both, eh, to me and to all the people who, eh, who, eh, are, eh, are from Dublin. I have the height of respect for, eh, the efforts and commitment you have for your county. Thanks again and well done.'

We gave him a good round of applause and a good cheer. I loved this about the GAA. The strange reality was that Bertie Ahern loved the game. No one knew about these visits. It was not a PR exercise. There were no photo ops. It was simply one man proud of the place he came from. As for his political legacy, well, that's a different book altogether.

After our meal we got back on the bus and headed up towards the Sunnybank Pub, a real Dubs boozer in Glasnevin. By the time we got there, most of the patrons had been drinking for seven or eight hours. We had a little room out the back where we were safe from the drunken fans. As we walked across the tarmac the chants began again. All manner of screams and hollers were unleashed as we made our way in. The revellers whistled, shouted and clapped us in.

'G'waaaaaan de boyas!'

'I say Boom Boom Boom, everybody say Jayo, Jayo!'

'Come on yew Boys in Blue . . . Gerrup yis bleedin boyas!'

I got right into the drinking. It was a free bar and Pillar had told us to enjoy ourselves responsibly. I didn't need to be asked twice. I had missed the gargle. It had been a long few weeks of sobriety: not a drop had touched my lips since beating Longford and I had a serious goo on me. After five or six pints I made my way out to the beer garden to have a smoke on the sly. I didn't smoke a lot except for when I drank. When I drank, I loved the combination with ciggies. I knew it was wrong, but I couldn't help myself.

It surprised me to see a few of the other lads come out to have a smoke. Everyone had the same story – it was a release when on the piss after a big game. As evening settled in I wandered back and forth between groups of lads in the beer garden and around the pub. The

drunkenness began to kick in and, mixed with the euphoria of winning, I felt fucking good. Some lads headed into town and some back
to their clubhouses and locals. I stuck with the lads who were going
on the rampage.

We made our way into the Arlington Hotel along Bachelors Walk
in the city. I met some friends who had been at the game and were
still out on the piss. I sat with them at the bar and had a great time. In
the excitement of it all I ordered a bottle of champagne for my group.
We were having the craic and the drink was flowing. As I stood up to
go for a piss Alan Brogan was doing some kind of moonwalk along
the dance floor. Then he spied the champagne and saddled up beside
me as I headed to the jacks.

'What's the story with the champagne, Lenny?' he asked me.

'Just celebrating today and seeing my friends, Brogie . . .'

He stopped me and looked dead eyed at me.

'Well, Len, we have won fuck all. Don't be getting carried away
with yourself . . .'

Quick as you like, he pirouetted away and slid back across the
dance floor, doing some kind of jig to the cheers of the lads. I was
quietened as I headed in for a piss. What the fuck, I thought to myself.
Couldn't I order a bottle of champagne and share it with some
friends? I could . . . sure I could, but Brogie thought it needed to be
said. It took the wind out of my sails a little, but in my heart I knew
I was not celebrating beating Laois. I was celebrating being alive,
being with friends and being part of the Dubs. That was winning
enough for me. I was celebrating life. For the first time since getting
the call from the Dubs, I pressed the 'Fuck It' button.

The night dissolved around me. I ordered Jager Bombs. I ordered
shots. I ordered more pints and bought a pack of cigarettes. My
friends and I left in a haze and then spent a few hours in Eamonn
Doran's, getting even more hammered. The night blended on into
disco music, flashing lights and a fizzy, boozy blur. I found my way
to Copper Face Jacks, where the party always ended. I was not sure
how I got there, but I met a few teammates on the street going in. We
had a free pass in Coppers and were always looked after, no matter
how boozed-up or obnoxious.

The security knew who we were and allowed us do our thing. That thing involved drinking furiously and acting the maggot. Eventually I found myself at a beer-garden table, smoking and drinking on my own. I stared around and no one noticed me. I blinked, opened my eyes and everyone had changed their seats. I looked to my right and saw a big group of my teammates standing and laughing in a group. I saw them look over at me. They all laughed. I blinked again and they disappeared. I blinked again and I was beside the dance floor, propped against a pillar, watching some girls dancing. They looked like giant gummi bears. I blinked again and I was trying to talk to a strange-looking man; he had a long, wiry chin, beady, black eyes and wore what I thought was a wizard's cape.

My eyes closed again and I took a long time to come round.

12

I took a new pair of Adidas Predator boots from my gear bag and dropped them on the concrete floor. The Leinster final was two weeks away and the dressing room was buzzing. Our three gear sponsors were Adidas, Puma and Umbro, and after some deliberation I had opted for the Predator over the Puma boot. New gear arrived every couple of months and it was always welcomed. Coman Goggins could be heard cackling in the other dressing room. He burst into our one, laughing:

'Right lads, who is it?' said Goggsy. 'If one in ten people are gay, then there must be at least two or three here, right? Who is it?'

Lads were chuckling nervously. I was hoping he didn't pick me out. Goggsy was quick-witted and fast to pick up on things. He caught eyes with me.

'Who d'ya reckon, Len? Ha? Who is it?'

'Not sure, Goggsy,' I answered.

He twisted away like a hyperactive cat, screeching at the next lad to enter. It was Vaughny.

'Ah, Vaughny, just the man we were talking about . . .'

The room burst out laughing.

'Whoht? Whoht?' Vaughny protested in his D4 drawl.

I made my way into the physio area and got a stretch and a strap. I was developing a little niggle in my shoulder. All the gym work, after years in recess, was taking its toll. I walked over to the weighing scales and made a note of my weight – 91 kilos. You weighed yourself before and after training to gauge how much fluid you were losing. It was a way of making sure you were keeping hydrated. I went up to the gym and did a light pre-training workout – twenty chin-ups, twenty squats and twenty bench presses of 80 kilos – then I went out to the pitch and carried on with my second warm-up.

This pre-warm-up warm-up was done before the pre-training

kick-around. It was done on the side of the pitch and was compulsory. It involved some light jogging, some core activation, some active yoga and some stretching. The science behind it was that there was a risk of getting injured in the warm-up if you began kicking balls without stretching first. It didn't happen with us.

When I was finished, I jogged over to the goal. The first outfield lads on the pitch were always the same – Mossy, Vaughny and Keaney. They spent the first twenty or thirty minutes going through kicking routines, slotting over point after point. They practised penalties and long-range shots. They practised shooting for goals against us. It was no surprise that they were the ones who stood up and took responsibility during matches. They put in the extra effort and knew the commitment that was needed to be a success.

The other person who was out there was my nemesis, Mr Stephen Cluxton. More often than not he was first on the pitch. When I first joined the squad I thought I could make a good impression by being first out there. What I didn't allow for was Clucko being more dedicated than anyone else. He was always there before me, slotting over balls from the 45. He would have a big bag of balls and would assiduously slot over ball after ball after ball. I couldn't believe how early he was arriving to be out, warmed up and already training.

So, as the season progressed, I arrived earlier and earlier until I would have to arrive almost two hours before training just to be able to get on to the pitch at the same time as him. I loved every second of training and being on the Dubs panel was something I cherished, but I was hoping to be able to stand out by my sheer and immense commitment. Clucko made that a very difficult proposition. It was as though he knew what my plan was and just kept raising the stakes.

It was widely accepted that Clucko was the best keeper in Ireland. He already had one All Star, and would go on to win another this season. I liked to think that Gary Matthews and I were part of his success – pushing him on, helping him reach his incredible heights. But of course Clucko's achievements were his own. As for me, being next in line to the best in the country was no small achievement – but it still wasn't enough.

I began my quest to be number 1 by matching his dedication and commitment. Then I tried to better it. On my days off I was practising on my own. But I was pretty sure he was doing something similar.

In training I thought I was pulling off better saves than Clucko. I had a better acrobatic range and better reactions. He had better technique, as he had been doing the correct training for longer. But I was naturally more gifted in this area than him. I could pull off saves that he wasn't capable of. I firmly believed I was the better shot-stopper.

But shot-stopping is not as important in GAA as it is in soccer. A team can win a game of Gaelic without putting a shot on goal. So while you might have the reflexes of the ninja, you may get very few opportunities to show these skills off.

I felt Clucko and I were very similar in dealing with the high ball. We made very few mistakes, were solid and dependable. It was hard to distinguish who had the advantage here. Similarly, commanding the area was something we were both excellent at. I was always loud, dominating and constructive with my defenders. Clucko was too. His advantage was that he already had the trust of the group. He had shown he could control the game in high-pressure situations. That was something you could earn only over time and by playing big matches. So he had the advantage here.

Probably the most important aspect of GAA goalkeeping is distribution. Nothing else a keeper does has more impact on the game. This is where Clucko had an advantage. His kicking was incredibly accurate. He was robotic in his technique and relentless in the repetitive practising of his methodology. There were no surprises when he pinged a fifty-yard ball into the chest of a running half forward at a key moment in a match – he did this every day in training. It was no surprise when, in the 2010 season, he took over taking the long-range free – he had been practising for years.

I have often heard it said by Manchester United players that they were never surprised to see David Beckham scoring free kicks or making incredibly accurate long-range passes, because of what they saw him do every day in training, outside of the normal training

hours. He repeated over and over and over again his method of strik-
ing the ball, and it was because of this dedication that he excelled.

I got a glimpse of this kind of dedication when I began training
with Clucko. He was relentless in his application and in the serious-
ness with which he approached everything. He was cool and calm
under pressure because he rehearsed everything over and over again.
An exemplary range of techniques was stored in his muscle
memory.

His pre-warm-up consisted of hitting twenty balls over from the
14-yard line. He then moved out ten yards and repeated the process
from the left and the right. Then he moved out to the 45. There was
no hidden secret, no enigma. He simply practised excellent technique
over and over and over.

The accolades rolled in for Clucko, and rightly so. He deserved
them all. He was cool under pressure, a good shot-stopper and solid
under a high ball. But what really made him stand out was that he
varied his kick-out. He revolutionized the perception of goalkeepers
in the GAA. You were no longer the fat lad with the long hoof. You
were the tactical orchestrator with vision and accurate range.

The bog-standard GAA kicking tees were either training cones
which had been cut with a scissors, or the funky-looking yellow
or green hedgehog-style ones. Neither of these quite suited Clucko,
so he had his very own kicking tee created by the dentist who
moulded the gumshields for our squad. The tee was custom-built for
his exact kicking swing, allowed him to strike the ball at a lower
point.

It was the nature of Clucko's ball-strike which allowed him to be
so accurate. Instead of the hoof under the ball, he employed a strike
down through the ball, which gave his kicks a lower and quicker trajectory. I thought about asking for my own custom-made kicking
tee, but chickened out. I continued using my hacked-up training
cone. The cone was dependable and I could always cut up a new one
if needed. But it just seemed unprofessional that I did not have a
specialized piece of equipment for the thing I did most often. My
kicking style meant I needed more loft than Clucko, but something
which presented the ball a little lighter than the hacked-up cone

could. I envisaged something like the rook in chess – the little castle that sits in the corner. The ball would sit lightly on the turrets on a slender base, the size of which could be changed depending on the kicker's style. My design ideas never quite made it past my daydreams.

Clucko and Shane Ryan had developed a great understanding on kick-outs. Shane jogged in one direction towards Ciarán Whelan's side of midfield, and then did a reverse roll around the back of his marker and sprinted the opposite way. He did this as Clucko placed the ball on his tee. Clucko could then stroke a nicely weighted ball into the vacated space, where Shane would gobble it up. It was all pretty simple stuff, but because new ideas in GAA are like polar bears in bikinis – 'let it go up the middle to hell' being the dominant ideology – Clucko's approach seemed revolutionary.

The following season I was asked to cover for Clucko when he couldn't play for the Leinster team in the Railway Cup. On the subs bench that day I got chatting with the other lads from around the province. They were all in absolute awe of Clucko and were probing me as to what secret methods there were for the psychic link-up he and Shane Ryan enjoyed. I laughed them off and pretended there was a little something they just couldn't guess. I helped shroud the mystery just a little more. In all reality though, Shane Ryan made a decoy run, Clucko looked up and kicked a ball into space for him. That was it – plain and simple. I found it hilarious that there were other possibilities existing in the minds of these footballers. I mean, what could they have been doing? A secret signal? A secret signal in front of 80,000 people which no one else picked up on? The truth was that Shane Ryan was extremely quick and mobile. The other truth was that Clucko was extremely accurate in his kicking.

I got my first glimpse of Clucko's notorious temper two weeks before the Leinster final against Offaly. Training that day began with a warm-up where the forwards, defenders, midfielders and keepers all broke up into small groups. The defenders went through some pretty heavy drills with Ski Wade marshalling them. Two of the keepers would kick balls out to the midfielders. The third keeper would head over to a goal with the forwards, who would practise shots on goal.

The forwards essentially ran in towards the posts and tried to beat the keeper. It was a fairly simple and effective warm-up in my eyes: the attackers loosened up while getting their eye in. I was usually the keeper sent to do this exercise, and I loved it. But it was a tough gig. The forwards would do a hand pass to each other and then shoot, close to the 14-yard line. No matter how much like Jorge Campos I was feeling, it was difficult to stop the shots. If the forward picked his spot and buried it low and hard across me, then it was a goal. Only the likes of Mossy and Jayo had the composure required to do this time after time. They had that consistency and clinical attitude that made them deadly in front of goal.

On this evening the drill was exhausting. I saved a few but spent most of the time diving through the air saving sweet fuck all. The ground was bone hard and the sun was still high in the sky. Finally Clarkey called a halt to the drill and put me out of my misery. At least the morale would be good among the forwards, I thought. I jogged back over to our keepers' corner to begin our training session. Clucko was fuming. He was cursing under his breath and lashing footballs into the net.

'What's wrong, man?' I asked him.

'What's wrong, Len? That fucking shite is what's wrong.'

I looked at Gary and Coper, and they raised their eyebrows a little and tried to seem a little angry too.

'What shite?' I asked him again.

'That fucking shite you were just doing. You think Colm Cooper is down in Kerry doing fucking drills like that? You think he is running in to the 14-yard line and burying a ball past a keeper with no one trying to stop him?'

'I don't know, what's wrong with it?' I asked.

'It's a load of bollix, Lenny, that's what it is. We bust our bollix over here, the defenders burst their arses over there and then the forwards prick around doing shite like that? It's no wonder we don't fucking win anything. I'm fucking sick of it. How the fuck are we meant to progress with that kind of shite?'

I didn't have an answer. I thought it was a tough drill on the keepers but a good one for the forwards. But when Clucko spoke, you listened. Gary stepped in and got us switched on to our own job.

'All right lads, quit the chattin' and let's get warmed up. Let's just focus on what we're doing and not on the forwards.'

'It's a load of bollix, Gary, we're wasting our fucking time.'

'OK, OK, let's just focus on ourselves, all right?'

With that we began training hard. We went through our usual routines and we trained as professionals would train. We pushed ourselves on and I forgot all about the little blow-up. But Clucko found it hard to let go. He fumed for most of the session and was still in a strop at the end. As we all walked off the pitch back to the dressing room, he had a go at Jayo and a few of the other forwards. Alan Brogan laughed it off and said to me, 'Lenny, what the fuck is wrong with your mate, ha? Have a word with him, will ya?'

But I didn't have any words with Clucko; he was not a man to cross in moments like this. He took it personally that the forwards were not doing the same level of intense warm-up. I was a little taken aback by it, but I respected him for it. He had standards and was not afraid to let people know about them. He was the first to take it to management and make his opinion heard. He did not do it as an ego trip or as some kind of personal crusade, but as a means to push Dublin GAA on.

Clucko was prone to blow-ups during matches, and a part of me was banking that this was something that had not completely gone from his game. I was hoping that his temper would fray in a big game and he would get himself sent off. I didn't mind admitting that to myself; every substitute felt the same. I wanted to play. I wanted to play, no matter what. If that required Clucko having a rush of blood, then so be it. It was a fact of my life – one that became clearer to me as that season went on – that Clucko would not be getting dropped for bad form. He was like some kind of robot. He'd be dropped only if he was injured or suspended. Either would do for me.

Clucko, it should also be noted, was also the first man I ever saw drinking Blue WKDs. I was blown away on our first session together in the Sunnybank Hotel. Behind the bar was a case of Blue WKD, chilling in some ice. Who the fuck drinks that shite, I thought to myself. I turned to see Clucko slugging one down. He was oblivious to slagging. His single-mindedness meant that in a room full of macho drinkers of stout, lager and cider, he could gulp back the weirdest-tasting alcopop of them all, simply because he liked the taste.

Five minutes before half-time of the Leinster final against Offaly, I thought my chance had finally come. Clucko had committed a cynical professional foul, preventing a certain goal for Offaly. In soccer it would have been a straight red card, no questions asked. In today's GAA it is a black card: the offending player has to be substituted for the rest of the game. But in old-school GAA, no one really knew what it was. The Offaly fans were screaming for the red. The Dublin fans were just screaming.

I sat there and watched as the referee marched over in slow motion, his legs like chicken drumsticks. Marty Duffy was the referee, from Sligo, the county of Yeats. *Send him off, Marty, and give me my chance. I am the second coming.* The crowd became white noise. Marty reached into the back pocket of his slippery, oil-black, referee shorts.

Clucko opened his hands out in the pose of a guilty man pretending to be innocent. His navy baseball cap looked too big for his head. My eyelids closed and opened once, twice and again. They felt heavy. My head felt heavy. I closed my eyes and listened. The white noise whirred. It screeched higher and higher and higher, until it popped into the most thunderous, deep-waterfall, exploding boom. A gigantic chorus of cynical boos rang out. I opened my eyes and saw a flash of yellow in Marty's hand. It was a yellow card. It was a fucking poxy yellow card.

Half-time was blown for shortly afterwards and we marched back under the stadium to regroup. I was gutted. Although there was no professional foul in GAA, I had been hoping Marty would set some kind of precedent. It was a chance for him to make a name for himself, and for me too. It didn't happen and the incident didn't get a mention until much later, when many pints had been downed.

The second half blurred along. It was a tight game and Offaly pushed us gently all the way. But we had a little too much for them. In the end we pulled away quite handily. Our superior fitness and speed made us impossible to live with and a Jason Sherlock goal at the end of a well-worked attack gave us the cushion that killed off the game.

When the final whistle blew, fans streamed on to the pitch and mobbed some of the players. We had retained our Leinster title and now there was a real reason to celebrate. I had finally picked up some silverware playing – or at least training and sitting on the bench – for Dublin. I stood on the steps in line with the rest of my teammates, watching Collie Moran make his speech and lift the Jack Delaney cup. The majority of the Dublin fans were crammed at the side of the pitch under the Hogan Stand. I looked back at them and soaked it in.

I heard my name being shouted from close to my right. I looked over and saw my three sisters and my mother, beaming and smiling. It was a sweet moment. The noise in the stadium filtered away any other words, but I could see the delight in their eyes. I was proud they were there for this moment. It was three months since my dad had died. This moment marked the beginning of a revival for us all. They had taken my dad's passing badly and I knew that they all understood the connection he had with me and the GAA. They shared this moment with me in the same way my dad would have. It lifted the gloom that death had planted on them. We were living in the moment, feeling deep connection and pure joy. This moment signalled to me that things were going to be OK for us all.

Each player took his turn to go up and lift the cup. When it got to me I was pumped. I was the last player in line for it. I took a split second to stand behind the cup and look at the fans below. As far as the eye could see was an ocean of faces. Semi-naked boys and girls flew flags in triumphant delight. Red flares flared in dazzled corners and 'Molly Malone' reverberated. Ten thousand eyes eyed me from the field. Ten thousand eyes required me to deliver.

I placed one hand on either side of the cup and brought it up to my lips, gave it a kiss and screamed, 'You little fucking dancer!' and raised the cup above my head. The fans below erupted and cheered. I savoured every second and tried to slow it down as much as I could. The moment was there and then was no more. As I turned away, someone tried to grab the cup from me. I was not sure what was going on as I was so charged with excitement. I yanked the cup away from the fan and jogged on in a panic, down the steps of the Hogan Stand and back to the dressing room. Beyond the concrete walls I heard the muffled chant of 'Championes, Championes, are we are we are we' coming from the dressing room.

There was a reason to get hammered now, and I was in full throttle. By the time we got to the Sunnybank, after our usual pit stop in DCU, my family had arrived to celebrate. My mother and sisters all joined in and they mingled with the families of the other Dublin players. The drink was flowing and I was in my element. It had been such a big part of my life, and I missed it. It was great to have a few drinks with my family and share the celebration with them.

Most of the squad ended up in Coppers, where the session went on late and long. The beauty of Coppers was that there was no hassle getting a lock-in. They really looked after us and at five in the morning there was a good spread of us still standing, with a heap of women and friends around us. I began to struggle as the hours went on, and I ended up stumbling out on to the streets at seven in the morning. I was a blurry mess. I hailed a taxi and made my way home for a few hours' kip.

I was woken by the sound of my phone. There were a few missed calls and I managed to get in touch with Mossy and Shane Ryan, who lived close by. We got a taxi out to Hollystown Golf Club, where some of the lads had been playing a round. I sat in the beer garden with the lads and we got right into it again, topping up where we left off a few hours earlier. Jayo finished his round and held court for a while, telling stories about the past. He was like a *seanchaí*. All he needed was an ould pipe and a cap. We made our way in to Temple Bar, carrying on in the Quays pub before making our way to Club M and then, no surprise, Coppers again.

I thought that women were looking at me a little differently now.

Whatever it was about being even slightly famous, it appealed to a certain type of girl. The women flocked around the main men, but ended up only being confident enough to talk to the peripheral lads like myself. It was the perfect scenario, really. It was the perfect scenario if you were able to do something about it.

For my part, I was in beast drinking mode. Beast mode entailed drinking until I could no longer speak. Beast mode meant drinking until I was oblivious to my bodily functions. This was when I would black out. The night would whirl away from me, only to be regurgitated through the various tastes I belched up the next day – Jagermeister, Sambuca and Red Bull. I had some vague flashes of skulling alcopops in honour of Clucko, who never made the lock-in on day two.

Tuesday evening came and we were back training. I took a taxi to my car, which had been parked in Parnell Park for three days. I was sick from drink, still a little drunk and absolutely feeble. I drove my car the short trip to St David's and hopped out and stared at the blinding white brightness of the pitch. I had left my gear bag in the Sunnybank Hotel but had asked Pillar to bring it to training for me. When I arrived I approached Pillar and asked him for it. Pillar looked blankly at me.

'Your gear bag, Lenny?' he answered, standing there beside Ski and Talts. 'I don't have your gear bag. Why would I have your gear bag?'

'I thought you said you'd put it in your boot for me.'

'No, Lenny, that didn't happen.'

Oh. OK. I told them I would swing up by the pub and be back as soon as possible. I turned on my heels but caught them all shaking their heads. By the time I got back to St David's the session was almost over. I made my way across the pitch and took part in some of the final exercises before doing the warm-down and turning back to the dressing room. I thought I had almost gotten away with it.

The team meeting was brief and, as we headed off to get some much-needed grub, Pillar pulled me aside.

'Johnny, we don't need lads who are going to turn up three days after a game still drunk. We don't need that shite. I had plans for our session, and you fucked them up. There's no place around here for that, all right? Get it together.'

I was shattered. It had been my first two-day bender in a long time and I was not able to handle it like I used to. To make matters worse, I either imagined asking Pillar to bring my gear to training or actually *did* ask him to bring my gear to training.

It was time to get the head down again.

13

At the team meeting after the Thursday session, we were spoken to about celebrating and alcohol. The point was made that we had responsibilities. We were adults, and we had to be allowed to celebrate when we won; but we also needed to know when enough was enough. This was directed at a few of us who were worse for wear after drinking for a few days running. I had little patience for it as my endorphin levels were still low from the overload of booze I had consumed.

There were a lot of team meetings with Team Dublin. After every training session we waited around afterwards to talk, analyse and learn. When you were not starting the games, it was harder to focus on these things. All the videos you watched in the weeks leading up to matches became an abstract exercise in looking interested.

On top of the video work were the brainstorming sessions. These normally happened a few Saturdays before big Championship games. We were put into groups of five or six and were given a whiteboard on which one player wrote up our ideas. It felt a bit corporate. The topic up for discussion before our quarter-final against West-meath was 'Being Strong Favourites'. We sat around and had a good giggle before getting serious about it. It was like being back in school. Ray Boyne collected all the answers, and three days later we had a nice shiny insert for our Blue Book containing the following suggestions:

Never underestimate any opponent
The 'favourite' tag does not matter
Being favourites does not win games
The tag is not important – the perfect player is not interested
    in outside views – the squad view matters . . . nothing else
Accept the tag, then focus on performance

It is 15 v. 15 — just win the battle with the guy in front of me
Routine mental preparation will avoid the mental weakness
    that comes with 'being the favourites' tag

This sort of analysis grated on me; it all just seemed like common sense, and it introduced an element of tedium that I thought we could do without. But there was no getting away from it.

We had a psychologist called Dave Whelan working with us. Dave was well groomed and spoke with a very soothing voice. He had the permanent tan of a man who thought that appearance was important. Pillar brought him in occasionally to speak to us as a group. He was a champion of mental preparation. He taught us various methods of visualization we could use when preparing for the game. For some it might be as simple as going for a walk and remembering a great game they had played. For others it might mean meditating on all possible outcomes for their performance, but always resulting in a positive showing.

This was something I naturally did. I always thought about playing well and saving incredible shots. I didn't find a 'special' place to do some visualization; I just did it when I was alone. As a sub keeper, I had changed my routine slightly. Now I imagined Clucko being sent off or getting injured. I imagined my name coming over the tannoy system. I imagined the nerves jingling inside as I ran on to the pitch. I imagined catching the first high ball that came in. I imagined kicking the first kick-out high and long to a Dublin player. I imagined pulling off an incredible save in the top corner.

I knew that lots of the lads didn't bother with this mental side. It was not for everybody. The lingo of sports psychology sometimes made it difficult to take it seriously. Most players didn't need it. They were confident and had a simple system which worked well for them. Other lads bought in completely. I took the line that if it helped one or two players out and we increased our performance level by even 1 per cent, then it was worth it.

It must have been tough standing up there as a psychologist, talking to a group of egotistical sportsmen. Dave was a nice guy, maybe a bit too nice. Maybe he spoke a little too softly and gently. Most footballers have a hard edge and operate at a pretty basic level. If a psychologist – or any outside expert – doesn't have that hard edge, he can fade in the face of the group.

One weekend Dave brought Niall Quinn out to talk to us before a game. It was an underwhelming experience listening to him. He spoke softly and nicely. I wanted a battling madman to tell me his secrets. Like Dave Whelan, he said all the right things, but there was a lack of conviction in his voice. I found both of them a little contrived and formulaic.

God knows good psychological advice wouldn't be wasted on me. I knew I had deep and long-running problems. I had spent years taking drugs and gargling heavily. Now I immersed myself in a world where I took all my meaning from sport and the occasional sexual conquest. While it was somewhat healthier, I was still living a very shallow existence.

There were four weeks of training before the All-Ireland quarter-final. In these few weeks the training really ratcheted up. There was a different feeling in the camp – I sensed it every time I arrived at training. There was expectancy and tension in the air. We knew we were on the verge of greatness. When we beat Westmeath – and we were completely confident that we would do so – we would be one game from an All-Ireland final.

We had some cracking A versus B games on the Saturday mornings. There was no love lost whatsoever in those matches. The first fifteen were battling to keep their places, and a lot of other lads were trying to break into the team or the match-day squad. The intensity in the games was heavy and the competition was fierce. I was outright number 2 keeper now and Coper got the last ten or fifteen minutes of the second half of the games. I was secure and confident that there would be no change in my status.

Another unorthodox feature of this Dubs squad was that each player was expected to write a match report after each Championship clash. Ray Boyne would have a DVD copy of the game for each player before we left DCU on the evening after the match. It was up to us to watch it and write down our thoughts.

In my report on the Leinster final, I focused on Clucko's

performance and made out some charts, breaking down how our kick-outs were won and lost. I observed that our kick-outs winning percentage was not much better than the opposition's. When you drilled right into the statistics, we came up pretty similar. Clucko had a great reputation in this area but, from where I sat, this area of the game was not actually a significant advantage for us.

True to the corporate style of running things, we all had KPIs (key performance indicators) for our positions. I painfully tried to work the KPIs into my match report. The KPIs for a sub on the bench were as follows:

Be aware of one strength and weakness of all 6 opponents in
    your zone
100% compliance with warm-up procedure
Positive communication with at least 6 players before the game
Distance yourself from the emotion of the game
Positively communicate with the man in your jersey

I would tick all the boxes for the above and add them into my report. The KPIs changed when you came on, but that hadn't happened for me yet. The goalkeeper KPIs included the following:

No goals conceded
Vary kick-out when you lose 2 possessions in the same
    target area
No handling errors
Complete 100% of passes
Communicate on all frees/45s

The list went on and on. I would analyse Clucko's game in terms of his KPIs and then I would write what I would have done differently had I been playing. If I saw a mistake he was making, I would write about it. If I thought management brought on the wrong player I would include it in the report. Although I knew the reports went to Pillar, I didn't write things which I thought might further my place in the squad – I just wrote what I thought.

I would have given my little finger to read Mark Vaughan's reports.

★

The build-up to the All-Ireland quarter-final was a little under-whelming. Maybe it was all the brainwork we were doing. There were no surprises when the team was announced the Tuesday before-hand. I retained my spot on the subs bench and was happy to be there.

There was a little work to be done on the training pitch in the weeks beforehand, to prepare to counteract the kick-outs from West-meath keeper, Gary Connaughton. He was blessed with an incredibly long kick. In order to acclimatize our half backs and midfielders to the inevitable onslaught of high balls around our 45-metre line I took my kicks twenty yards further out than normal in our practice games. I was embarrassed that I had to play off such a big handicap! It gave me more incentive to work harder and gain those extra yards which could propel me into the next category of keeper.

In the event, it was Connaughton who was the standout performer in the game. He pulled off an incredible save after ten minutes or so. Mossy Quinn was clean through, but Connaughton managed to extend an arm and tip the ball away from his control at the very last second. His kicking was exemplary, but our half backs and midfield were well prepared. They had an answer to everything. Nothing typi-fied what our regime was about more than the ability and play of Paul Griffin.

Griff was a great defender. He was quick, agile and teak-tough. He rarely gave away more than one or two scores in a match. Against Westmeath he pulled off two of the most incredible blocks. The first came midway through the first half. He flung himself full length to parry a ball, which deflected into a Dublin hand, and from this result-ing possession we drove up field and scored an excellent point. On the subs bench we all laughed to each other: 'Ski is gonna love that!' One or two did a quick impersonation of Ski's orgasm face while whispering the words 'Griff, Griff . . .'

Five minutes before the end of the game he pulled off another incredible block, tipping a ball away from the blind side. When you watched it again in slow motion you realized how good it was. The game was dead and buried at that point, but Griff's effort typified the resilience we had. There was no room for anything other than com-plete commitment. Griff was such an unassuming fella off the pitch and he spoke very gently and quietly. When he got going, though, he was a complete animal.

After the match, we followed our usual routine, heading to DCU for a warm-down and a meal. There was a two-week turnaround until the All-Ireland semi-final, and the decision was taken that we wouldn't be heading out for a celebration; it was too close to the next round. We were allowed to head out for a few quiet pints in our clubs or locals, but there was an explicit ban on ending up in Copper Face Jacks. Pillar warned us he had eyes around the city of Dublin and that any breaches would not be tolerated.

I was itching for a serious session. As a never-used sub, I trained like the first fifteen, prepared like the first fifteen, but never got to release any of that energy. A team that gets to an All-Ireland final will be training for ten months. Training sessions would average out at two hours per day, six days per week. That works out at a very basic fifty hours a month, five hundred hours per year. A team that reaches the All-Ireland final will play on average six matches – that's ten hours including stoppages. Looked at in this light, a starting player and a never-used sub do 98 per cent of the same things per annum. The commitment to train and not play was almost greater than the commitment required of the starting fifteen and the subs who regularly got on the pitch.

Being in my position was a bit like wining and dining a beautiful girl every week, knowing she would never go home with you. I poured so much energy into it but got nothing back. I needed a release. So I took my gear bag and got home to Portmarnock. The lads had been at the match and I carried on drinking with them before heading into Malahide.

The problem with staying local was that everyone knew me. I was entitled to have a fair few drinks, though. I was sure most of the lads would be having a good session and I wasn't going to miss out. We spent a few hours in Gibney's before making our way to the most infamous nightclub of them all, Tomangos. Tomangos was a north Dublin institution and a great place to get drunk and meet women. It came complete with DJ, who talked over the music, a slow set and lots of local lunatics running amok. Better yet, it was only a ten-minute walk from our house.

The night passed without anything of note until a few minutes before home time. I was having a smoke at the front of the nightclub as we waited for a friend to go home. I got talking to this girl who happened to be smoking too. We had a good laugh and I thought it would be a good idea to invite her back for a drink. She accepted the invitation. My friends had found a taxi and were shouting at me to hurry up. I jogged over, jumped in the back with the lads and told the girl to hop in the front.

They both looked at me.

'Lads, this is Mary; Mary, the lads . . .'

They looked again at her and back at me as the cab drove away. Mary was only three or four foot tall. For some reason this made Joxer very uncomfortable.

'I'm not having any part in this,' he said. 'Pull the cab over.' With that he jumped out of the taxi and stormed off back to get another one.

I laughed, and we got back to the house, where we got a bottle of spirits out. At this stage it was just me, Mary and Stevie. It turned out that Mary was extremely drunk; I just hadn't realized it, as I was pretty hammered too. Stevie called me into the kitchen.

'Lenny, you can't.'

'I can't what? She's a woman, not a child . . . just because she's small doesn't mean she can't be loved.'

'Nah, man, she's too pissed . . . Come on. Let's call her a taxi and get her home.'

He insisted on calling her a cab. When the taxi finally arrived, it pulled right in to the driveway. I helped Mary out to the front of the house and Stevie followed me. She stumbled along the path towards the cab. I looked up at the taxi driver and I caught the strangest of looks.

God knows what he thought had been going on.

In the All-Ireland semi-final we'd be playing against Mayo, the Connacht champions. They'd scraped into the semis after a replay against Laois. We'd hammered Laois. I wasn't sure how much to read into that, but certainly we had no fear of Mayo. The next two weeks would be spent ironing out injuries, recovering our energy levels and having our minds in the best place possible. There would be no dramatic changes to the team. There would be no surprises.

It had been four years since Dublin reached an All-Ireland semi-final. That match had ended in heartbreak against a strong Armagh side, when Cossi missed a last-minute free to tie the game. There were a fair few survivors from that time and they knew only too well how hard it was to get to this stage of the competition. Before 2002, Dublin had not won a Leinster title since 1995. So there were no thoughts of us taking anything for granted or getting carried away. We were in the semi-final on merit, but so were our opponents.

The bulk of the hard training had been done by this stage. Our gym sessions during the week were stripped right back. The general instruction now was just to top up a little. The instruction from Clarkey was to do your favourite workout when you went. It was all about getting the head into perfect shape now. My trips to the gym were still something to look forward to. I was addicted to the routine.

I still saw Eamonn Fennell in the gym at this stage of the year. Even though he was not in the squad he was still training away on his own, getting stronger and staying in shape. While a lot of lads might have packed it in after being dropped, Eamo worked harder than ever on his own. It was no surprise to me that he lifted an All-Ireland a few years later. He deserved it for the sheer dedication he showed in the difficult times.

The challenge now for us was to raise our performance-level to beat Mayo. We talked about what it meant to all of us as a group. Playing and winning an All-Ireland final was the goal of every player. We were surrounded by coaches and staff who supported us and believed in us. It was all about tweaking the little bits now. It was all about ensuring the first fifteen and the impact subs would be as mentally fresh as possible.

My family and friends understood what it took to be involved in this team. My mother and sisters had been part of the conversation about football in our house for nearly thirty years. They knew how intensely my dad and I had talked about it. They experienced the highs and lows with us. They knew what I needed to do to be there, and they helped push me on.

In our final A v. B game on the Saturday before the team was named, the energy levels were high. Everyone expected the same starting fifteen to be chosen for the semi-final, but guys were giving it everything. The game was a particularly fiery one and Pillar blew it up before half-time with the A's winning well – I was sure he was worried about guys getting injured. Mossy and Brogie were in top form and buried me for a goal or two each. It was the first A v. B game which was won heavily by the A's.

In the week of the game the training sessions were short and sharp. The excitement built steadily all week. There were groups of fans coming to the sessions now, and TV crews out doing interviews with players. As Ciarán Whelan chatted on the sideline to RTÉ, we took aim with about ten footballs from sixty yards away. Vaughny got the closest, missing the camera by a foot or two. Whealo was a serious man and wasn't too happy.

As the summer progressed I got my first taste of one of the major stresses facing inter-county players from the top counties: the huge demand for tickets. We got four complimentary tickets for each game, and could buy as many more as we wanted – within reason. People in the pub asked me for them. Friends asked me for them. Extended family asked me for them. People who didn't belong to a GAA club asked me for them. Work colleagues asked me for them. They weren't looking for freebies: they were happy to give me the money. They just wanted access to tickets that, as the summer progressed, were increasingly hard to buy. I found it hard to say no.

For the first Championship game in Croker I got my four complimentary tickets and I bought two for the lads I live with. For the All-Ireland semi I had a list of 16 Hill tickets and 24 Stand tickets. I now had to think about collecting a lot of money and delivering a lot of tickets. The day after the quarter-final I sent out a text to those I had been looking after until now. Everybody increased their order a little. On the Tuesday at training I wrote up the orders on a chart. The total value of the tickets came to over €1,000. I sent out more texts to ask people to drop money in to my work.

In the end I had to stump up half the money myself, as a few people were too busy to get in to see me. On the Thursday night and

Saturday before the game I was dropping off tickets and collecting cash all over Dublin. It was a stress-fest and a waste of energy, coming up to the biggest game I had ever been involved in. There was no other way to do it, though. In the future, I would learn to just say no to certain people.

The morning of the semi was slightly overcast, with pockets of blue to the west. As I drove along the Malahide Road en route to Parnell Park, I saw the signs of a city that was ready. There were flags hanging from windows, blue-and-navy bunting flapping gently in the early-morning breeze and barmen stacking kegs at the front of the pubs. The roads were empty, early on a Sunday morning. I put on some deep progressive house and cranked it up. I felt good and I felt charged.

As I got close to the turn for Parnell Park, I spied none other than Clucko walking along with his gear bag on his shoulder. It was his match-day ritual to walk to Parnell Park. He lived relatively close by. I slowed down a little, rolled down my window and hurled some abuse at him. He didn't flinch. He stared ahead and kept on walking. I laughed to myself and sped off. He had heard it all before and had learned how to tune everything out.

The usual championship match-day ritual was in full swing in Parnell Park. The physios arrived early and had a long list of people who needed strapping and stretching. There were some light snacks and fruit available. The mood was light-hearted.

Myself and Clucko were the first out on to the pitch to get our warm-up done. We worked on all our usual routines: quick feet, quick hands, high balls, low balls, snap shots, reflexes, long-range shots, getting set, reacting, kicking and stretching. We both went through the exact same warm-up: if he pulled a muscle or broke a finger, I needed to be as ready as he was. After the warm-up was finished we went back into the dressing rooms and got ready for the journey to Croke Park.

I didn't bother changing from my training gear. I just took off my boots and slipped on to the bus. I sat beside Conal Keaney and, as we waited for the Garda escort, we chatted away. Keaney was a cool operator and had the quiet confidence needed to perform at the highest level. We chatted about Damien Dempsey and his music – we were both fans. It was the sort of conversation you might have at any time.

As the bus moved through the city, I stared out the window and thought of my dad. I thought about him being gone and I imagined how happy he would be that I was on *the* bus on a day like this. So many times I had pushed him along Jones's Road on the way to see the Dubs play . . . so many times we got excited to see the team bus pass by. My mind drifted to the memories of him for a few long seconds. My emotions swirled and then I let them go. I snapped back into business mode.

We made it to the stadium in good time, and I took a stroll out to the pitch with some of the lads and watched a little bit of the minor game. Clucko and Gary were in early to the warm-up room and began pushing it hard again. I took a back seat as Clucko needed the attention more.

As the clock ticked down we took a few, last minutes to ready ourselves, and then Pillar brought us into the training area for his pre-match speech. We huddled around, arms locked shoulder over shoulder. Pillar took his time with the speech and it had us all a little pumped. Then, as was his tradition, he sent all the mentors and subs out of the room, saving the last few words for the starting team. We made our way outside to the corridor to wait. I bounced a ball on the ground. The noise from the stadium was deafening. It sounded like thunder and mayhem out there.

Stadium officials scurried around the corridor, animated by some drama.

'Mayo have gone down to the Hill!' one of them shouted, looking panicked.

The cheeky feckers had left their dressing room first and taken up position where we normally warmed up, in front of our fans. There was no panic in our lines. Paul Clarke and Dave Billings had a quick chat at the front of our group and turned to inform us succinctly: 'Fuck them, lads. Let's go!'

As our first fifteen came out of the dressing room, we clapped and

cheered their names. The noise of studs on concrete was barely aud-
ible as we turned out the corner and on to the pitch. We posed for
our photo and then clamped together to jog slowly together as a
group, arms on shoulders. The energy was nuclear, the crowd electric and the noise insane. As we reached the Mayo lads warming up,
bodies began crashing into other bodies. A Mayo staff member took
a tumble after receiving a shoulder. Gary dragged me and Clucko
away to the left so we could do our final warm-up on the grass. Then
we headed to the goalmouth, where, ordinarily, we'd kick out some
balls for the midfielders.

This was when the absurdity of the situation hit me: there were
four goalkeepers in the goalmouth, all trying to do the same thing. I
shouldered the Mayo keeper a few times, tussling for position. Any
Mayo ball which came my way was hoofed over the safety netting
and into the Hill. The Hill would swallow up any Mayo balls. While
the kerfuffle was slightly distracting in terms of normal routine, my
sense was that it was only increasing our energy levels. The adrenalin
was surging, and if anyone ever needed a final burst of motivation to
play their hearts out, then this was it.

As I jogged back into the dugout and sat down, my mind relaxed.
I was here to do a job – today could be the day that Clucko went loco.
Today could be the day that he cracked a metatarsal.

I watched the game as dispassionately as possible. It was a scrappy
first half and although Mayo opened up a small lead, a Conal Keaney
goal after some great work by Alan Brogan brought us right back
into the game. We hit the crossbar and Mossy missed a few frees
which could have seen us take a big lead into the half-time break.
Mayo battled hard and had some good scores themselves.

The dust settled a little as we gathered ourselves. There were sore
bodies and hectic minds. Pillar took the time to settle everyone down
and get us focused on our jobs. The medical team patched up the lads
and got everyone ready to battle again. There were a few enforced
switches and the lads were in full battle mode as we stepped out for
the second half.

We managed to go seven points up with fifteen minutes left. But
Mayo got back into the game when, with Shane Ryan operating at

the unfamiliar position of wing back, he was caught wrong side for a through ball and deflected the resulting shot past Clucko.

As the last few minutes ticked down, I hoped and wished and prayed like every Dub fan in the stadium. The momentum seemed to swing to Mayo. The scores were level as we entered the last minute of play. Then a ball broke to Mayo forward Ciarán McDonald. He took the ball down the line and after a series of passes he took a shot, running at full speed from a ridiculous angle, almost forty-five metres from the goal. I was in direct line of the ball and as soon as he kicked it I knew it was over. It was a sublime piece of skill from an incredible footballer. The score put us one point behind in injury time.

There were still a couple of twists yet. We got two frees from over fifty metres out. Both times Mark Vaughan had a chance to make himself a hero. The first he swung high and long, but the ball dropped a few inches short. The resulting break of the ball saw a Mayo man block a shot which would have tied the game. Vaughny got one last chance with another free from a long distance out. The tension was incredible. Sitting on the bench was a nightmare. I knew Vaughny. He didn't feel pressure the way most people did. He would just put this down and hit it. That's what he did. He put it down and hit it high and hard, but ten yards wide. The referee blew up the match not long afterwards and the stadium erupted with the sound of Mayo delight.

The dressing room was a broken place. Bodies were slumped around. Heads were buried in hands. Eyes were closed and no words were spoken. There were no words to be said.

As our bus made its way out to DCU, the Dubs outside the pubs clapped their hands above their heads for us. The Mayo fans danced slippery, gleeful jigs and laughed in our general direction.

Pillar asked me if we could go to the pub that I ran instead of our usual Sunnybank routine. I arranged it, and we made our way into town and proceeded to get absolutely demented drunk on the premises of The Church, a bar and restaurant in a converted church on Mary Street in the city centre. It was a complete contrast from the usual GAA pubs we frequented and it was a relief to be far away from it.

I don't remember anything that happened at The Church.

I woke up at home in bed. There was a girl beside me. I didn't know who she was. She was sleeping and I was semi-clothed. My head was pounding and my mouth was dry. I made my way downstairs to get a drink. I sat down on the couch and shook my head. The memory of defeat flashed up in my mind. It was the first thing I thought about. I sifted through my jeans and found my phone. There were a number of texts and missed calls between 4 a.m. until 7 a.m. One of the texts said there was a session on in The Straw Hall, a great little pub near the Phoenix Park. I made a note to myself to get there. I got a drink of juice and poured a glass for the mystery girl upstairs in bed.

I went back upstairs and the girl opened her eyes ever so slowly.

'Hey.'

'Hey,' she answered.

'I got you some juice,' I said, and put the glass on the locker beside her. I slipped across the bed and dived back in under the duvet.

'Thank you,' she said.

She had black hair and pale-blue eyes. She was not Irish – she spoke with some kind of East European accent. I edged closer to her side of the bed and reached to touch her. Her body was warm and she was almost naked. I gently stroked a finger along her shoulder, her back and down to her top of her panties.

'Mmmmm,' she moaned. 'You are awake now, Mr Sports Star?'

I was awake and ready all right. The misery session with the lads would have to wait a few hours.

14

The papers hammed it up as one of the games of the decade. We were so close to the big time, but we bottled it. A lot was made afterwards about the Mayo tactic of going to the Hill for their warm-up, but it made no real difference to the game. We made crucial mistakes and were not clinical enough. Watching Mayo get destroyed in the final was no consolation, even though I had a fair few quid on Kerry to win that match. Mayo shot their bolt against us in the semis.

The All-Ireland, like an animal long used to handling by countrymen, had slipped away again. Another year demeaned and gutted by the coarse greed of the Kerry battalions, gluttons for more and more.

I stroked my fingers through the stubble on my chin. Ha! Three months at least until a drug test. I had studied drugs for years. The one which lingered the longest in your urine was my old pal, Mr Cannabis. It stays in the system for thirty days after smoking. The rest were far more sport-friendly. Cocaine, speed and ecstasy all left the urine in less than a week. The object of the next few months would be intoxication. Get the drugs in as often as possible. Get the gargle in as much as possible. For in December, it began again.

My friends away from the GAA had other interests. There were clubs to go to. There were women to shag. There were drinks to be drunk. I took the foot off the brakes and sped away, full steam, into debauchery. I still had some club commitments with Sylvester's. There were some league matches to be played. But there was nothing I needed more now than lots of drinking and messing. The roller-coaster intensity of the last six months had taken its toll. I needed my mind to relax, release and explode.

Dublin was a mad city. It was full of mad characters. There were women from all over the continent here. There were bars and clubs, and they were just waiting for you. Having spent months training like a demon, I was entitled to release my new, bulked-up persona on to the streets. My confidence was up. I looked stronger and more muscular than I ever had. I had gone from being a nobody twelve months ago to being the back-up to the best keeper in Ireland. I had a few quid in my pocket and one thing on my mind.

I told myself that, operating at the highest level of sport, it was right and proper that I be shallow, garrulous and carefree in the off-season. I became a pretty vapid fellow.

The cocaine I got in Dublin was a particularly brutal cut. Often it was mixed with novocaine so that it gave you that numb feeling, but with less of the high. It was also mixed with baking powder and lots of other crap – all to give more profit to the seller. Even still, if you dumped enough of it up your nose, you got some kind of kick. The typical bag sold was worth €100 and you got three grammes for that. After five pints, two lines and three Morgan Spiced Rums, you had zero problems talking to any woman. They just might not want to talk to you.

The pills in Dublin had plummeted in price, but also in quality. Back when I was doing them in the mid-'90s, the pills cost up to £25 each. But they were strong. You would take one in a club and maybe a half at a party afterwards, and all night long you would dance like a lunatic in a euphoric state. You would feel energy, delight, connection and an access to incredible thoughts.

Now the pills were €5 each and even cheaper in bulk. They were cut with every kind of crap imaginable. There were no epic come-ups or come-downs. They gave you a little burst of something; the net effect was that they kept you alert and wired, no matter how long you'd been drinking. Being someone who liked to drink, they became an essential part of my short-term party mindset.

Hitting the town in Dublin meant carnage. The city salivated, chewed you up and spat you on the dance floor. I jiggled my furry hips against the rural and the foreign, impersonated hip-hop dancers Irish-style, flaunted Jackie Chan moves in staccato strobe effect.

I took women. They took me.

I trained a little and I worked. I met random people while out of my mush who knew who I was. It was a worry. I had to be careful. Lots of the time I was smoking and on some kind of drug. Word was quick to spread in Dublin. You can only create one reputation in life. I was the blip on the radar that was going off course, the flashing green dot that wanted to be lost. I drifted away from my family again. I think we all needed a break.

In October I received a call from Paul Clarke. There were a group of lads meeting every Saturday morning in Darndale to do some boxing training. I was invited along. A part of me was relieved; this phone call confirmed I was in the plans for the next year. It also meant I would have to temper my Friday night sessions. A 9 a.m. boxing session with fifteen fit and strong lads who were out to prove themselves was no place for a hangover.

I had to work late the night before the first boxing session, and I didn't get to bed until 3.30 a.m. But four hours' sober sleep was better than eight hours of drunken. I had a bowl of muesli and a quick drink of juice. My gear was ready to go. The year had been spent constantly washing football gear. Day after day, clothes horse after clothes horse, never-ending and thankless. Thank fuck it was finished for now. Today all I needed were shorts, runners, a T-shirt and an uppercut.

Darndale was a different world. The remains of a burnt-out car sat on a large patch of grass at the front of the estate.

I looked beyond the wrecked remains and saw some young kids riding horses bareback, with ropes as reins. The horses were tall but skinny, with ragged manes. The boys were no older than twelve or thirteen. They cast long, flickering shadows as they galloped along the green in the winter morning sun. They were lords of their domain.

I slowed down to drive through the first chicane. The chicanes had been built to prevent joyriders from abusing the area too much. I took a right into the community centre area and parked up. Old supermarket trolleys lay upside down. Giant weeds grew through the cracks in the pavement. I saw two girls no older than seventeen or eighteen pushing prams in their pyjamas. One of them, wearing a pink, silky set with a strawberry and cherries print, was shouting at a little toddler who was running away, 'Come eeeeeyyyyaaaaar, Romeoooooooo, ya little blaydin bolliiiix!'

I smiled in their general direction but was ignored, and I carried on walking towards the community centre. The gym was upstairs in a run-down, dilapidated building. There were giant black-and-white photos of some of the boxing greats on the walls. The room was bright from the sunlight streaming in through the dirty windows. It was a closed session just for us Dubs this morning. I took up a position at the end of the room with the rest of the lads.

Clarkey was here to do the introductions, but the boxing trainer took the session. There were about fifteen of us, most of us not in the starting team. There were a few tired-looking heads and definitely a few signs of nerves. We warmed up with skipping, running on the spot and various aerobic exercises. Then we worked on punchbags and on the stomach with medicine balls, sit-ups and core work. Then we shadow-boxed and skipped. It was exhausting. The trainer took absolutely zero shite and no excuses. There was no favouritism or going nice because of who we were. The session ended with one or two rounds between lads who had boxed before. The idea was that after a month or two of this, we would all step in the ring to slug it out with a rival.

It took thousands of hours to get to the level that the top boxers boxed at. We were spending two hours per week for a few months to get to some kind of fighting level. I loved the training. It brought out a new monster in me. Working the punchbags was a joy. I imagined what it must feel like to punch the head off a rival. It appealed to some deep and instinctive aggression which I never really knew existed in me.

After a few weeks I felt I was getting the hang of it. Jabs, hooks and uppercuts were slowly fed to us. We started working on combinations. I developed a powerful left-jab–right-hook combo. When I say powerful, I mean that I could do it without falling over. But the punchbag didn't punch back. I admired the lads who got into the ring, and I looked forward to the time when I was asked to step in.

My thirtieth birthday fell on a Friday night and I arranged the night off work. It was the end of October and I had boxing in the morning, but I couldn't fail to mark my thirtieth. The drink flowed and a little bag of devil's dust was gobbled. Midnight turned into 3 a.m., which turned into 6 a.m. and a house party. I had time enough to get home and lie down for an hour. I stared at the back of my eyelids while trying to get some sleep. My alarm went off around fifteen minutes after I nodded off. I had a shower, brushed my teeth, ate some fried eggs for soakage and jumped in the car. I guzzled an energy drink, chomped a banana and dropped some Optrex into my eyes.

The first person I met at the gym was Ross McConnell: 'Holy shit, Lenny, the bang of gargle off you . . . did you come straight from a lock-in?'

'Had a few last night all right,' I answered, the sweat already bleeding out through my skin. It was going to be a long, nasty session.

Ross was a decent lad. He was athletic, tall and strong and was vying with Denis Bastick for a place in the starting team. Bassy was an absolute machine. He had the body of a Greek god on steroids and the mind of a silent killer. As luck would have it, the management team paired the two of them against each other for some sparring.

The sparring happened at the end of the session. While the lads slugged it out, the rest of us were meant to keep working away in the background. We all stopped for this fight, though. Pillar and Ski Wade were here today and I watched them out of the corner of my eye. They gave each other a kind of 'Well, let's see what happens here' smile.

The fight kicked off and the aggression was magnificent. Bassy unleashed a volley of vicious haymakers, aimed at Rosco's head. Rosco blocked them and responded, lashing jabs and hooks back at Bassy. The bangs, grunts and slaps of gloves against heads were relentless. This was no cultured spar, where lads experimented with techniques. These were two rivals trying to injure each other to advance their own position. It was intoxicating to watch. Bassy seemed to be getting the upper hand as he relentlessly threw punch after punch after punch. But Rosco defended and took all that was thrown at him.

They were given a short breather at the end of the first round and then were straight back into it. The referee pulled them apart a few times, calling for more technique. But, once he let them go again, the flailing of powerful arms was all there was. If there was a judge, then Bassy and his aggression would have won on points.

I was in a dehydrated and dishevelled state. I had sweated out all the booze and intoxicants and was looking forward to getting home and collapsing for a few hours. The call went up: 'Lenny and Collie Prendeville.' Oh, Jesus – today of all days. I was physically shattered and about to step into the ring for the first bout of my life. I sucked in the dank, warm air of the gym. I put on some of the sweatiest, smelliest gloves known to man. The referee put on my headgear and I slipped in through the ropes and started hopping from leg to leg, shaking my shoulders. It was only as Collie shaped up across from me that I realized how small a boxing ring is.

Collie was a tough, quiet lad. He was on the fringes of the squad, and there was no rivalry between us. On the other hand, he was standing in front of me and was coming to hurt me. I tried to access that concentrated aggression which helped me play sports. Shadow-boxing and skipping was all well and good, but when someone was a few feet away and looking to hurt you, the game changed completely. The referee gave us a few instructions and the round began.

It was intense. I kept my guard up and tried to keep him at arm's length. I had a slight reach advantage and I tried to use it. I swung some wild jabs and hooks and connected with the side of his guard and the top of his protective padding. I was trying to wind him and soften him up. I then worked it the opposite way, trying to get him to lower his guard and then smash through his face with all I had. I connected with one punch: a jab slid through his defence and connected with his nose. Blood spurted from his nostrils. My adrenalin levels shot up. The sight of blood made me angrier and thirstier. I launched in at him and tried to hurt him more. At the same time my poor, abused body was going into shock. I was exhausted, and the three minutes' fighting had completely wrecked me.

The referee called the round over and someone signalled to end it completely. I staggered out of the ring and found a chair to sit on. My heart was pounding blood at a dangerous speed around my body. My temples were bleating inside the skin. Noises echoed behind my eyes. My lungs burned and wheezed. Pillar came up to me. His face seemed unusually oblong, like Desperate Dan's. He shook hands with me and said something. I couldn't hear him over the blood and static in my head, but I gathered I had done some kind of good. They were satisfied. I gave a feeble thumbs-up and shuffled slowly back to the lads warming down.

No more late-night sessions before boxing.

The next week I fought against Derek Murray. Derek was a nippy corner back. I was around six inches taller than him – and much slower. He punched the head off me. For every jab I threw, he landed two. My nose took a good cracking but he didn't draw blood. It was as though I was punching through water and he was in the air. I learned how to use my guard that day. All I needed was to land one big, solid haymaker. But I was far too slow.

We boxed all the way until Christmas. I was in great shape, coming into the festive period. I was flat out in work, too. The bar was heaving as the nights got colder and the darkness set in. Henry Street was awash with revellers buying presents and celebrating the general time of the year. They poured into the bar; we filled them up and then poured them back on to the streets. It was a beautiful symbiotic relationship.

Christmas Day brought us all together again as a family. It was a strange time: the first Christmas since my dad died. We all put on brave faces and tried to be as cheery as possible. But the world was a much emptier place without him. It would take some getting used to.

After Christmas we were back in the swing of it. It felt as though we'd had no time off at all. Coper had been dropped from the squad, and no third keeper had been called in. It meant I was outright number 2, with no immediate squad competition. This was a massive weight off my mind.

We were up against DCU in the first round of the O'Byrne Cup. This competition is ordinarily seen as a chance to give your squad members a run out; but they selected Clucko, an All Star keeper. I soldiered on as best I could. I put on a strong front. But my failure to get a game even in the least significant of competitions damaged my confidence. With Clucko in goal for all four games, we picked up our first silverware of the season.

The National League kicked off. Still I couldn't get on the pitch with us playing Tyrone under floodlights in Croke Park. By this time I had mastered the art of the warm-up and stretch. I excelled in the pep-talk handshake. I was the steely-eyed substitute, resolute and ready. The frustration built.

One day in the gym at DCU, Ski Wade came up to me. He gestured over to a skinny young guy I didn't recognize.

'Lenny, show this lad the ropes, will ya? Take him through the programme and routine you do.'

'No problem, Ski,' I answered. 'Who is he?'

'Diarmuid Connolly – the most talented footballer in the country is who he is.'

'Oh yeah?'

'Yeah, unbelievable talent. Bit of a head case, though . . . He has a few issues, but not as bad as you, Lenny.'

Ski looked at me with a glint in his eye. You must be good if Ski is vouching for you, I thought to myself as I looked at the skinny little youngfella. And you must have problems if they think you are like me.

We flipped and flopped through the league. The pitches were sodden and lumpy. Cold northern gales ripped into us. The blood circulated intermittently through the fingers of my keeper gloves. My toes numbed and I sometimes found it hard to follow the progress of games.

I left my job; I couldn't deal with the late nights and also meet the demands of training. I had done a TEFL training course back in 1999, and now I blagged myself into teaching English to foreign students. I was a joke of a teacher. My classes consisted of playing hangman and countdown, and watching DVDs.

Pillar took us on a training weekend, away down in Wexford, after the league. It was cracking May weather. The sun was luscious as we did a session at some rural GAA club. As the evening set in we returned to the hotel, played some poker and began cracking into some beers. It was just what we needed. The porter was flowing and before long there were calls for a sing-song.

'Come on, Lenny, get us started,' shouted Mossy at me from across the bar.

I thought for a quick second and launched into Johnny Cash's 'Folsom Prison Blues'. At the end of the first verse I whistled and screamed and started dancing. Whoops and whistles went up from the lads, and once the ice was broken there was no stopping us. The night carried on long and hard. I plunged deep into drunken oblivion. I sat outside with Dermo Connolly and chewed the ear off him for a few hours. I was smoking away and I let my guard down completely. Lads were flying around the hotel and making the most of the boozing green pass we'd been given. I drank and drank and drank and passed out at some ungodly hour . . .

The knocking on my door wouldn't stop. It was early morning and bright outside. Who the fuck was it? Eventually the door opened and in strolled a bright-eyed and bushy-tailed Ray Boyne, Mr Stat Man himself. He moved purposefully to the blinds and opened them, letting the sunlight stream in.

'Ask not what your county can do for you, but what you can do for your county,' he pronounced in a JFK voice. 'Let's go, Lenny, time to rock and roll.'

I was deep in a world of pain. My head thumped, my eyes bulged and every part of my body was tight and stiff. Eventually I managed to sit up. Ray took a second look at me and shook his head, laughing. I was still fully clothed. I grabbed my gear bag and stumbled after Ray towards the exit and down to the team bus, where everyone else was already on board.

Within a few minutes, before I could get to sleep, we had arrived at an epic-looking beach that was straight out of an ad for desolate Ireland. The sun was blinding. As we got off the bus I could make out some giant mounds which I would soon know better as sand-dunes. There were some flags dotted along a path and someone began shouting instructions about what was happening. I was still drunk and was feeling very old and frail. We were put into groups and sent on our way.

I couldn't breathe and could barely see. The sweat poured from me, and before long I was stumbling through the dunes on my own, far from the speeding young heroes ahead. I took a sharp left off track and slowly edged my way up to the top of one of the dunes. I could see for miles in either direction. A cool breeze sliced across my face, cooling me down. Behind, I could make out some speckled figures close to the bus. Beyond, I could see my teammates running far into the distance, then turning and running back down the strand in front of me.

I stayed up there and gathered my thoughts, watching the waves lap in gently. I wasn't cutting corners; I was just staying alive. I waited, high in the dunes, until the last group struggled past me. I then ran down like some kind of monster from the planet of the shapes. By the time we got back to the bus the rest of the lads were as fucked as me.

We drew with Meath in the first round of the Leinster Championship, then beat them by a few points in the replay. There was nothing spectacular about either game. Our preparation didn't change. Our team talks hadn't changed. Our personnel hadn't changed. We had tweaked one or two things. We had worked on a strategy for closing games out. With ten minutes to go, the management gave the half backs and forwards the ten-finger, open-palmed signal. Those players then signalled the same to the players immediately around them. It was a crude but effective way of making sure everyone knew we were in the endgame. It was a direct reaction to our late capitulation against Mayo.

After beating Meath we had a raucous session in the Quays Bar in Temple Bar. We met some American students who were in Ireland for the summer. The match was being replayed on TV and they were suitably star-struck. There were four or five of these girls, and I think all four or five of them went home with one of us. I pulled a cute twenty-one-year-old blonde who thought of me as though I was a place-kicker for the Chicago Bears. The illusion might have been punctured when I dropped her home in a beat-up old VW Golf the next morning.

We cruised through the rest of the Leinster campaign. We beat Offaly quite easily and a few weeks later rolled over Laois in the final. It was an underwhelming experience this time. Although I was chuffed to be part of a squad that had won Leinster two times in a row, we had bigger fish to fry.

It was now over a year since my dad had passed away. Time was healing things. My family were caught up in my journey with the Dubs almost as much as I was. Being involved with the Dubs brought a magic to life, an effortless sparkle to existence.

We were drawn against Derry in the All-Ireland quarter-final. We had no real history against them but had a lot of respect for them. We watched videos and studied how they played. We earmarked their danger men. We planned as meticulously as you might expect. We trained hard. Keeper training had gone up a level. Just having Clucko and me meant a lot more focus and attention from Gary.

Clucko had a great game against Derry. He pulled off a few fine saves, and we managed to win by a few points. It was a massive relief more than anything else. Next up: Kerry.

It didn't get much better than Kerry in an All-Ireland semi. There was no need for any kind of motivational tools from the management team – no Jedi mind-tricks, no newspaper clippings pinned to the wall, no wild battle-cries. With a two-week turnaround we could do little more than rest, recover and clear the minds. The squad knew there would be no changes to the first fifteen. There was nothing to do but get ourselves feeling as fine as was fathomable. We had some light and sharp training sessions. We tanked up on good vibes that were pulsing through the city.

Our routine on the Saturday was the same. Our video work was the same. Our analysis of the statistics available was as thorough as usual. We talked about ourselves in the same way. There was a little more media around, looking for interviews, but we were shielded well away from most of that by management. From where I was training and preparing, we were as ready as we had ever been.

There was a big sense of occasion on the morning of the game. My family and friends were excited. The people on the streets were excited. I was excited myself. But it was also a time to feel that alligator blood coolly saturating your veins and arteries. It was time to breathe in excess oxyhaemoglobin to populate those cells. There was a gargantuan battle on the horizon. And it was the most imperious champion of them all who was calling us out.

By the time I stood on the sideline of Croke Park, with '*Amhrán*

Na bhFiann' being sung by 82,000 people in unison, the decibel level was higher than at any other game we had played that season. The sight of the Kerry team brought out that extra inspiration. They were the standard-bearers of Gaelic football. At the same time, it was just another game. We had spoken for two weeks about approaching it with that clear and simple mindset: it was just another game.

As I jogged up and down the sideline, keeping the muscles limber, I had a strange sense of calm. Bodies and limbs were flying into each other, players were running at impossible speeds and the crowd were furious in their abuse and encouragement. But I was in a sweet and lovely zone. I was patiently and silently going through my thought-process for what happened when Clucko got injured. I imagined the sight of the ginger lollipop kid, the Gooch, bearing down on me, one on one, with a minute to go and Kerry two points behind. He tries to dummy solo around me, but I spring into him and claw the ball away . . .

The game swung back and forth in the first half and we managed to go in, one point ahead, at half-time. Kerry came right at us in the second and scored a nicely taken goal. From then on, we battled and fought and scrapped, but they just had too much for us.

After the final whistle, I sat for a second or two on the squishy comfort of the subs' bench and smelled the air. It smelled of defeat, as unmistakable as the bang of rashers frying on a Sunday morning. It smelled like fresh air, country clothes, cheap fabric-conditioner, car-seat sweat and ham on a sandwich. It turned like an eel down my throat into my gullet and burrowed in there. It wriggled around, and something told me it was laying eggs.

The dressing room was blown apart. The lights seemed too bright and the walls seemed to have moved closer together. Bodies were heaved over on top of themselves. Lads sobbed gently into their hands. I shook my head and muttered banalities like 'Let's keep the heads up.' One or two others trotted out some motorized crap about it not being our day and having left it all on the field. It was lip service. There was no hiding the hurt and it had to be felt.

We showered in Croke Park. The DCU warm-down and meal was abandoned. It was no time for ice baths and saunas. It was no time for chicken fillets and spuds. There was only one substance that would help at a time like this – drink. We went straight to the boozer and let the handbrakes off. It was the kind of chaotic shot-drinking, pint-skulling mayhem you might expect when you have just failed at the only thing that truly matters in your life.

15

Halloween 2007

Eating with some teammates in a fancy Italian joint in Manhattan, I spotted a familiar face. I walked over to the table and extended my hand.

'Ronan,' I said, 'I won't take up too much of your time, but I just wanted you to know that there is another group of underachieving Irish sports stars here in New York and they are eating and drinking at that table over there.'

I pointed over to a round table on the far side of the room. Collie Moran, Shane Ryan and Paul Casey waved over and laughed.

'There are a few of us from the Dublin GAA team here and we'd like to invite you over for a drink.'

Ronan O'Gara smiled back at me. Ireland had just had a meltdown at the rugby World Cup. I thought he might like to drown his sorrows with us. He said thanks and that he would drop over at a later stage. I marched back over to our group and we got into the cocktails and the rest of our meal. Later on, Ronan came over to our table with his wife. The old romantic in him had other plans.

'Lads, I would love nothing more than to come out on the beer, but sure haven't we booked a moonlight horse-and-carriage ride around Central Park. Best of luck to ye though!'

The lads had booked this trip well in advance. At the last minute, I had booked a flight, taken a taxi straight to Times Square, ordered two Coronas and two shots of tequila, and hadn't stopped since. We went from bar to bar, guzzling and carrying on. We ended up in a lock-in at an Irish bar. The owner plied us full of drink all night. By the end of night one I was completely baloobas, and stumbled through the streets with Collie Moran towards home.

At some point we got separated, and instead of going to bed I ended up in some bar, drinking with a one-armed Vietnam War vet. I went with him to some Russian bar where they threw me out mid-afternoon. I stumbled into a peep show and took solace looking at some young lady bend over. I found another bar and drank on until they realized I was out of my mind and they threw me out too. I crawled back to my hostel and passed out.

Later in the day I woke with a head on me and caught up with the lads. We ended up in a bar in Brooklyn. I was deranged drunk. After one Jager Bomb I almost collapsed. I accused the bar owner of spiking my drink. The lads were in tatters laughing at me. I mumbled curses at them and stumbled out on to the street, where I lay sideways on a bench and began puking. They came out to check on me, but all I could hear were more howls of laughter. I was wearing 'I ♥ NY' socks. Some GAA hard man I was. Eventually I got it together and followed the lads around like a broken sheep. My head pounded and my thoughts were paranoid. I ended up passing out on Shane Ryan's hotel-room floor. I don't think he minded, but his girlfriend wasn't too happy.

I had a new job: as a Brand Ambassador for Guinness Mid-Strength. The job entailed visiting pubs, putting up promotional material and organizing sampling sessions. It was a pretty handy number, especially when everyone wanted to talk about GAA.

I took to having a pint when I was working a promotion, and I was promoting three or four nights a week. I was meant to give out twenty or so pints in each pub. I would sip one myself and ease myself into it. Although I was driving, the Mid-Strength was lower in alcohol and I could drink one or two over the course of an evening without repercussions. This was not the official line from Diageo, but I was making up my own rules.

Working for Guinness was amazing. We had meetings inside St James's Gate and it felt like going inside Willy Wonka's Chocolate factory. I had worked here many years before, when I first returned from Australia. I saw an ad looking for taste-testers. I applied and went in for a trial. They called me the following day and told me I had the job. Although I was not the most accurate taster, they told me I was the quickest at discerning taste changes. Three days a week we were collected and driven to Guinness HQ, where we were taught all about the beers and stouts and what goes into them. It was a dream job: taste-tester for Guinness! The only issue was that on Tuesdays, Wednesdays and Thursdays I was tipsy by lunchtime. This wasn't good for me because, once I got my goo on, I couldn't stop. After work I would carry on my own individual samplings in various licensed premises in Dublin. It resulted in me being a complete drunken mess and I had to put a halt to it.

In the winter of 2007–8 we took up Kung Fu for pre-season Dublin training. While it was a tough workout, there was no fighting at the end of it; sparring in boxing was manageable, but flying kicks and elbows would be going too far. The training was solid, and coming into the Christmas period I felt in the best shape of my life. I was still going to the gym once or twice a week. I had every reason to be cheerful: a cushy job, a fast car and a fit body. I was seeing a cute girl. What more could a man want?

How about a start for Dublin in the annual Blue Stars game? Yes, please. The Blue Stars game kicked off the Dublin GAA calendar. It was a match between the Dubs and the best Dublin club-players of the previous year. I was delighted to finally get a start for the Dubs. It was a nothing game, played at a slow, post-Christmas-pudding pace, but it was a game nevertheless.

Pillar decided to give me a run in every second game of the O'Byrne Cup. For squad members it is a chance to shine, to show you could be trusted.

We beat a good Wicklow side with Clucko in goals in week one. I started against Westmeath in the next game. But you could have had a big sack of spuds in goals instead. Westmeath were brutal, a pale imitation of the side who had rattled us a few years previous. We beat Carlow in the next round after a replay and then, lo and behold, I was selected to play for Dublin against Longford in a competitive final, under lights in Parnell Park, with the TV cameras rolling.

It was a proud moment for me. My mother, sisters, cousins and friends all came to the game. It was a great feeling to be able to give those who knew, loved and supported me the opportunity to see me play in a match with some kind of competitive consequence. I had been preparing and training for this moment for a long time, and they had been encouraging me for just as long.

I had a solid game. I pulled off one nice save and then conceded an opportunistic goal. I kicked decently and marshalled my defence well. We ended up winning the game with a dramatic couple of goals in the final minutes from Jayo. As the final whistle blew and the kids and fans streamed on to the pitch I had a microphone thrust into my face for an interview. This was more like it.

As the National League rolled in I expected to get a game or two. But Pillar and Clucko had other ideas. I was back to being the sub keeper again – game after game after game.

It was getting to me. At a meeting in Guinness with some of the bigwigs we talked about all things beer, and then turned our attention to the world of sport. After hearing that I hadn't been selected for any league games, one of them turned to me and said, 'Have you asked for a game?'

I laughed. 'It doesn't work like that,' I said.

'Why not? You think people get the jobs they are meant to in life? You think the people workng for me are the ones who have the most talent? In my experience people who ask and are hungry for things are more likely to succeed.'

I digested this and concluded that I had nothing to lose. After the meeting I phoned Pillar and told him that I wanted to play some games. I needed to show what I could do.

'You'll have to be patient, Johnny, that's the way things are. Let's see what happens.'

He left me with the impression that he would at least think about it. But nothing changed. I spent a few months dragging myself around the country, clad in the warmest of protective clothing. I got to warm up Clucko in some new and wonderful locations. We managed to scrape our way into the Division 2 final, where we lost a lacklustre game against Westmeath.

To add to my misery, a new keeper had been drafted on to the panel. Michael Savage had just won a club All-Ireland with

St Vincent's. He was in his early twenties and had a lot going for him. I had watched the club final while having a few quiet ones, and he had been one of their star players. He was a quiet and humble chap, too. Keepers have a reputation for being lunatics, but Savo struck me as a very studious and decent young lad. It was a worrying time.

With Savo in the squad the training changed a little. I began to feel under pressure. It was a very subtle difference, but it made me question everything.

It was at times like this that I really missed my dad. He would have known what to say to me. He would have had some good advice, some nuggets of wisdom to keep me balanced. He knew how to re-focus my mind. Without him I felt a sort of emptiness, a hollowness.

Faced with the challenge from Savo, I upped it. I had to respond. I was more committed than ever. I put in more effort and wanted to prove I was still good enough. I felt I had enough talent and maturity to keep Savo out in the cold.

I did struggle in a few areas, which began to irritate Gary Matthews. One of those areas was drop-kicking.

Keeper training involves a large amount of repetitive exercises. You work on accuracy of movement, speed of movement and flexibility, to replicate match situations. To do this, you need someone who can kick the ball straight, over and over again. The best straight-line kick is the drop kick. It was never something I had a problem with while growing up. But I began to mis-hit shots, which meant that training exercises went a little longer and slower than they were meant to.

I really noticed how inaccurate I was when Savo came along. He and Clucko were like robots. They never seemed to hit a stray one. This got to me a little. On top of this, my kick-outs had lost a few yards due to a problem in my hip flexor. I had improved my kicking distance through a lot of hard work, but now I was back to kicking fifty to fifty-five yards.

I knew that the pressure was on me. I knew that Savo was here for my spot. It was a silent battle. Well, it was a silent battle until Pillar called it at a team meeting.

'You two are playing for your place in the Championship squad,' he informed us in front of everyone.

During one of the A v. B games, Talts and Gary Matthews were to the side of the goal, watching what was going on. I had played for most of the game, and I thought I had played well. I turned to Savo, who had been waiting to be told to go in. I felt bad for him, and when the ball went out for a goal kick at the far end I turned and asked him, 'You wanna go in, Savo?'

Savo said nothing but just jogged in for the last few minutes. I trotted off to the sideline and was thinking nothing of it. As I went past the coaches, almost out of earshot, I heard Talts remark, 'That's the difference.' My stomach did that weird dropping, sinking thing. What the fuck had I just done and why had I done it? Who gave their younger competitor a chance without being told to? Who did that? Most people would tell you I was ultra-competitive. You cannot get to the heights of any sport without that streak. But something in me went that day.

A week later we were playing in a challenge game against Sligo. The build-up was inconsequential for most of the team. It was a nothing game against a nothing team out in the back arse of North County Dublin. But for us on the subs' bench it was prime time.

I had been seeing a Swedish girl, and I invited her out to the Sligo game. She was interested in sports and I thought it would be nice to have her there. She sat in the car and watched from the sidelines.

Before the match I took a walk with a few of the lads into the centre of the pitch. A gale-force wind was blowing from one end. We all looked at each other and laughed – no one wanted to be playing into that. I was starting the game. We lost the toss and were playing into the wind. It was the worst beginning possible. Pillar reminded me in the pre-match pep talk that we were playing for our places: some fucking pep talk that was.

I struggled kicking into the wind. My kicks were landing between the 21 and the 45 and putting us under immense pressure. I don't think Savo could have done much differently in that wind; it was just one of those natural phenomena which the big man/woman/hobgoblin upstairs puts in your way.

About five minutes from half-time a ball was driven in to their corner forward. He slipped past Davey Henry and drilled a shot which squirmed underneath me as I spread myself to block. My first-half analysis: no clean sheet and rubbish kick-outs.

We got a grilling from Pillar at half-time. I was gutted. I sat in the dressing room as the team tromped out for the second half. I could do nothing but hope that Savo fucked up in the second half. But the wind was at his back literally and metaphorically. His kick-outs sailed over the halfway line. He pulled off one solid save and caught a few balls which dropped in the wind. He did everything you would expect. I knew it was enough. When that final whistle blew I knew I was gone.

A fuzzy light inside me went out that afternoon. As I drove away I cursed and muttered to myself, thumping the steering wheel. The Swede was oblivious and thought I had done great. She didn't realize that my time was up, and I couldn't really articulate it.

We drove past a sign for a fairground outside Swords.

'Oh my, let's go!!' she screamed. 'I love them . . . please, please, please let's go in . . . it will cheer you up!'

We pulled in to get some cash from an ATM, where I met Ger Brennan. He had played in the game too, and he was livid as he had been taken off. He said he was packing it in under the current management. And he did – a man of his word he was. I wished I had the same confidence.

So, half an hour after one of the most depressing games of my life, I was screaming and laughing like a maniac at a fairground. We went giggling through the hall of mirrors and played some shooting games where I won a giant teddy. I almost shat myself on some of the rides – they seemed like they were about to fall apart. We went back to her apartment and I slipped away from thinking of Dublin.

A few weeks later the squad was named for the Championship first-round match against Louth. I sat there and hoped against hope as Pillar listed the outfield players. He paused as he got to number 16. My heart stopped, my mouth went dry and my stomach fell up inside itself. He named Michael Savage. I was gone and it was official. I felt like crying. Two seasons of playing second fiddle had turned into the nightmare of playing *third* fiddle.

I was hurt. Savo wasn't a better keeper. He might have been younger and more consistent . . . but he wasn't better. He had a good temperament, though. He worked hard and fastidiously on his game. He was soft-spoken and confident. From the outside he deserved it. But from the inside, from the point of view of someone with my talent . . . well, I felt I was being cheated. But I just picked myself up and got on with it. After the season was over, Gary said to me that I took it well. He said most keepers sulk and train less and lose interest. I had worked harder and trained more. That was something at least.

Off the pitch I was in a whirlwind of emotion. I was ashamed to be out of the match-day squad. I was embarrassed to talk about the Dubs to clients and customers. I was out of the loop now. I felt that I had let everyone down, that I had failed. Telling my family was tough. While they were positive and supportive, it still felt as though they had a lesser opinion of me now. The person I was trying to be since my dad died had lost some of his sheen. It was a tough time.

The practical reality for those who were not in the match-day squad was that on match days we watched everyone warm up in Parnell Park. We then got on the bus with the lads and watched them warm up under the stadium. We made our way out and took up some seats in the stand, just behind the dugout. We sat there with the supporters, them oblivious to us and who we were. I watched the kids walk past us, asking the new unknown subs for autographs, and I wanted to be beamed up to anywhere but there. It was a sickening and tantalizing experience. I wanted them to win, but I was disgusted that there was not even a theoretical possibility that I could influence the result.

I cared less now. I still went to the gym and I trained hard when I was there, but I knew I wasn't going to be playing or togging out on match day. This meant I could have a few beers when I liked. So I did. And hey, if I wasn't going to be playing, then I wasn't going to be drug-tested, so I could have a few lines. So I did. I didn't know what else to do. I had given everything and it wasn't enough. Now they wanted to drag me around like an extra head of lettuce at a barbecue. I should have just walked away, but the addict in me couldn't quit. Clucko getting suspended and Savo breaking a leg was still a possibility. But all the mental preparation in the world wasn't going to make that happen.

We battered Louth in the first round and then scraped by Westmeath in the semi. We then hammered Wexford in the final and hit the town. I might have been out of the match-day squad, but I still felt entitled to get battered drunk when we won.

We were leaving a pub on Dame Street and heading up towards Coppers. Savo was slipping into a taxi with some friends he had been drinking with.

'Where are you off to?' I shouted at him.

'I'm heading off to meet some other mates in a McGowan's,' he answered.

'Are you not sticking with your teammates tonight, Savo?'

He just laughed and shook his head as he opened the taxi door.

'You'll never make it as a sub keeper like that!' I shouted.

'I don't want to make it as a sub keeper,' he shouted back.

That summed it up nicely, I thought to myself. I fingered the bag of Bolivian in my Johnny pocket and vowed to get absolutely deranged.

We were pitted against Tyrone in the All-Ireland quarter-final. While players and management cranked the emotional level up slowly during the weeks, I dealt with that acidic taste of rejection. It felt like my head was going to explode.

Tyrone played us off the park. We made mistakes at crucial moments when we could have kicked on and left them chasing us. Losing Alan Brogan after less than five minutes was a huge blow, and a few minutes later Diarmuid Connolly was clean through but Mossy overcooked a hand pass. We lost momentum and the game drifted away from us. The defending that allowed Tyrone in for two first-half goals was loose and passive. The second half was more of the same, and we ended up getting a right good skinning.

There was something definitive and final about being hammered in that way. It completely destroyed that sense of 'what if?' that always followed a narrow defeat. In a way it was a good thing. There was no doubt or shimmering regret laughing at you in your dreams.

Pillar brought us all into the main training area after we were showered and dressed. In an honest and typically understated speech he thanked everyone for their commitment and hard work. He said we had left everything out on the pitch and that today just wasn't our day. It happens. He told us he was stepping down as manager. We huddled in a big circle, arm around arm, and he told us he was proud of his time with us all and that he would continue supporting the Dubs as a fan. There were a few watery eyes as we clapped his last words to us as a group.

I can't be sure of what happened after that. I pressed the giant 'Fuck It' button. At one stage I was scooping cocaine up my nose at the side of the Sunnybank Hotel, when I looked up to see Ski Wade crossing the road. I had a pint and a smoke in one hand and a bag of drugs in the other. He power-walked past me, either oblivious or in a state of not giving a fuck. I took it as a sign that I needed to leave the environment I was currently in. I pressed the ejector seat and rocketed off into the chaos of the night.

I took a week off work and went to the Electric Picnic with a big group of friends. I consumed a fistful of pills and speed, and on day three I went completely la-la. The drugs had deprived me of the power of speech. I made up my mind that I had to find a tree and climb up to the top to be OK again. On my way to find that tree I spied Diarmuid Connolly and some friends sitting around. I went over to say hello but couldn't speak. He looked at me quite puzzled as I squirmed away.

I found a tree, a giant oak, and climbed to the top. There I clung on to the thinnest of branches and swayed like a koala. I began making weird, alien noises at the people walking below for an hour or two before I felt a bit more normal. I got myself down to terra firma, but I was still scatter-brained and delusional. Driving home from the festival I nodded off a few times, only to be woken by the sound of the tyres hitting the lane dividers. I was an apple crumble without the cream, the apple or the plate.

Guinness moved me into a new job as a sales rep in Meath and Cavan. This was a much busier and more stressful job, but I was still getting paid the same wage, and I felt like I was being taken for a ride. I asked for more money and a few extra perks but was refused. Fine, I thought to myself. If that's the way they wanted to play, then that's how I would play it. I fell back in love with my old friend, Señor Hash. I began to smoke a little in the evening and on my days off. I also took a little piece with me in the car for the long drives home from Cavan and Meath.

My work ethic slumped. I would drive out to Meath and call into a few pubs. Then I would pull into a service station and buy a big breakfast roll and the papers. After eating I would roll myself a little one-skinner spliff and have a smoke out the window. My next hour or two would be spent dozing with the seat down, listening to the vroom of cars whizzing by and the moos of cows in fields.

Tyrone eventually won the All-Ireland, beating Kerry in the final. In October Pat Gilroy was appointed as the Dublin manager. I had played against Pat many times in club games. I knew him and he knew me. Mickey Whelan was going to be his coach. Mickey was a highly regarded coach, but he was also the man who had overlooked me way back when I was the Dublin U/21 keeper and John O'Leary was retiring. And he was a Vincent's man, the same club Michael Savage was from. Game over.

There were still occasional games for Sylvester's, but I was bereft of any motivation. The hashish dragged me back into a lazy, apathetic lifestyle. I was now smoking straight after breakfast while I checked my work emails and had a Tommy Tank. On one occasion I went into a meeting with my marketing manager and opened my laptop – revealing two or three pages of porn I'd forgotten to close. It was a swallow-me-up-and-die kind of moment. She looked away and I blabbered something about email viruses while turning fifteen shades of stuttering and stammering red.

A call came through from the new Dublin set-up. I went to a meeting in Parnell Park and they outlined their plans: a few tweaks and an All-Ireland next September. There would be some fitness assessments and a panel would be named. I went along to the fitness tests. After two months' drinking and smoking hash and doing zero training, I was a joke. I ran around like a long-legged bird that was trying to fly but couldn't. It was pathetic and I knew I was in trouble.

I got on with life. I played some golf. I smoked some hash. I shagged some women. I played some poker. I took some pills. I drank some booze. I still went into work occasionally. It was coming up to Christmas, and this was time for a Guinness rep to earn the coin. Or, as was the case with me, time to do what a poorly paid, badly trained, frequently stoned waffler would do: struggle. I lacked the big balls it took to get publicans to buy booze they knew they wouldn't sell.

I was in a pub in the little town of Athboy one evening, waiting to speak with the bar manager. It was dark and the streets were bustling with folk coming and going. The smell of turf wafted through the air as the fires were lit to bring the heat. My phone rang. I looked down and saw the name of Pat Gilroy flash up. I stepped outside on to the street and answered.

'Hi, John, Pat Gilroy here.'

'Hi Pat.'

'Listen, I'm just calling to let you know you are no longer on the Dublin squad. We are making a few changes, and I'm afraid you don't fit into our plans.'

There was a pause. I sighed out loud. A lorry carrying live sheep wheeled noisily by. Static echoed on the line. Two old ladies hurried by me, talking about the cold setting in.

'The reasons you are not involved are that your kick-out is inconsistent and your decision-making at times is questionable. As a shot-stopper you are probably the best in the county, but overall we think you are not stable enough.'

I tried to be cheery.

'No worries, Pat, thanks for the honesty. I had a feeling this call was coming. Best of luck with everything, and I hope you bring home the All-Ireland.'

'Thanks, John, all the best.'

The phone went dead. I stood there, looking around in a daze. It was over. It was officially over.

I walked straight to my car with my eyes down. A fury gathered inside me. A sense of injustice welled up in my stomach. My hands were shaking as I reached up to my tie and ripped it off. I reached for the glovebox and pulled out my skins and hash. A wailing and a sobbing curdled deep in my gullet and escaped through my mouth and eyes.

Speckles of snow began to fall slowly from the purple sky.

16

I lay with my eyes closed, on the flat of my back along the couch of the rented house in Spiddal. Around me a New Year's party was in full swing. A delusional paranoia had crept into my thinking. All conversations were about me. Everybody was ridiculing me in some weird way. I was deranged and psychotic and all I could do was close my eyes and hope everything went away.

It didn't go away. When I woke on New Year's Day, I stormed around the house and packed up my things. As I was about to jump in the car and drive away, my sister came out to see what was going on.

'Are you all right, John?' she asked. 'What's wrong . . . where are you going?'

I looked at her with disgust.

'What's wrong? What's wrong?' I questioned rhetorically. 'You know perfectly well what's wrong . . . I heard you all yapping away last night. Fucking sick of it. I'm out of here.'

She looked at me in puzzlement.

'I don't know what you think you heard, but no one was talking about you. You are over-reacting.'

There was nothing quite like telling me I was over-reacting, when I was over-reacting, to cause me to over-react some more. I looked back at her and shook my head.

'Yeah, right. I'm going, I can't handle this shit.'

I slammed the door behind me and sped away. I smoked a spliff as I drove. The empty, open road soothed my addled brain. By the time I reached Athlone the fog began to lift. I pulled the car over and turned off the engine and began to sob. I held my head in my hands and wailed big, lonely, desperate tears.

I made a decision then that I had to get away. Every conversation I had with people went back to the Dubs, to my failure. Every thought

I had drifted back to the Dubs. I was swimming in a world of pain and I didn't know how else to drag myself out of it.

My contract with Guinness was finishing at the end of January and I had no desire to stay on and drag myself through hell. I would see out the end of my contract, but I knew I was finished with Dublin. It was back to sunny Australia for me, where the streets were paved with gold.

The last month in Ireland was insane. I went on a rampage. I was seeing a few different women, all of whom needed attention. On top of that I had to say goodbye to my friends over and over again. I was smoking and drinking every day and couldn't stop myself from driving around in some intoxicated states. I was a shameful mess, out of control.

On my last day in Ireland I spent an afternoon in bed with one girl, saying goodbye. I then left her before dinnertime and went on the razzle with my friends. There was drinking and smoking and plenty of pills being consumed. In the height of it, another girl I was seeing called to say goodbye. I dropped her home in my car in a heavy state of intoxication, shagged her in the back of a parking lot and returned to the party. I carried on into the early hours.

When my mother came to pick me up and drop me to the airport, I had just double-dropped some pills and was out of my mind. I couldn't maintain eye-contact and my face was like something out of a Munch painting. My sister and mother knew what was going on, but maintained silence. When we arrived at the airport and I discovered I had no passport on me, my mother couldn't hold back.

'Arrah for feck's sake, John. Look at the state of you! You're an embarrassment to yourself.'

It was true. I was a repugnant mess. I could mask nothing now. One part of me felt deep guilt leaving them behind, but I knew I couldn't survive in Dublin now. I called a couple of the lads who were at the house and they managed to find the passport, jump in a taxi and bring it to the airport in the nick of time. I still owe them for that one.

In Sydney I stayed in the spare room in Joxer's, and spent a lot of time at drinking and gambling with a friend of his from Cork, Seán Mac. He was a racehorse aficionado, and we spent the days and evenings in pubs that had bookies inside them. We won money, drank heavily, lost money.

When Seán moved on a few weeks later I took to hitting the casino on my own. I was a good poker player at this stage of my life, and in the casino I was able to earn some good dollar. My problems arose when I went in drunk. Any of the money I won playing poker I would blow playing blackjack and roulette, and on the pokie machines. After one session where I blew almost $2,000, I left the casino in a haze of anger. I stormed through the streets, arriving at the Pyrmont Bridge, which is a pedestrian bridge over Sydney Harbour.

I found a workman's site and jumped the fence. The site led to a section which connected to the giant metal girders underneath the bridge. I climbed in here and began to climb the girders. Close to the end of the climb I began to tire, and as I swung myself over a large gap I lost control of my hands. I managed to propel a leg forward and flew, chest first, into a giant metal column, cracking some ribs in the process. I wrapped my arms around the column and regained control. Thirty metres below me the shallow, rocky, shark-infested waters of Sydney Harbour lapped and waited.

I spent a week or two afterwards in a pitiful state. I had blown half the money I had in the world. I had no visa to work and was living off the grace of my friend, rent-free for now. I had some cracked ribs and I took to drinking more heavily to deal with the pain of this. I met a girl and went on the pills with her. The pills in Oz were still very strong and speedy, relative to the ones in Ireland. While others were bedding down of a Sunday evening with work to think of, I was off scouring the streets looking for action.

It went on like this for a few weeks. Joxer was busy working and running his business and he left me to it a lot of the time. As luck would have it, he was bringing over the Irish singer and songwriter Damien Dempsey an Australian tour. I was excited about the prospect of meeting Dempsey, whose music I enjoyed.

'So, is he staying in a hotel close by or what?'

'Not exactly,' replied Joxer.

'Where is he staying then?'

Joxer looked a little awkward. We were sitting, having a few schooners in a local bar called the General Gordon.

'Well, he'll be staying with us.'

The penny dropped. He would be staying in my room. Damien Dempsey would be kicking me out of my bed. I acknowledged that this was the natural order of things, seeing as I wasn't paying rent and had been a drunken, useless messer since I had returned. Joxer offered me the floor of his home office, which had a soft carpet and plenty of space. I graciously accepted.

Damo's arrival sparked a series of sessions. He was a real salt-of-the-earth Dub and had some great stories to tell of his times, singing and touring. At the end of the night's drinking and debauchery, I would retreat back to the office, close the door and place down my pillow on the ground. I was sleeping directly on the carpet with a little sheet on me.

I slept quite well, all the same. Some mornings I would awaken to the sound of Damo practising his songs, two rooms away. I would lie there and listen and take it all in. After a while he would stop singing and I would hear the door to his room open. Down the wooden hallway I would hear his feet pounding, the reverberations ricocheting up through my body. Some days the door to the office would creak open as he walked. He might pause at the door and look in at me lying on the floor.

'Howaya, Lenny,' he would say in his deep, Dublin drawl. I would look up to see him standing there with his shower bag in his hand, naked save for a skimpy little light-blue towel. His shoulders and upper torso looked like a stone carving of some ancient colossus.

'Howaya, Damo,' I would answer as he strode off to have his shower, the floor shuddering from his giant steps.

I had about $1,000 to my name, and it was running out fast. I had to find some kind of work, but without a visa and with a constant hangover it was tough. There was always a reason for a few jars and, even if there wasn't, I went for some anyway.

Damo played a gig up in Brisbane and a few of us went along for the craic. I hit the Guinness hard at the gig. Afterwards, back at the hotel room, we carried on with a couple of other musicians who were on tour. I threw one lad's box of smokes off the balcony for no reason. I started having a pop at another for being a nationalist Scotsman. I arced up at Damo for trying to calm me down. In the end I stormed off to the casino to gamble and drink on my own. They were long and miserable drinks. I knew I was just being a nasty and belligerent git, but I couldn't help myself. The drink was changing me. When I met the guys again to fly back to Sydney, I was apologetic and tried to make a joke of it all. Apologies were accepted, but damage had been done.

On April Fool's Day – which is also my dad's birthday – I was in various bars, handing out flyers promoting Damo's upcoming gigs. To help me through the process I had a beer in each bar. After a couple of beers I ordered a shot of whiskey. Before long the flyers were in the bottom of my backpack and I was shifting from bar to bar, downing beers and whiskey. I got a train back to the local boozer and met up with my old friend Billy.

We talked about our dead fathers and shared stories of our past. I offered him a whiskey, and when he refused I bought him one anyway. He was driving but I was too drunk to listen to his reasons. When he refused to drink it, I snapped. I faced off against him, hurling insults. He stood up and I shifted my weight and aimed a kick at his nuts. He just took it, shook his head and walked away. I cursed after him and slammed the two whiskeys down my throat. I stumbled out of the bar and followed the bright lights to the next bar along the street.

I woke up in the early hours of the morning, face down in some big black sacks of rubbish behind a rubbish dumpster in an alleyway. My T-shirt was up over my head. My back was covered in mosquito bites, hundreds of them. I sat up and looked around me. The sky was lightening as the early sun rose. My jaw felt stiff and sore, my head throbbed, and when I went to check for my phone and wallet I realized they were gone. I had no idea where I was or how I had gotten there.

I had always suffered blackouts – always. A good ould blackout meant a good ould night. Almost always, I would manage to get myself home or to a bed. There had been times in Greece when I woke up on the side of the road, using a rock as a pillow, but that didn't seem as bad as this. This was a new low. I went home in the horrors, and I couldn't even sleep there as Joxer was using his office. I showered and felt excruciatingly sorry for myself.

After another Damo gig a short time later, a group of us went from bar to bar and then to a nightclub in Kings Cross. We sat out in the beer garden and the devilment was mighty. As Joxer walked by me I thought it would be funny to pour a glass of water over him. He didn't see the funny side and turned for me. We grappled with each other, and a mini-melee ensued. Security ejected a few of us from the venue and we went on to Taylor Square to the twenty-four-hour bars there.

We arrived at the infamous Courthouse, an institution from which I had been banned for life during my previous Aussie sojourn. But that was almost ten years ago, and they let me in.

As we settled into the drinking I asked where Joxer was. The others looked at me incredulously.

'He's down in St Vincent's Hospital, man . . . he slashed his hand open scrapping with you . . . don't you remember that?'

I didn't. My friend and benefactor was in hospital because of me, and I hadn't even registered the fact.

I ran out of the pub and jogged down to the hospital, which was only ten minutes away. I got into emergency, and found Joxer there with his arm all bandaged up. He had slashed his forearm on a broken piece of glass when he went for me.

'Jesus, man, you all right?' I asked.

He stared me down. He was angry.

'It's nothing, man,' he answered.

'I'm sorry, man, it was meant to be a joke.'

'That was a joke? Who finds that shit funny? Who finds pouring a glass of water over someone's head funny? We're not fucking teen-agers any more, man.'

I didn't have an answer. I told him I would sort myself out and get some help. He accepted my apology and I headed back to the pub to carry on drinking.

I got a job working in a bar. I used my old tax number from years earlier. It was a risk, but I was sure that nothing would come of it unless I got into trouble with the law. The first week's pay was a sweet relief. Having money coming in again would give me a little breathing space.

A call came through one afternoon from Seán Mac. He had left Sydney and had spent the last month out in the bush, training some racehorses. He told me that they had a horse running at a harness meeting at Menangle the following week. The horse was a sure thing. They reckoned it would start off at 50–1 and the price would move inwards and settle around 25–1. I wanted in. He told me the name and the date, and he asked me to come out to watch the race live.

On the morning of the race, I took all of the money I owned and went down to the local bookie and placed various bets on the horse. I placed $50 on a win, $100 each way. I went to another bookies', close to the train station. I put $100 on the win and $50 each way. I went into a pub with a TAB and placed a stomach-tingling $200 on the win. I saved another $200 for out at the racetrack. All in, I had $700 riding on this horse. I left $100 at home just in case it all went wrong.

I took a train to Menangle, in the outer suburbs, and dozed off a little, staring out the window at the city's hinterland of scrub and scorched earth. I felt that I was going somewhere deeper than just a racetrack.

I woke up just as the train was leaving Menangle station. I tried to get off, but the doors had shut. Some ten minutes later we pulled into a deserted little stop and I hopped off. There was nobody around, save for a lady who was speaking to someone on a phone and seemed to be arranging a pick-up. She finished talking and a deep silence filled the air. Except for a few cicadas which were singing on some trees near by, there was no sound.

The woman turned to me.

'Are you lost?' she asked.

Here I was at some desolate, Aussie outback halt, with practically every penny I had riding on a horse, and a belly that was screaming for beer. Was I lost?

'No, I got off at the wrong stop,' I answered. 'What about you?'

'I'm going to a retreat,' she told me. 'It is run by some nice and gentle people.'

We got talking. She was a tall, striking-looking woman, with long, black hair and pale, white skin. She told me she had been abused all her life. She had fallen into addiction, heroin and alcohol and anything else she could get her hands on. She had met these people and they had saved her, brought her back from the brink. They were spiritual people who lived in a commune and she was going there to spend some time . . . maybe a few years.

I told her my story as quickly as I could. She smiled and told me that we were going in the same direction, that I just didn't realize it yet. Her lift arrived and she said goodbye, leaving me alone with a sense of regret and foreboding.

I sat there, waiting for a train to come back in the opposite direction. Giant eucalyptus trees swayed in a soft breeze. The sun heaved down heavily upon me. The gravel track leading from the station was empty. The cicadas sang their tune faintly, far away. I was heading down the wrong path. I knew it. The girl I had randomly just met at a train station knew it. The cicadas in the trees knew it.

I caught the next train back and made it just in time for the race. Seán Mac was downing double vodkas to deal with the stress, and I quickly joined him. I placed my last bet and said a little prayer. The price came in to 16–1.

Myself and Seán stood and watched the first lap. Our horse was nestled at the back, but Seán insisted it was all tactics. As the bell went and the final lap kicked in, I let out a few roars. Fuck those tactics, I thought to myself. Our horse began to move a little and, as they turned the corner for the home straight, it pulled out wide to overtake the three front-runners. We screamed in unison – a violent and desperate roar. The horse pushed and pushed, but the first three pushed and sprinted too. They passed the final post in a blur of wheels, legs, jockeys and dust. I didn't know where we had come. I turned to Seán, and then I knew.

Seán had walked away from me and was doubled over a metal barrier. He seemed to have collapsed. I went over, grabbed him up by the shoulders and looked at him. His eyes were gone, glazed over with a look of complete horror.

'I'm sorry, Leno . . . I'm sorry, kid,' was all he could say.

I released my grip and turned to look at the result on the screen. We had come in fourth. There were no prizes for coming fourth and I stood there for a minute or two, wondering how to win back that $700. There was nothing. It was all gone. The last few quid I had was left at home in case this happened. I turned to Seán and shook his hand.

'I'm going home. Seán, I'll chat to you sometime.'

'I'm sorry, kiddo,' he said again, shaking his head and staring off into his own world of pain.

I got back to my house in the late evening. I went into the room, took my last $100 and went down to the pokies in the local pub. I put in my first $50, and it disappeared in ten minutes. I put in the second, and it went just as quick. I sat there, and my stomach emptied and a rage built up inside me. I was disgusted with myself. I had blown everything I owned and I didn't even have enough left for some food or a drink.

I got paid the next day, a few hundred dollars, and it was enough to keep me going. But life seemed meaningless. It all seemed too hard. I couldn't drink right, gamble right or meet the right woman. I was working illegally, was officially broke and living on my friend's floor. My drinking was destructive and the gloom of my Dublin mentality was following me around.

The drinking was the root of it all for me. Most of the bad decisions I had made in life had been made when I was drinking. It wasn't as though I woke up in the morning and couldn't survive without a drink; but if there was no explicit reason not to drink, then I would drink. And when I drank, I drank in order to be drunk. I wanted to be away from the reality I lived. This was the crux of it: I was deeply unhappy with who I was. I saw myself as an abuse victim for many years, a degenerate poet for other years, and a sporting failure for the past few. All of those identities dismayed me, and I used drink to deal with it. That would have to stop.

Initially I wanted to ease myself out of it. I spoke to my mates in

Australia about it. I told them I was cutting down for a while. I wanted to just stop the rot. They were all very understanding. I cut out the drugs completely. I still had a few beers and glasses of wine, but I made a conscious battling effort not to get drunk.

The hardest part was talking about it to people. I had to change myself inside. Most of my confidence had been linked to booze and drugs. But booze and drugs dragged me down into a world of pain and remorse. I had to rebuild myself as a sober man. I had to discover a love for myself again. The Dubs had given me a short-term blast of something, but that was long gone now.

One afternoon I was sitting with Julie, Joxer's wife, in the house. We were watching *Masterchef* and chatting lazily. She had just returned from being away for two weeks and had yet to see Joxer. Joxer and Damo were out, doing a radio interview to promote the final gig of his tour. We heard the front door opening and we expected to see Joxer come in through the door. Instead this incredibly cute girl popped her head around the corner.

'Do you mind if I borrow the toilet?' she asked with a cheeky little grin.

'You can as long as you give it back,' I quipped and pointed her through to the bathroom.

Julie turned to me. She didn't look too happy – nor would I, if I was her.

'Who the fack was that, Lenny?' she asked.

'I don't know . . . but don't worry, Julie, I'll take care of her for you.'

The mystery girl came out from the toilet and introduced herself. It turned out she was the DJ who'd interviewed Damo. They were on their way out to the gig, and she had hitched a ride with the lads. She sat on the edge of the couch and looked like an angel from heaven, a Polynesian princess. She had the deepest, darkest chocolate eyes, with a sprinkling of freckles on her sallow skin. We looked at each other and I fell right in love at that moment.

The gig went off like a rocket. Damo was incredible. The only blight was that the mystery DJ girl spent the evening with the curly-haired Irish musician, Declan O'Rourke, in her ear. I watched them from afar and thought my chance might be slipping away. As we walked through the streets of Newtown after the gig, the mystery girl produced a bottle of vodka from her bag and offered it to me. I took a little sip and laughed at how similar we were.

There was karaoke in the next bar we went to. I got up and belted out 'Walk the Line' by Johnny Cash. I saw her watching me in the distance. I smiled and wiggled in her general direction. I sang the chorus, and I sang it to her.

After the song was over I made my way closer to her as she played some pool. I took up a seat beside her and we chatted. I was blown away by her natural beauty and warm, flirty nature. She oozed sweetness and confidence.

'So, you're staying with Joxer and Julie, are you?'

'I am,' I answered.

She leaned in close and whispered into my ear. I could feel her breath exhaling slowly.

'Would you like to stay with me tonight?' she whispered above the racket coming from the karaoke blaring in the background.

I looked at her steadily. I think I said something but wasn't sure. I know I didn't even have to answer. She smiled the naughtiest smile at me and turned away to take her pool shot. We stayed a while longer in the bar, then took a taxi back to hers in Bondi. Before the cups of tea had been made we were in the bedroom ripping off each other's clothes.

The next morning she cooked me some eggs and we lazed in each other's arms. I borrowed her flatmate's swimming trunks and we went to Tamarama Beach. We bought a salmon lunch and lay back in the sunshine, enjoying the beautiful Australian summer. We talked for hours. Her name was Serena and she was a Kiwi DJ, business coach and entrepreneur. She ran music festivals, set up charities and was in the process of launching a dating service. She had been born in Hong Kong, where her father had taken up a position working for the Hong Kong government. Her family returned to New Zealand when she was eleven.

We went for a long walk along the coast with her little Staffy puppy. She told me about her life growing up as a teen in small-town

New Zealand. She had moved to Australia when she was twenty-one, spending four years in Melbourne, before moving to Bondi. We had listened to the same music, danced to the same DJs and been on similar journeys. The ocean waves lashed up against the rocks, spraying us with mist. The dog barked and we laughed in slow motion at each other. It was like an alternative reality, Technicolor and gaily saturated. I was falling heavily for this girl and it seemed like she was falling for me too.

We became addicted to each other. Over the following few weeks I stayed in her house every night. We became inseparable. I felt inspired again. The desire to write came flooding back. I moved my meagre earthly belongings and went from living on my mate's office floor to living with a gorgeous, intelligent, creative girl in a fine house in Bondi. I felt blessed to have met her. I felt like nothing could stop us.

Well, there was one thing.

17

I sat in a circle with seven other people. We were in the house of an Israeli girl, in North Bondi, on top of a cliff. I was drinking the last of the beers I had brought. A guy to my right, Broderick, was reading a poem of his. It was about minestrone soup and buggery. I was next – the next poet in line to read a little of my work. I was calm externally, but inside my skittled nerves could be calmed only with alcohol. Everybody clapped as Broderick finished and took a bow.

'Wow, Broderick ... amazing analogy, so risqué and yet so gauche,' laughed Ariella, our host. Her face wobbled in the candle-light that held the room aglow. The scent of weed and incense filled my nasal cavities.

'How about you, John, are you ready to read us something?'

I looked down at the ground and coughed. I smiled and nodded to say yes. I picked up my pages and began at the top. The papers wobbled, my hands shook. I opened my raspy throat and began reading:

> Livin on a warm floor
> Gettin no bed sores
> Taking time from drinkin
> Tryin to do some thinkin
> Livin in the slow lane
> Recession turns us all the same
> Governments are panicking
> Candlelights are flickering

I rattled through the poem and sighed a gulp of relief when it was over. I stood up, acknowledged the applause and returned to the kitchen, where I filled a glass with some wine, slammed it back and then filled it up again. The booze flew around me, tickling me. I wandered back into the room where the others were. I looked left and right.

The giggles went high and low. My brain began to cave. I had to make an exit.

I hastily muttered an awkward goodbye and staggered out into the night. I called Serena and arranged to meet her at a café on Bondi Road. I stomped through the darkened streets. *Fucking poetry readings*, I thought to myself. *Shower of fucking thespian wankers*. I didn't fit in there. I was confused and irritated. The drink helped the nerves, but also opened up the dark side. It sang to me of nihilism and of the useless vanity of life.

At the café Serena and I ordered a pizza and a couple of drinks. I was happy to see her but was drunk and brooding. A dark, gloomy cloud floated blearily above me. I could feel bleakness and suspicion rising within me.

'Are you OK?' Serena asked me as we sat there, waiting for our food.

I mumbled responses to her while looking away into the distance. I couldn't maintain eye contact.

'Have you been drinking?' she asked me.

I turned and locked eyes with her. 'What if I have?' I replied petulantly.

'It's not a problem, you just change when you're drunk . . . I've never seen you like this before.'

I thought about it. I stared away again. That's just what my mother and sisters used to say. That's what most people said, but especially those who loved me and knew me the most. I changed when I was drinking . . . well, of course I changed when I was drinking! I was getting drunk and then I'd be drunk – why could people not understand that!

The waiter came and brought us our pizza. I looked down at the cheese and pineapple sitting atop the dough. I had tried cutting down on the drink, but now, sitting across from Serena, I decided to go cold turkey. I wanted to be truly who I was, not some drugged-up parody of someone I thought I should be. I knew it would be hard. I knew that people would question me. I would have to reinvent myself a little. I looked at Serena that night and saw the future.

I hibernated to begin with. I had to get the head down and keep it down. I stayed away from my mates in the pub. I wasn't strong enough to go to the pub and not drink. I didn't yet have the conviction that I could enjoy myself while they were getting sloshed and I was drinking lemonade. I told them I was taking a complete break from the drink. This meant I couldn't be around them for a while. I think they were fine with that.

It was hard. Every social event had revolved around drinking. I worked in a pub, for fuck's sake! I saw people drinking around me, all day, every day. I battled it, though. I wrote about it, I thought about it and I got great help and support from Serena. She didn't care if I drank or not – she just didn't want me to be a paranoid, gloomy asshole.

I began to dream heavily. In one recurring dream I spoke with my dad under a giant oak tree in the middle of a field. There were little pink flowers blowing everywhere. He was smiling at me, telling me I was on the right track. I would begin to cry and then I would wake up from the noise of my own tears and sobbing.

My love for Serena was an immense power of light in my head and heart. It was conquering all my fears and my troubles. My dad always told me that one day I would just know – and I did. I just knew she was the one. My heart and head told me instinctively. There was nothing to consider. It was the most natural thing to be with her, and I wanted to confirm that to the world.

I got down on bended knee and proposed to her. She said yes and we planned a simple yet beautiful wedding. We planned it all one day in a park, while I was on my lunch break from work. We would invite a small number of immediate family and friends, and we planned to have a bigger celebration sometime in the future.

We went into the registry office and sat with a staff member who showed us the available dates. One was a Friday afternoon, which coincided with Serena's radio show on Bondi FM. It was a three-hour show and had a real mix of elements: she interviewed musicians and artists, played live music and some cool, laid-back tunes. As we pondered this possible date, Serena was taken by an idea: instead of getting married in the registry office, why not get a celebrant and get married live on the radio show? I smiled and shrugged my shoulders and said, 'Why not?'

She called the station owner there and then, and he was keen on the idea. We could have the small reception in the newly opened café, adjacent to the studio. We would be able to do interviews and shout-outs live to people around the world who couldn't make it and wanted to listen in. We would set up a Skype link for friends and family to gather and watch online in a house in Dublin.

I was still battling hard with sobriety. Cold turkey was a standard I struggled to meet. Our engagement drinks were a torrid affair in this respect. I sipped a glass of champers over the course of a day. Otherwise I drank soft drinks and spoke politely with everyone. I stayed calm and felt a bit underwhelmed. It was a real acid test. My previous life would have involved a two-day session for something like this.

My stag night involved heading into Kings Cross with my brother, who had come over for the wedding, and my three old mates – Joxer, Bomber and Billy. I sipped a few beers with them and had a few tequilas. Fuck it, I thought – I'll only have one stag night. I stayed controlled the whole night, though. I never got pissed, just mildly merry. It was a revolution for me.

The day of the wedding was fantastic, spent with family and loved ones. I married the woman of my dreams and managed to stay sober for the whole day. It was a turning point for me, a moment when I chose the clarity of responsible happiness over the recklessness of booze and uncertainty. I felt strong with Serena at my side, and the battles I faced inside seemed easier to win with her.

As the spring became summer in Sydney, I was training hard, looking tanned and fit, and people were remarking how much happier I seemed. I was writing, and was happily married. I really felt I was out of the danger zone.

Serena was asked to participate in a bikini pageant called Miss Bondi. The girls paraded in front of hundreds of people, mainly lascivious men. I encouraged her to go for it, but inside I was struggling with the idea of my wife being ogled at by drunken louts. On the day of the event I hit the drink and I hit it hard.

As soon as Serena left to get ready for the show, I opened a bottle of vodka and drank four or five doubles. I met Bomber and we headed down to the pub. We hit the lash hard, and by the time Serena came on stage I was leering and hollering as much as the next man.

The next thing I knew I woke up. I was in bed beside her. It was morning. I leaned over to give her a kiss and she stopped me.

'You don't remember last night, do you?'

'Eh . . . not really.' I had some recollection of her strutting down the catwalk, but everything after that was fuzz. I had gone into the blackout zone.

Serena filled me in. After the pageant was finished, I had hijacked the evening's festivities with some drunken antics. I poured drinks over friends and interrupted conversations. We all went for dinner, but I proceeded to throw the spaghetti and bread I ordered at other people on our table. I danced by myself at the side of the table, dry humping a fire hydrant near by. It turned out the owner of the bar I was working in was sitting at the next booth. He didn't care – 'What happens on your days off in different establishments has nothing to do with me.' But Serena cared. She was embarrassed. She told me to quit it or go home. Somehow I had the drunken sense to leave. But on my way home I rang her phone over and over again, leaving insane messages, making weird, animal noises and cursing violently at her. When I got back to our house I had no keys, so I tried to climb in a side window. Our flatmate, who was at home, thought we were being robbed. She came out, saw me and let me in. She had just returned from a winery and was packing away a box of wines she had bought. I spied them and helped myself to a couple of bottles, while twisting the caps off others.

I sat there, drinking her wine, and I asked her all kind of weird personal questions. She fled the house and left me there, talking to myself. She called Serena and told her I was steaming drunk and possibly dangerous. Serena returned home later that night to find me passed out, naked, in the kitchen.

As she told me the story of my drunken shenanigans, waves of guilt and anger flooded over me. I had not changed. The passing of a few months meant nothing. I could still no longer handle my drink. I felt as low and miserable as I ever had. Hearing the harsh reality of my madness come from the woman I loved really hammered my situation home to me. It would have to end.

The rest of the day was spent grovelling and apologizing. Flowers were bought and meals were cooked. I headed off into work, feeling broken. I wanted an end to this kind of crap. I was a married man in his thirties! I needed to move on. I made a decision that day that it was over. There would be no more days feeling like this. There would be no complications, no confusion and no going back. That day I beamed myself into a new world: Planet Sober.

That Christmas Serena and I decided not to buy presents for each other, but to make them instead. I made a cartoon comic book for her. She made me a website: Sober Paddy.

Sober Paddy was something we had talked about – a new persona for me, and a platform to do something useful. The tag line on the website was 'Be Yourself, Be Cool, Be Sober'. The idea was that if I could help just one person with my story in their own journey, then it would be worth it. I started blogging on the site, charting my experience of getting sober. I did interviews and researched articles on sobriety.

My view of my own drinking was that it was not a disease for me. It was something I had chosen.

I didn't call myself a recovering alcoholic – I hated the term. I preferred to call myself a sober person. I wasn't comfortable with the AA idea about giving yourself up to a higher power. AA has helped millions of people over the world, but their approach was not how I wanted to fix myself. I wanted to be in charge. I wanted to be a cool, crazy fucker who chose sobriety. That was it for me.

In a funny twist of fate I took up a manager's job running the Cock and Bull in Bondi Junction – the very same Irish pub that a decade earlier I had vowed never to set foot in again. Now here I was, sober and loving the craic in the place. I felt a huge connection with my staff and customers, felt the camaraderie between the Irish people. I fed off it. When I was a drunken, drugged-up messer, years before, it had repulsed me, but now I welcomed it with open arms.

Life changed. Sydney changed. The world changed. I was no longer thinking about drinking, avoiding my friends or struggling to be me. I was winning. I felt free. My mind opened up to reading about the world again. I studied politics and religion and history. I was open to learning and changing in a way that had been impossible while I was drinking.

For the first time in Australia, I felt a calm connection with the people and the beach and the outdoors. Now I could go to the pub for a few hours, have a great night and not feel like I needed to be the last one standing. It was powerful.

Emails began coming in from Sober Paddy readers around the world. They shared their own stories, asked for advice or simply encouraged me to keep doing what I was doing. I was humbled by the response. I was making a difference for some people and that felt good. It felt like there was some meaning in my life again.

I interviewed plenty of interesting sober people, including Des Bishop and Christy Dignam. They sat with me and told me about their own battles with their demons. Christy, who had quit heroin, had one salient piece of wisdom for me. I asked him about replicating that high from drinking and drugs. It was something that I felt would be very hard to replace in the future.

'I don't look at it like that,' he said. 'If you look at it being a forever thing, then it becomes too big of a deal . . . All you have to do is wake up and say "Today I won't drink." Make it through, one day at a time or one hour at a time.'

That made sense to me. Take it hour by hour, day by day, and after a while it builds up. Before long it is months and then years, and the crippling and destructive habit becomes a memory.

My desire to play highly competitive sport had disappeared completely. I still loved watching the Dubs. I knew most of the squad and wanted nothing more than for them to succeed. In 2009 they were hammered by Kerry in the quarter-finals, and in 2010 they were beaten narrowly by Cork in the semis. By 2011 they had perfected their new style of play as laid out by Pat Gilroy. They bludgeoned their way through the Championship and came up against the might of Kerry in the final.

I watched the match with Joxer early on a Monday morning in Sydney. When the Gooch put Kerry four points ahead with only seven minutes left I slumped down on the couch. A sickening feeling crept inside my stomach. My deepest Dublin fears were being realized: losing to Kerry in a final. I knew how hard the lads would have worked to get where they were, and how gutted they'd be. The writing was on the wall. And the regulars in the Cock and Bull would not let me hear the end of it either.

Then came a magic goal from Kevin McManamon, a brace of points from Dublin, a huge point from Kieran Donaghy and then . . . well. It was as though Clucko reached inside my mind and stole my dream. To kick the winning point into the Hill, with the last kick of the game, against Kerry, to win Dublin's first All-Ireland in almost twenty years? Who wrote this script? As that ball sailed over, I cried real man tears of unfettered and sweet happiness. I was thrilled for him, and for all the lads.

Echoes and rumours of all kinds of parties drifted through the internet to me on my laptop. I followed the blips and squibs online, where legends collided in dance and in song. Twitter produced photos of Jayo, Clucko and Damo drinking together in late-night revelry. It was a most magnificent celebration. These men had earned it. They had been on the longest, hardest road in GAA and finally won the big one.

A month or so later, Clucko was the skipper of the Irish team which travelled to Australia to play in the Compromise Rules series. Serena and I took a flight to Melbourne to meet him and his girlfriend, Joanne. The day before the game we went for some lunch down by the banks of the Yarra.

Before long I asked him the obvious question: 'What was it like kicking over that point, man?'

'Ah you know . . . not a bother,' he answered, deadpan. 'I just kicked it over, Len.'

'Fair play, man . . . I never doubted you for a second.'

It was great to see the old square-jawed man himself. What people didn't always understand about Clucko was that he was just a regular lad who was very talented at football. He worked as a teacher and was a shy, introverted person. He had incredibly high standards, and that was why he was elected captain of his county and his country. He led by example.

I asked him about what had changed over the past three years.

'All that shite stopped,' he said. 'All that pricking around in training went. The intensity went up. There was no room for lads acting the bollix. Some of the early-morning training had me in an absolute heap afterwards. I was puking, lads were in bits, but it sorted out all the shite. We got rid of the messers and that's what pushed us on.'

'Got rid of people like me, you mean?' I asked, joking.

He laughed. 'No, Len, you were one of the good ones. It was all that other shite that was going on that was the difference.'

Clucko's standards were the highest. He had been through so many years of disappointment, and he knew better then anyone what separated the All-Ireland-winning team from the teams I'd been part of in '06, '07 and '08.

We got chatting about a few other stories, like when he made the front and back pages for punching Irish soccer legend Jason McAteer at a charity soccer game. I asked him did he really have a swing at him.

'Len, the thing was we were having a right go at each other in the middle of the park. All fair enough. He was a mouthpiece though, giving it loads the whole time. I bundled him over as we were tussling for a ball. Then he jumps up and throws his head in to stitch me a loaf. I just stepped back and smacked him one. He dropped like a stone. Fuck him. Then they call me out, saying I should apologize. Ask me, bollix!'

It was typical no-nonsense Clucko. I laughed away at his stories. He was being attacked in the press over here for not speaking to the media. The Aussie media were making a big deal out of the silent Irish captain.

'At the end of the day, Len, I am an amateur sportsman who plays the game he loves. I don't want the media or the attention. I am a school teacher who has to go into his class on a Monday morning. That's it in a nutshell. I don't get paid to talk to the media. It's not my job to speak to them. It's my job to teach kids science. The rest is all bollix.'

I got it. I really did. I understood his side of it. But fuck me, we were different. I loved the limelight. I loved talking to media. I loved the attention.

We went to watch the game the next night, and Ireland trounced the Aussies. I was as proud as any man in the stadium. Here I was, watching my friend captain an Irish team to a win over Australia in their own back yard. The world seemed a great place that night. It seemed small, warm and easy.

Serena and I moved into a cool, one-bedroom apartment in Bondi. I was now co-hosting her radio show on Bondi FM. This was a great outlet for me. For three hours every week we got to play some great music, interview great guests and talk nonsense presenter-talk.

Being married gave me a sense of security that I'd never really had before. I was enjoying the relative tranquillity and simplicity of things. Serena was an entrepreneur and business coach; she had just written a book called *How to Retire in 12 Months*. It began to do well in Australasia and her websites were becoming quite popular. She was getting noticed in mainstream media. The ideas that she blogged about forced us to take a look at the way we were living our own lives. We had some big conversations about what we wanted to get out of life.

Her mission was to make her income earnable anywhere in the world so that we could travel freely. She could write from anywhere and coach her clients via Skype from any internet connection. We talked about spending some time in Latin America. For months we did nothing about it, but one day we walked past a travel agent, went in, sat down and booked two tickets to Caracas. We gave ourselves five months to finish up work, sell all our possessions and be ready to go. It was exhilarating to be thinking about hitting the road again. I was excited, but part of me was a little worried. I had a good job, a car, a nice place to live in Bondi; I was saving a bit of money and living as healthily as ever. Jacking it all in would mean a completely new beginning.

Two months before we left, Serena went to a blogging conference in Melbourne one weekend, and there she met with a woman from a charity called World Vision. They talked about some of the work they were doing in Latin America. Serena mentioned we would be travelling there and that maybe we could visit some of the projects and report back on what was going on at ground level. Before I knew it, we were blog ambassadors for them and plans were being drawn up for us to take to the field.

Our other plan was to make documentaries as we went. We wanted to show the places we went to and the projects we visited. We wanted to create some beautifully shot, inspirational videos which would tell the world about the people we encountered.

There were a few difficulties with this beautiful vision. We had no cameras, no editing software, no microphones, no lighting – no equipment of any kind. We had no experience in film-making, no idea how to script and storyboard a documentary. To top it all off, we had no idea how to coordinate all these aspects with real-life people in remote locations in a language which neither of us could speak. We had a lot to learn and we had very little time in which to do it.

But we carried on. I worked long hours over the busy holiday periods. We had a couple of garage sales, gave our excess to charities, sold the car, gave up our apartment and booked a place to stay in for the first few nights in Caracas. We bought a camera and managed to get some sponsorship for some of our equipment. On 1 April 2012 we left Australia to embark on another chapter.

18

Arequipa, Peru; Sunday, 22 September 2013

I hurried through the dusty early-morning streets. My head was scrambled: I had walked these streets a day before to make sure I knew where to go, but now I was running ragged, lost and sweating hard, dragging Serena behind me.

Finally I found the café and ran inside – only to find that the internet was down. I stormed out and ran down the street to another internet café. The place was packed full of gamer kids who wouldn't let me connect my laptop to their cable, and all their computers were taken.

I stared down the long, empty road. The centre of town was ten minutes away in a cab. There were no cabs. I was close to exploding.

Serena pointed to a fancy hotel. 'What about going in there?' she suggested.

We skedaddled across the road and into the foyer, where I put on my most elegant and posh impersonation of someone else. The receptionist didn't care. She just motioned me to an extremely comfortable-looking couch, where I took out my laptop and connected to the internet, just in time to stream the All-Ireland final. Dublin versus Mayo.

Serena sat beside me, and the bellboys and the maître d' all gathered around. They were fascinated by the game. I told them the rules and explained that I used to be a part of one of the teams playing. They loved the physicality and the speed of our sweet GAA. I was like a proud father watching his firstborn head off to school as I described in my gibberish Spanish the ins and outs of Gaelic football.

The game was an epic battle. Mayo had their keeper to thank for three outstanding saves which kept them in the game, but some incredibly tough and smart football won it for Dublin in the end. As the final whistle blew I let out some crazy yelps and yips, fist-pumping and shouting and high-fiving the bellboys. The high ceilings and grey stone finish of the hotel lobby echoed drifts of 'The Boys in Blue' as groups of wealthy tourists sneered their way past to the elevators.

I had played with eleven of the lads who played on the day. It still felt personal to me. I felt as if I had made some kind of vague and distant contribution.

As Serena and I returned to the streets, the sun was higher now in the sky. I skipped up into the air and screamed, 'Come on, the Dubs!!!! Gerrup yis boyiz!!!'

We had been travelling for a year and a half by that point. In Venezuela we'd spent a few weeks in a highland town called Merida, high in the mountains. Here I immersed myself in learning how to use a camera and edit video. My freedom from drink and drugs gave me an abundance of time and clarity, and I learned quickly.

We travelled to Colombia and stayed in a small coastal town called Santa Marta. Here we volunteered in a school in the slums, and after three weeks we created our first mini-documentary. It was a mammoth task for us, but one which we took on as professionally as possible. Three years earlier, if you'd told me I would be in Colombia and not try their most famous export, I would have bounced you all the way around the padded cell you were staying in. But I was done with it all, and I was happy for it. It was dead and buried and I intended to keep it that way.

We sailed from Cartagena in Colombia through the San Blas Islands and over to Panama, and spent a year travelling through Central America, Mexico and Cuba. We visited sixteen different charity and conservation projects – schools in slums in Colombia, turtle conservation projects in Costa Rica, women's rights groups in Nicaragua, soup kitchens in Guatemala, animal refuges in the Ecuadorian jungle – and made mini-documentaries about them. Time and again we witnessed people who were operating with little, helping those who had nothing. It was a humbling and inspiring time.

Serena's book *How to Retire in 12 Months* became a bestseller in Australasia, and when we got good internet connection she would work with her coaching clients via Skype, so the dollars kept coming in. We launched our new website, FivePointFive.org, while on the road. On the site we shared our travel experiences and documentary videos. We also began to create videos for hotels, tour companies and cruise lines.

Meanwhile, I was also able to make a bigger contribution through poker winnings. Sober and with plenty of time on my hands, my game had been improving. I began to win a few tournaments – small-stakes, large-field competitions where you could turn $20 into $5,000. Over the course of a few months I was able to win four of these relatively small tournaments. Along with Serena's income, my winnings helped us to live freely and travel far.

In a small town called Tulum on the Caribbean coast of Mexico, Serena and I sat down at a café. It was nice and busy, with a band playing local music. A high globe of sun poured its heat on to the Earth.

An elderly American man I had met earlier walked past. He was wearing short blue sport shorts and a dress shirt, with a denim floppy cap and long, wispy beard. 'Hey, there he is!' he shouted as he walked by, shaking his fist and laughing at me.

I laughed to myself and shook my head, thinking that this man must have done some amount of drugs. As I smiled and looked around, I noticed two tables down to my left a guy with wild hair and a goatee, staring at the American man and then back at me, and then twisting his eyebrows up and giving me a knowing look. I eyebrowed back, then turned away. It was a second before I realized: that's Billy Connolly.

It was uncanny. Billy had been sober for many moons, and he was the man I most wanted to talk to about being sober. I had been trying to contact him for years – via emails, Facebook, agents and all sorts – and had got nowhere. Now he was sitting in the same café in the Yucatan. I wasn't certain I could believe my eyes.

When Serena returned from *el baño* I said, 'That's him, isn't it? I'm not going crazy, am I?'

She assured me that it was him – how could you actually mistake Billy for anyone else? I scribbled my email address and website on a bit of paper, fixed my eyebrows, bushed up my hair and hopped over to his table, where he was sitting with a friend.

'Ah howiyah, lads, sorry to interrupt, but my name is John and I have a website called SoberPaddy.com and I was wondering, well hang on a sec . . . you are Billy Connolly, right, I'm not hallucinating, am I?' I asked.

Billy looked at his mate and they both cracked a smile.

'Ayeee, it's me,' he answered.

'Well, I have this website and I interview people who are sober, to show you can have a great life and be sober. I was wondering if you'd do an interview with me? It would only take half an hour and we'd just chat about booze and being sober, just get your story . . .'

'Aye, sure, we're both sober,' he said, nodding to his buddy. 'Sober Paddy, eh? Great name . . . a sober Irishman . . . aye sure I'd do an interview.'

My fingers were twitching with excitement.

'Great, what about later on today?' I asked.

'Achhhh noooo, nae can do it . . . we're goin' deep-sea fishing out in the ocean fer a few days.'

'When are you going?' I asked.

'Right now, after this.'

'Right now?'

'Ayeeeeee,' said Billy.

'Fuckit . . . when do you get back?' I asked

'After the weekend,' he replied.

'Bollix – I'll be in Cuba . . .'

'Nae a bad life you have there, eh?' Billy quipped.

We all chuckled.

'It's a pity, man, it'd be great to interview ya . . . people need to hear from people like you about drinking. I've posted an interview you did with Parkinson about every man having a certain amount he can drink in his life and that you just drank yours quicker than everyone else.'

'Oh ayeee, that's one of them . . . another time I knew I had to stop was when I was stuck in a telephone box. I was turning around inside it and couldnae get out. Now I knew the side with the telephone wasn't a door so that narrowed it down to three, but I still couldnae figure it . . . so I had to call ma manager and he had to come down and get me home. It's a true story.'

We all laughed on this side-street in Mexico. His friend asked where I was based. When I told him we were on the road, shooting documentaries about people making a difference, Billy started chuckling.

'Ayeee, a friend of mine used to work in Derry with a group called MAD – Making a Difference. I used to tell him he should call it MACOY, Making a Cunt of Yourself.'

We all cracked up laughing at this. Billy's friend suggested we do an interview on Skype. We swapped emails and I gave him the web-site address on the back of a napkin.

'This is really bad,' I said. 'I was trying to reach you for years, and then you just pop up in a small café on a side-street in a small town in Mexico. And you agree to it and I am thrilled, but then it turns out, I can't interview you anyway.'

'Aye lad, you know what that is now?' Billy asked in a hushed, conspiratorial tone.

'No, what's that?'

'That's the devil!'

He never did answer my emails, the ould codger.

We spent almost two years in Latin America. I learned basic Spanish. I was enjoying a simpler side of life. Little moments of life dazzled me now. I climbed volcanoes, sailed the Caribbean, rode horses with cowboys and explored lost cities. I smoked cigars and danced salsa under the open sky in Cuba. There was enough in the day-to-day sights and sounds of Latin America to keep me satisfied. For the first time in my life I felt completely at ease with who I was.

Watching the Dubs win another All-Ireland meant so much to me. I loved the team and loved the lads. Getting rejected by Pat Gilroy and his team hurt me and sent me to the bottom of the greasy pole. But the beauty of it all was that I found a way out. And I became a better man for it.

I followed them now as a fan. The former player who could have, should have and would have . . . had some things been different. As I watched Dublin lift those two All-Irelands I took some satisfaction that I had been involved with some of the players. But another part of me was less indulgent. The other part said that the reason they won was because they got rid of the dead wood like me. That was the deep gut feeling. I was never good enough and I dragged the rest of the squad down.

In the dirty Peruvian streets, little kids with no shoes ran past, chasing a ragged little dog. Old women with missing teeth and blackened feet leaned over fruit stalls, chatting and laughing. Beyond, in the distance, I could hear the sound of some band starting up in the town square. There always seemed to be a band starting up, no matter where we went in Latin America.

Very occasionally I wanted to give up and get wasted. I wanted to go on a three-day bender and see where it ended up. Serena still enjoyed a drink and I had no problems with her drinking in front of me. She had no problems with me drinking or anything else, as long as I didn't become a paranoid, twisted asshole. But that was the part I couldn't guarantee. The new me was all about being honest, and I just didn't think it was possible for me to get fucked up and not be a bad person.

What would I do if I came round with the walls wobbling and my mind a fuzz of nothing? What if there was a young lady snorting lines off my belly, looking up at me with a naughty smile? What if I got robbed and jumped on the first mode of transport I had seen, and came round in a village where no one knew my name? What would be the point of it? Why ruin a good thing?

All my life I had been hiding from the truth of being abused. It had haunted me as a teen and throughout my adult life. The only times I was free from its shackles were when I was drunk, drugged or playing for the Dubs. I had spent fifteen years of my life in a haze. I was either coming up or coming down: drunk, blacking out or hungover. I had given enough of my life over to the priest who had abused me. I had wasted enough of my time hiding and running and dodging. The big, fat elephant in the room was there and I was going to scream my fucking head off until everyone else knew about it.

That was the power of my new sobriety and I didn't want to give away any more. I was happy to be a former Dublin squad member. I was happy to be a former abuse victim. I was happy to be travelling the world with my beautiful wife on the trip of all lifetimes. I was happy to be sober now. I was happy to have come full circle and to be at peace with myself. I was happy to be a hippy, growing my hair long and with no job to go in for. I was happy to be a vegetarian who lived day to day and moment to moment.

The marching band pumped on by, celebrating some patron saint that must have been forgotten about during the festival the week before. How crazy was life on this little blob of blue and green circling our star known as the sun? How incredible that I could sit at a laptop and watch a match over 10,000 kilometres away, via some invisible force.

I picked up my pen and began to write. A strange energy clamped itself around my pen and my hand. My mind's eye accelerated away and drew me to a thoughtful world. I asked myself question after question with no one to reply:

Is writing these thoughts a proper way to celebrate the Dubs' success?

Surely ten pints of Guinness and some 'Molly Malone' would be sufficient?

Can I return someday to Ireland and regale them all with tales of my battles and my scars?

Will I become some tanned hippy, waffling on about some Guatemalan coffee bean that stole my heart?

Will arguments flutter to and fro among those who try to understand the madness that had befallen me?

Will they laugh at my story?

Will they say that the worst thing about my abuse was having to listen to me talk about it, like some kind of old shitehawk?

Can I ever blend back in among the noise of Ireland?

Was it all just a dream, an epic hallucination?

I put down my pen and looked up again. I was in Peru, in a side-street and full of caffeine. Serena had gone to do some shopping. I had ordered coffee after coffee after coffee. Three espressos was my limit. Any more than this and I got angry, intense and irritable. Any more than this and my pen became the master of me. Any more than this and I failed to be balanced and controlled.

I made a little side note on my copy book: 'One last crack at it'. Part of me thought I still had more to offer, that there were a few years left in the old dog yet. The competitor in me reckoned that one last year at senior level would make me know for sure. There was a club championship to be won, and after that, who knew? You always heard of the old guy at the club who soldiered on, defying all kinds of logic and physical torture. Surely that could be me?

Maybe I would return to the family home one last time. I would sit in the garden in the summertime. We would all gather – my mother, my sisters, the new wives and husbands, the kids – and recount the old times. We'd lean on each other and laugh and point and cheer. We would raise our glasses to the spirit of our ancestors. Maybe that was all that was left to do.

Maybe it would end the dream I'd been having. The dream always started the same way. I was back in Dublin, training. The sky was always grey, with dark, curly clouds pocketing the horizon to my right. The fields were always three or four times the size of regular ones.

Sometimes in the dream I would approach the lads who were running around and kicking balls at each other. I would run up and they would seem confused that I was there, as though I had interrupted them. I would try to join in, but my feet would move a little too slowly. I would try to shout at them, but they would always turn their heads away just a few moments before I could catch their eyes. Other times I would see the managers at the side and they would greet me heartily. I would stop and chat with them. They would all ask me the same thing. Was I back? Was I really back? And I would always think, how fucking weird is this, I am talking to you all, of course I'm back. Where the hell else could I be?

But no matter what happened, no matter how many times I have had the dream, no matter if I talk to the managers, the players or am just training away, the same result always occurs. I am distracted by something – a shoelace or a tree or a bird flying by – and when I'd look around, the team bus would be pulling away. I would stand there, mouthing words, and try to scream for them to come back.

Come back, turn the bus around, I should be on the bus.

And then I'd wake up.

Acknowledgements

Writing this book has been a real journey into the past and present. I could not have done it without the help of some very special people.

First and foremost, I want to thank my mother. You have been the absolute rock who has held our family together over decades. You raised five kids and looked after Dad with a rare strength and power. You always encouraged me to be creative and to speak my mind. Your love and energy have driven me on in the world and I thank you from the bottom of my heart.

I want to thank my brother James for always finding a way to look after me, no matter how tough it was. You paved the way for me.

I want to thank my sister Vanessa. You have always been there for me and, with your ideas, laughter and spirit, inspired me to keep on trooping in life.

I want to thank my sister Ellen for being such a fun and light person in my life. You have always been a ray of sunshine, no matter what was going on inside my turbulent self.

I want to thank my sister Ava for being such a live wire and such a loving person. Your quick wit and banter have been a constant source of comfort and happiness.

For all my cousins, aunties and uncles down the Wesht I say thanks. You all helped shaped this Jackeen into something different than the norm. *Go raibh maith agaibh.*

The friends who have put up with me over the years are too many to mention. I have had to change your names in this book in order to protect your identities, but you all know who you are. We have lived and laughed hard for many moons. Thank you all for providing the spark that keeps the fires burning.

To all my teammates along the years I want to say thanks. In the Baldoyle, Sylvester's and Dublin dressing rooms I have found a sanctuary and a healthy buzz that balanced out the madness of my life.

To all the coaches and managers along the way. Paddy Morrissey at Baldoyle showed grit and loyalty that marked him as one of the best. Brian Talty showed me the level of intensity needed to compete at the top. Pillar Caffrey brought me on to the Dubs' senior set-up and went close to cracking the winning formula.

A special mention for Dave Billings, who passed away shortly after I finished this book. He was the first Dublin manager to give me a Championship start. He showed faith and belief in my abilities and was the finest gentleman you could ever meet. Thank you.

I want to thank the team at Penguin. You showed confidence in my writing and in my story. Thank you to my editor, Brendan Barrington, whose keen eye, advice and expertise have helped shape my chaotic ramblings.

To Denis Craven, who gave me a real love of the English language way back in the nineties. His teaching helped me understand complex literary ideas and he showed me how to write in a simple yet vigorous style.

To Hunter S. Thompson, Jack Kerouac, Tom Wolfe, William Burroughs, Charles Bukowski, Ken Kesey, James Joyce and Flann O'Brien I tip my hat . . . You are the true masters who have inspired me to write.

To Stephen Cluxton I must say thanks. You are the top dog for a reason, and even though I often wished you'd get injured while I was in the squad, I am proud you have gone on to lift Sam and be a true champion. You deserve all the success you have for your dedication to your craft.

To all the other goalkeepers in the Keepers' Union, I say 'respect'. We are the crazy ones. Thank you to all those I have trained with over the years: Hustler, Coper and all the rest who have helped push me on.

I must give one final mention to my dad. You were the driving force of my football and my education and always made me reach higher in life. You would be shocked by the contents of my book, but happy I finally wrote something worth publishing. Thank you for putting in the graft all those years ago.

And last but not least I need to thank my wonderful wife, Serena. You are the woman who made everything make sense. You inspire me, drive me, love me and send me to places I never thought possible. You helped me write this book by giving me the space and mindset to do it. Thank you for your advice, support and love.

You have made me be a better man.